PLANNED RESIDENTIAL ENVIRONMENTS

JOHN B. LANSING
ROBERT W. MARANS
ROBERT B. ZEHNER

A report prepared for
the U.S. Department of Transportation,
Bureau of Public Roads

1970

Survey Research Center
Institute for Social Research
The University of Michigan
Ann Arbor, Michigan 48106

Library of Congress Card No. 76-632967

Printed by Braun-Brumfield, Inc.
Ann Arbor, Michigan

Manufactured in the United States of America

PREFACE

The research reported here has been directed at two objectives: first, an assessment of people's overall responses to selected, planned residential environments and their responses to particular features of these environments; and, second, an investigation of the transportation requirements of people living in planned residential environments and a comparison with similar demands of people living in more typical residential surroundings.

The rapid population growth in our metropolitan areas over the past two decades has been accompanied by construction of new housing at a rate unsurpassed in the history of the United States. Continuing population growth in the metropolitan areas and rising incomes will require continued high rates of construction for the next two or three decades.

Three ways in which the demand for new housing in metropolitan areas can be satisfied include the development of vacant suburban land; the restructuring of land use, housing, and transportation patterns within the central city, and the building of completely new settlements at or beyond the fringe of the metropolitan area.

The method of inquiry has been to select ten communities to represent the different types of planned and less planned residential environments and then to conduct intensive personal interviews with carefully selected probability samples of their residents. The scope of the study has been restricted to people living in single family houses and townhouses. A total of 1253 interviews were taken, distributed as follows:

iii

Community (Region)	Number of Interviews	Response Rates (Ratio of Interviews Completed to Families Selected for Interviews)
Columbia (Baltimore)	216	92.3%
Crofton (Baltimore)	98	91.6
Glen Rock (Northern New Jersey)	106	82.2
Lafayette-Elmwood (Detroit)	106	85.5
Montpelier (Baltimore)	105	86.1
Norbeck (Washington)	99	83.2
Radburn (Northern New Jersey)	103	85.1
Reston (Washington)	203	89.0
Southfield (Detroit)	110	87.3
Southwest Washington (Washington)	107	73.3
Total number of interviews	1253	86.1%

The sample of each community was selected to represent a cross-section of respondents exclusive of apartment dwellers. The interviews were taken in November and December, 1969, and lasted about an hour. The arithmetic mean length of interview was 63 minutes, with 35 percent lasting under 50 minutes, and 17 percent, 70 minutes or longer. The person interviewed in each family was either the head or the wife of the head, the choice between them being randomly determined in advance with no discretion left to the interviewer. This report is based on these 1253 interviews supplemented by other data from maps, photographs and visits to the communities studied.

This report continues a line of inquiry pursued by the Survey Research Center for the Bureau of Public Roads. Earlier studies have been based on national samples of the population living in metropolitan areas (exclusive of New York).[1] This study attempts to meet a criticism made of the earlier work: that people in those studies were responding only to the places where they lived without knowledge of the new environments being developed elsewhere. In this project we have attempted to include some of the best known examples of planned communities existing in the United States. We anticipate the criticism

---

[1]*Residential Location and Urban Mobility*, by John B. Lansing and Eva Mueller with Nancy Barth, Institute for Social Research, The University of Michigan, Ann Arbor, Michigan, June 1964; *Residential Location and Urban Mobility: A Multivariate Analysis*, by John B. Lansing and Nancy Barth, Institute for Social Research, The University of Michigan, Ann Arbor, Michigan, December 1964; *Residential Location and Urban Mobility: The Second Wave of Interviews*, by John B. Lansing, Institute for Social Research, The University of Michigan, Ann Arbor, Michigan, January 1966; and *Automobile Ownership and Residential Density*, by John B. Lansing and Gary Hendricks, Institute for Social Research, The University of Michigan, Ann Arbor, Michigan, 1967.

that these communities are not yet completed; they will be further developed and others of better design will be created. Further inquiry will then be appropriate. Meanwhile, we hope that this research may contribute to an understanding of how people respond to their residential environments and, hence, to the process of community development.

There is an extensive literature on urban planning in general and on new towns in particular. There is also a voluminous literature on urban transportation. Some of the more important references are cited in the bibliography. As far as we know there have been no projects directly comparable to this one, that is, no studies which have included personal interviews with probability samples of residents of matched planned and unplanned communities.[2]

A project such as this one represents the work of many people whose names do not appear on the title page. We wish to acknowledge at least some of these individuals by name. This study is a project of the Survey Research Center. The Center is a division of the Institute for Social Research, which is directed by Rensis Likert. The Director of the Survey Research Center is Angus Campbell. The sample design for this study greatly benefited from the work of Irene Hess. The field work was directed by John Scott, assisted by Jeanne Keresztesi, with the hiring and supervision of the interviewers in the eight eastern communities under the direction of Lilian Kleinberg. Coding was under the direction of Joan Scheffler with the particular responsibilities for editing and map work handled chiefly by Nancy Cole, Francoise Duesberg, Cynthia Meredith, Steven Pinney, Lynn Redlin and Georgina Rice. The computing section was under the direction of John Sonquist and Duane Thomas, with responsibility for computing on this project carried primarily by Joseph O'Neill. The manuscript for this report was typed by Anita Ernst and Priscilla Hildebrandt. The text's readability has profited from the editing of Douglas Crase. For the Bureau of Public Roads the contract managers have been Carl N. Swerdloff and Sydney Robertson, both of whom have contributed actively to the development of the project. We also wish to acknowledge the Social Science Research Council who in part supported the work of one of the authors, Robert W. Marans.

---

[2]Three of the empirical studies which come closest to being direct predecessors are the following:
1) *The Community Builders*, by Edward P. Eichler and Marshall Kaplan, Berkeley: University of California Press, 1967. A useful account of the development of selected communities, but it is not based on interviews with residents.
2) *The Levittowners*, by Herbert J. Gans, New York: Pantheon Books, 1967, A stimulating account based on the personal observations of the author who lived for a time in the community he studied.
3) *Planning and the Purchase Decision: Why People Buy in Planned Communities*, by Carl Werthman, Jerry S. Mandel and Ted Dienstfrey, University of California, Berkeley: Institute for Urban and Regional Development, Center for Planning and Development Research, Preprint No. 10, July, 1965.

CONTENTS

Page

SUMMARY

This study is based on interviews in ten communities selected to represent different levels of planning. Only people living in single family homes or townhouses are included. The bulk of the interviews were taken in six new suburban communities selected to represent three different levels of planning. Two communities are highly planned, Columbia and Reston; two, moderately planned, Crofton and Montpelier; and two, less planned, Norbeck and Southfield. In addition interviews were taken in two new highly planned inner city communities (Lafayette-Elmwood and Southwest Washington) and two older communities, one planned (Radburn) and one not highly planned (Glen Rock).

The median family income for residents in the ten sample communities is high, approximately $18,700. In the newer communities, the higher the level of planning, the higher the educational level. In the two highly planned suburban areas about 42 percent of married couples both have college degrees; in the least planned it is 18 percent. The median age of people interviewed in the six newer suburban communities is within the range from 36 to 42 years, while median age is 50 in the older communities.

Overall satisfaction with the community in the suburban areas is highest in the new towns, Reston and Columbia. Sixty-one percent rate Reston "excellent," but only 18 percent rate Montpelier, one of the moderately planned areas, that highly. In all communities the item most often mentioned as a source of satisfaction with the community was the nearness or accessibility of work, shopping, and other facilities. The extent of a community's planning was mentioned more often as a reason for moving to the community than as a reason for satisfaction once people had lived there.

Facilities for outdoor recreation tend to be more available and participation in outdoor recreation higher in planned communities than in less planned communities. In Southwest Washington, for example, everyone is within half a mile of a swimming pool and 65 percent of all adults swam in a pool five or more times last year. In Crofton, 12 percent live that close to a pool and 53 percent swam that often. Not all outdoor activities are influenced by distance to facilities. The number of golf courses available within ten miles and within two miles does not attect rates of participation. An internal walkway system does affect the number of people in a community who hike or walk. For example, in Reston and Columbia, 7 out of 10 are frequent walkers, but in Montpelier and Southfield, only 5 out of 10. Internal walkways, however, have little effect on number of people who go bicycling.

Residents' responses to their immediate environments indicate that dwelling unit density underlies many factors important to neighborhood satisfaction including privacy in the yard; neighborhood noise level; and the adequacy of outdoor space for family activities. Density, however, operates indirectly through these factors and the correlation between density and satisfaction is not high. Whether a neighborhood is "well kept up" is the best single predictor of neighborhood satisfaction. The compatibility of neighborhood residents is the next most important factor.

The proportion of families owning two or more cars is related to the level of planning in the six suburban areas. Multiple car ownership is about 20 percent higher in the least planned communities than it is in the most planned areas.

In-town residents drive fewer miles per year than those in suburban communities. For the communities studied, about 11,000 to 16,000 miles is typical in the inner city areas compared to roughly 21,000 in the suburbs. At the time of our study the degree of planning made little or no difference in total miles driven in different suburban areas.

The average journey to work is about three miles for the two inner city communities and twelve miles for the peripheral communities. The average distances are slightly higher for the two new towns. In all the newer peripheral communities but Reston, more than 90 percent go to work by car. In the centrally located communities public transportation is used more often but more people drive to work than use public transportation. In the older communities in New Jersey two family heads in ten always use public transportation.

The mean number of vehicle trips per family in a 24 hour period across all ten communities is 7.6. Variation within communities is large relative to variation across communities. There is no evidence that the total number of vehicle trips is appreciably influenced by the level of community planning. The average number of person trips reported is 11.5 per family when husbands report compared to 10.4 when wives report for the family. Studies which rely on reports from wives may be biased downward as a result.

Contrary to expectations a slightly larger proportion of people in the highly planned peripheral locations take weekend trips of 10 miles or more than of people in the less planned communities. The statistics for those reporting such a trip on the weekend prior to interview are 63 to 69 percent in Columbia and

Reston, compared to 51 percent in Norbeck and 42 percent in Southfield.

Bus service exists in all communities except Montpelier and Crofton. Among the six suburban communities frequency of reported use is comparatively high in Reston, reflecting patronage of the Reston commuter bus. Areas of most frequent bus patronage are the two inner city locations. The extent to which people who live in a given community use public transportation to get to work is related to measures of the degree of scatter of their places of work. This finding applies both to inner city and suburban communities. The proportion of people who value having bus service available is higher than the proportion who use it.

A surprisingly high proportion of the adult population in some communities report that they ride bicycles. About one adult in four in Southfield and Crofton rode a bike in the last week to get somewhere from their home.

PART I
THE SELECTION OF COMMUNITIES

1

INTRODUCTION

This project is a study of people's responses to residential environments which differ in the extent to which they are planned. Part I of the report, accordingly, is concerned with the specification of what is meant by the degree of planning of a residential environment and with the selection of actual communities. This chapter sets forth the principles used in the initial selection. This study has been conceived as an attempt to compare highly planned communities with other communities of similar age and economic level. It was intended that the communities be as similar as possible in characteristics other than those related to degree of planning, and Chapter 2 is concerned with the success of this effort to achieve comparability on other dimensions.

The other two main sections of the report concern people's responses to the residential environments. "Responses" for these purposes include both social psychological material, what people tell us directly about their attitudes toward the places where they live, and behavioral responses, what people tell us about what they do. We are especially interested in transportation, and Part III considers in some detail the difference in transportation behavior of people living in different residential environments.

The question as to why transportation planners should be interested in a project such as this one has been asked on occasion. It is generally agreed that the effects transportation and land use decisions have on one another necessitate a joint approach. One way to state a fundamental choice for urban development has been mentioned briefly in the *Preface*. The rapid population growth in our metropolitan areas over the past two decades has been accompanied by construction of new housing at a rate unsurpassed in the United States. Continuing population growth in the metropolitan areas and rising incomes will require continued high rates of construction for the next two or three decades. During this same period much of the housing stock in central cities will become

1

obsolete and deteriorate to a point where clearance and redevelopment and large scale rehabilitation become important possibilities. There are three ways in which the demand for new housing and residential environments in metropolitan areas can be satisfied: the suburban development of vacant land contiguous to the edge of existing development; the restructuring of land use, housing, and transportation patterns within the central city; and the building of completely new settlements at or beyond the fringe of metropolitan development.[1]

The predominant means of meeting housing demand in recent years has been suburbanization of vacant land at or near the edge of metropolitan areas. Development has varied from one or two single family lots to large areas containing single family detached houses, apartments and supporting shops, commercial services, and recreation facilities. For the most part each development has occurred within the framework of a land use plan and zoning ordinance which presumably reflect the goals of the particular political jurisdiction within which the land is located, as determined by the local balance of political forces.

During the 1950's sections of large cities containing "sub-standard" housing and other obsolete structures were razed as a means of eliminating blight and providing land for new commercial and residential development. These federally assisted redevelopment projects resulted in the creation of many residential environments which were strongly influenced if not controlled by professional planners and urban designers. The projects also uprooted large numbers of people characterized by low status, low incomes, ill health and unemployment. Increasing awareness by the cities and the federal government that these projects had high social costs slowed renewal activities which emphasized clearance and population displacement during the 1960's, and emphasized instead rehabilitation of residential structures and neighborhood preservation. However, it is probable that existing land use and transportation patterns will not continue indefinitely. To the extent that present central city residents disperse throughout metroplitan areas vacant structures and vacant land will appear in central locations, present resistance to large scale clearance will weaken, and programs of central city redevelopment which emphasize new housing may again become important.

The building of completely new communities at and beyond the fringe of metropolitan areas has received increasing attention in recent years. The highly publicized communities of Reston, Virginia, and Columbia, Maryland, along with several retirement communities have helped form a popular conception of a new community. Unlike many European governments which have initiated the

---

[1]See the discussion by Anthony Downs, "Alternative Forms of Future Urban Growth in the United States," *Journal of the American Institute of Planners,* January 1970, pp. 3-11. For a more critical appraisal of new town development, see William Alonso, "The Mirage of New Towns," *The Public Interest,* Spring 1970, pp. 3-17.

building of new towns as a means of relieving population pressures in their large cities, the federal government in the United States has played a relatively inactive role in the development of new communities.[2] Private developers have been responsible for new community efforts with little federal assistance. However, Title IV of the Housing and Urban Development Act of 1968 envisages a more active federal role in encouraging the development of new communities through subsidies in the form of low interest loans for land acquisition.

Thus, all three general types of urban development are realistic possibilities—continued development of suburban communities, redevelopment of substantial tracts of land in the central parts of metropolitan areas, and the construction of complete new communities beyond the periphery of the metropolitan area. The appropriate transportation system for the nation will depend in some degree upon the mix of these three types of development. One of the basic concerns of this study is with specifying the differences in transportation requirements of people in different situations. We are also concerned with exploring what patterns of residential development are likely to achieve public acceptance.

Another basic issue related to transportation planning has to do with the density of residential development wherever it takes place. A transportation planner who knew what the future density of residential development was to be in an area could be more confident of his plans than one who did not. Choices for urban areas are sometimes put in terms of combined transportation and land use plans differ basically in assumed densities. Density, however, is a planner's concept which must be translated into other terms in order to get people's reactions to the subject. When, in Part II, we are concerned with whether people want to live in a townhouse or a single family house, how important privacy is to them, how often they interact with their neighbors, and the like, we shall be dealing indirectly with the density question.

A. *Defining Planned Residential Environments*

This study is to focus on "planned residential environments." The terminology in the field is in a state of some confusion, and it is necessary to explain what is meant by the phrase. The terms "new towns," "new communities," and "planned residential environments" have been used interchangeably so often that it may be worthwhile to begin by reviewing their similarities and differences. The best recent practice includes all "new towns"

---

[2] For a recent review of the government's role in new town development, see Jonathan B. Howes, "The Shape of Federal Involvement in New Community Building - 1970," paper presented at the New Towns Research Seminar sponsored by the Center for Urban and Regional Studies, University of North Carolina at Chapel Hill, May 4, 1970. A case study of federal involvement in the planning of one new community is provided by Martha Dethrick, "Defeat at Fort Lincoln," *The Public Interest*, Summer 1970, pp. 3-39.

among "new communities," and all "new communities" among "planned residential environments." The flow of inclusion goes only one way, however. In other words, all "planned residential environments" are *not* "new communities," and all "new communities" are *not* "new towns." Eichler and Kaplan offer a clear approach to distinguishing between new towns and new communities:

> The principal difference between a subdivision as such and a new community is scale. As a rule, a 100-acre subdivision is considered very large; but as we shall see, the smallest of the new communities has at least 2,500 acres. Scale is not the only difference. Other differences to be discussed include such matters as the range of facilities proposed or offered, the number of years of projected involvement, and the institutional framework created for the process. . . . The critical difference between a new town and a new community is in the degree of "self-sufficiency" of each, which means the percentage of the population expected to live and work within the area. . . . Thus a new community is much less self-sufficient than a new town. A new town is an attempt to break the pattern of urban growth, and at the same time to shift development to different places and to control it. A new community is a way of ordering the business of land development at the fringe of American metropolitan areas.[3]

The category of "planned residential environments," thus, may include projects having a smaller area than the new communities (less than 2500 acres). Whether a small residential area is "planned" or not becomes a matter of the physical and social facilities provided by the developer.

It is not clear at what point a particular project has sufficient facilities to be considered as "planned." We have not found any single characteristic which is easily recognizable and widely accepted as distinguishing "planned" from "unplanned." We find it more useful to think of environments as ranged on a continuum from more to less planned.

At first glance, one possibility would have been to make the distinction on the basis of whether a developer considers and "plans" for the availability of non-residential as well as residential community facilities—e.g., recreation, shopping, education—even if these were *not* to be built by the developer. Unfortunately (for the purposes of a neat dichotomy), virtually *any* individual or developer must address himself to these basic questions of "planning" when deciding to locate in a particular place whatever the size of the land parcel to be developed. Since zoning regulations in this country were initiated and upheld in the 1920's, residential development usually has been based on plans and regulations controlling land use, lot coverage, setbacks, and street and utility

---

[3]Edward P. Eichler and Marshall Kaplan, *op. cit.,* pp. 23-24.

layout. When such controls exist, "unplanned" seems a misnomer.

Once the idea of an underlying continuum is accepted, the problem arises of how different environments are to be placed on the continuum. For this purpose one basic consideration is the size of the development. What is the extent of the area which is considered by a single authority? The importance of scale arises from the fact that the smaller the scale the more limited the opportunities for planning, while the larger the scale the greater the potentialities. We may distinguish at least three levels of planning objectives appropriate to different scales. The three scales we consider here are the individual house; the neighborhood, by which we mean in this context an area comparable to an elementary school district; and the community, by which we mean roughly an area large enough to include several elementary schools, or, following Eichler and Kaplan, over 2500 acres.

1. *Housing objectives.* Development is aimed at meeting the housing needs of individual families with little attention paid to the larger residential environment. Emphasis is placed on providing an attractive dwelling with associated outdoor space at a given price. The developer may be a man who wons one vacant lot on which he proposes to build. A developer with just a few lots is in a similar position. He will accept as given the existing land use patterns, zoning restrictions, transportation and water and sewer facilities. If needs for shopping, recreation and other facilities are considered at all, they are met by strategically locating the development so as to give the residents access to existing (or envisioned) facilities.

2. *Environmental objectives - neighborhood scale.* In addition to basic requirements for housing individual families, attention is given to the larger residential environment in which the dwellings are located. Provision may be made for local shops, recreation, and schools either by land allocation or actual construction by the developer. Beyond such basic requisites, the housing provided may include a mixture of dwelling types including detached single family units, townhouses, garden apartments or a combination built at a variety of densities. A hierarchy of streets may be provided to meet different levels of traffic operating in the environment. To provide for pedestrian movements, walkways may be designed to link up housing with nearby facilities. Where walkways intersect streets having heavy volumes of traffic, grade separations can be used to separate the pedestrian from the auto. Land characterized by woods, hills, water or marshlands may be retained in its natural state for recreation or ecological purposes. If man-made development does occur on such land, it may be integrated with the landscape so as to preserve scarce natural features. Attempts may be made to convey a sense of identity with the place, to those within or passing by the environment, by locating a distinctive physical landmark at a site in the environment which offers maximum visual exposure.

These possibilities exist because of the larger scale of development being considered.

3. *Environmental objectives - community scale.* To a significant extent physical planning objectives at the community level are possible only when even larger areas are considered. Thus, rather than concentrating on the needs of residents for convenience goods, provision may be made for larger or more specialized stores. Consideration may be given to the provision of land for a number of churches, large recreation areas, secondary as well as elementary schools, and various medical, cultural and entertainment facilities, all of which depend for their success on either a large or a captive population. Where the community includes several residential units (e.g., neighborhoods), increased attention may be given to the articulation of the pedestrian and vehicular transportation systems linking the residential units and community facilities. To provide a larger tax base and to allow residents to work near their homes, attempts may be made to lure commercial and industrial establishments into the area. Finally, plans to provide regional centers for education, retail shopping, or other purposes may be included as well.

Although scale is important, it is by no means the only determinant of the degree of planning. Even a cursory review of existing residential environments suggests great variety in the extent of physical planning actualized at each of the three levels of objectives. For instance, the Levittowns, built since the Second World War, as well as Columbia and Reston, have all attempted to satisfy a range of environmental objectives at the community scale, yet the observable differences among the communities are numerous. Scale is a necessary but not a sufficient condition for some kinds of planning.

It is not easy to reduce the degree of planning to a single dimension. One suggestion would be to try to specify such a dimension in terms of the degree of comprehensiveness of the objectives of the planner. The broader his objectives, the greater the degree of planning. This approach, however, has the limitation that there may be some uncertainty as to the exact nature of the objectives of those who planned a community. Definitive written statements may not be available. Objectives may change; they may represent compromises.

For our purposes, it is necessary to distinguish only approximately between planned and less planned environments. Our concerns are with the overall responses to existing planned communities, viewed as wholes or "Gestalts" in contrast to less planned areas, and with the particular responses to particular attributes of planned areas. We have found it helpful to specify a list of characteristics of planned communities which are more or less directly observable. One or another characteristic of existing, more planned environments may be widely diffused in the future. We would like to understand the response to each of these attributes, to the extent that they can be separately considered, as well as the responses to the communities viewed as wholes.

The following list summarizes 15 characteristics of planned environments. We regard those places which possess a larger number of these characteristics as more planned. We do not regard this list as definitive, but we hope most urban planners would accept it as a useful indicator. We have included a statement of the objective which each characteristic is intended to achieve. It should be recognized that a given characteristic may be intended to achieve more than one objective. It should also be recognized that a given characteristic may have unintended as well as intended consequences. As the reader will note, there are some characteristics about which observers may differ, especially those involving aesthetic judgments. The list of characteristics of planned environments is as follows:

1. At a minimum, parcels of land are designated for a single residential use and subdivided into units that are equal in size and subject to the same set of building regulations. The objective is to provide an area for one type of dwelling which is protected from the intrusion of "undesirable" land uses such as factories and warehouses.

2. In the community as a whole, provision is made for a variety of housing types (single family detached, townhouses, high rise, etc.) and unit sizes (efficiency through four-bedroom) with a wide range of costs. The objectives are to foster diversity in appearance of the environment; to provide living accommodations for a mix of individuals and families of varying sizes and incomes; and to facilitate interaction of populations which are diverse in their socio-cultural-economic backgrounds.

3. In neighborhood units relatively homogeneous housing types of the same cost range are provided. The purposes are to foster neighborhoods which are relatively homogeneous socially to facilitate congenial interaction, and to lower dwelling unit construction costs.

4. Contiguous buildings are attractively designed and relatively "harmonious" in appearance. The objective is to create an attractive place to live.

5. Shops, schools, swimming pools, playgrounds, and other facilities for outdoor recreation are provided within close proximity to one another and to housing. The purposes are to provide for a variety of facilities which are accessible to residents; to facilitate contacts among residents through the agglomeration of the facilities they use; and to reduce needs for many intra-community vehicular trips.

6. Cluster housing units are surrounded by open land which is used for parking, recreation, or play space. This arrangement has many

purposes: to preserve land and avoid duplication of driveways, parking lots, and other facilities; to maintain wooded areas, water or attractive open land; to facilitate social interaction by creating units in close proximity to one another; to create a "place" with which residents can identify; and to remove the responsibility for maintenance from individuals.

7. Pedestrian and vehicular traffic are separated through the provision of walkways away from streets and grade separations where streets and walkways must cross. The objective is to facilitate safe and convenient movement of pedestrians throughout the environment.

8. A variety of modes for vehicular movement are provided to interconnect places within the environment. The variety is intended to accommodate the various transportation needs of the residents and to limit dependence on the automobile as the sole mode of transport.

9. Trees are preserved or provided; they may be either indigenous or introduced into the environment. Objectives are to create an attractive place to live and to provide for shaded areas and cool temperatures.

10. Water bodies such as lakes, streams and marshlands are preserved or created. The purposes are to create an attractive place to live, to provide for recreational use, and to maintain an ecological balance in the area.

11. No visible overhead utility lines are permitted. The purposes are to create an attractive place to live and to limit long term maintenance costs.

12. Landmarks and visual symbols are provided. These symbols are intended to provide a means of identifying key facilities in the environment (e.g., the main commercial center) or the community itself.

13. Community newspapers, TV, information exchange centers, and cooperative associations are established. These are intended to facilitate the flow of all forms of information to all segments of the population and to foster participation and involvement in community life and the process of community planning.

14. Commercial and industrial corporations are provided for and are recruited. Two purposes are intended: to increase the community tax

base, and to enable those residents who so desire to both live and work in the same community.

15. Expected growth patterns are programmed to follow a hierarchical nesting of residential units, from dwelling unit to neighborhood to village to community to city. Objectives are to provide needed facilities as conveniently as possible as warranted by the population base; to foster a sense of identity at each hierarchical level; and to encourage formal and informal social intercourse between identifiable residential units.

This list might be thought of as an attempt at a concise statement of a planning ideology which might be accepted or rejected, analyzed or elaborated. For our purposes, however, its major purpose has been to serve as a guide in the selection of communities. Some of the ideas it contains have also played a part in our analysis of people's responses to highly planned and less planned environments.

B. *The Experimental Design*

The basic ideas which guided the design of this research come from the statistical theory of the design of experiments. The approach taken to the study of planned environments began with the idea that it is not enough simply to study planned communities themselves. Comparisons based on similar measurements undertaken at the same time using the same procedures in other communities offer better bases for generalization. The communities selected as controls should be similar to the planned communities in every respect except the degree of planning. There should be at least two communities of each type to provide some measure of the variations among communities within the categories being considered.

These considerations and an initial budgetary limit of 800 interviews led to a preliminary desigh of the following form:

I. Highly Planned Environments	Number of Areas	Interviews per Area	Total
A. Peripheral locations in metropolitan areas	2	200	400
B. Central locations	2	100	200
II. Less Planned Environments			
A. Peripheral locations	2	100	200
Total	6		800

This strategy provided for a basic three-way comparison with two environments in each of the three cells. It departed from the usual statistical practice of equal numbers of interviews in each cell of an experimental design by doubling the number of interviews in the two planned environments in peripheral locations. This departure was intended to allow for comparisons between the two environments in this cell. There was also special interest in comparisons between the data to be collected for these two planned environments versus existing data for cross-sections of residents of metropolitan areas.

This design was later expanded and strengthened by the addition of 400 interviews. Two considerations were judged to be vital: the need to increase the sample in the control communities and the need to take into account the dimension of time. People's responses to communities are often asserted to depend on the age of the community, and it seemed highly desirable to include at least one planned environment which was not new. An older community would have had a chance to develop stable behavior patterns and there would have been time for the initial effects of publicity in the development stage to have worn off.

The final plan, therefore, is essentially as follows:

	Number of Areas	Interviews per Area	Interviews
I. Highly Planned Environments			
A. Peripheral locations in / metropolitan areas, new	2	200	400
B. New environments in central locations	2	100	200
C. Older planned environment	1	100	100
II. Less Planned Environments			
A. Peripheral locations, new	4	100	400
B. Older less planned environment (to match I.C.)	1	100	100
Total	10		1200

This scheme was modified in one respect at the stage of actual selection of the communities. The four new less planned locations were subdivided into two categories according to degree of planning, so that two communities may be described as moderately planned, and two as characterized by a low level of planning. It is possible, thus, to think of three levels of planning among the peripheral areas.

C. *The Communities Selected*

The next step in the research process after the development of the sample design was the selection of communities to fill the different cells in the scheme. We would be less than candid, however, if we gave the impression that the design was completely fixed before we began to think about communities. The possibility of minor modifications in the design was kept open until the communities were finally selected. For example, the distinction between moderately planned and least planned communities did not emerge clearly until the selection process was well advanced.

The search for communities to match the design was a time-consuming process in which every source of information open to us was used, including literature in the field, personal contacts with informed people such as local planning officials, and personal visits to areas which seemed possibilities. Several areas which at first seemed appropriate on closer inspection had to be rejected. For example, one less planned new suburban development which seemed at first an excellent choice turned out to contain a heavy concentration of people from one ethnic group. If we had selected it, any special attitudes or behavior characteristic of the members of that group would have tended to be confused with those more generally to be expected from people who live in communities with a low level of planning. Another in-town planned development seemed excellent until it turned out to be too small. We would have been unlikely to obtain 100 interviews.

The communities selected to fill the places in the sample design are shown in Table 1. The reasons for the selection of these ten places may be indicated briefly.[4] There was only a limited choice of highly planned new communities, and we came to the selection of Columbia and Reston without much difficulty. They both meet all of the criteria implied by our list of 15 characteristics presented earlier in this chapter. We did consider the possibility of including one or more communities from California, Arizona, or one of the other western states. A logical extension of our work would be to obtain comparable data from that region as well as from communities in other countries. For our purposes, however, there was no need to search elsewhere to locate two highly planned environments and it was economical to work in the two new towns in the Washington area.

The number of highly planned in-town areas is also limited. Given the choice of Columbia and Reston, it was appropriate to select an in-town area in Washington, and the Southwest Redevelopment Area meets most of the criteria of the list of 15 characteristics of planned environments. It clearly does not include characteristic 14. "Commercial and industrial corporations are provided for and are recruited," but this objective does not apply as clearly to in-town areas.

---

[4]For a precise definition of communities and their boundaries, see Appendix B.

Table 1

The Sample Design and the Communities Selected

Classification	Location	Number of Interviews	
I. Highly Planned			
A. Peripheral, new	(1) Columbia, Maryland	200	
	(2) Reston, Virginia	200	
			400
B. In-town, new	(1) Southwest Redevelopment Area, Washington, D.C.	100	
	(2) Lafayette Park-Elmwood Park, Detroit, Michigan[1]	100	
			200
C. Peripheral, old	Radburn in Fairlawn, New Jersey	100	
			100
	Subtotal		700
II. Less Planned			
A. Moderately planned, peripheral, new	(1) Crofton, Maryland	100	
	(2) Montpelier, Maryland	100	
		200	
B. Least planned, peripheral, new	(1) Norbeck area, Montgomery County, Maryland	100	
	(2) Southfield area, Oakland County, Michigan	100	
			200
C. Least planned, peripheral, old	Glen Rock area, Bergen County, New Jersey	100	
	Subtotal		100
			500
	Grand Total		1200

[1]These communities will be referred to as Lafayette-Elmwood and Southwest Washington in the remainder of the study.

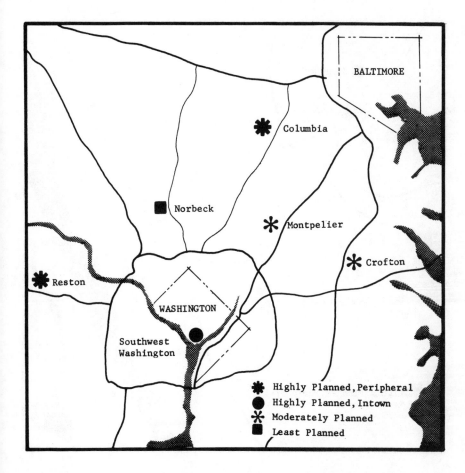

Map 1. Locations of Communities in the Baltimore and Washington Regions.

In the same way there is no provision for further growth following a hierarchical nesting of residential units, but growth is limited by the character of the site. The Lafayette Park-Elmwood Park community contains two contiguous urban renewal projects located near the center of Detroit; it also meets the requirements for a highly planned development. Here again considerations of expense entered: it happened to be more economical to take interviews there than in other, similar communities in other cities.

The number of older planned residential environments in the United States is strictly limited. We found few candidates in addition to Radburn, which is famous among planners as the community in which Clarence Stein and Henry Wright first applied to an area of single family homes the idea of a superblock

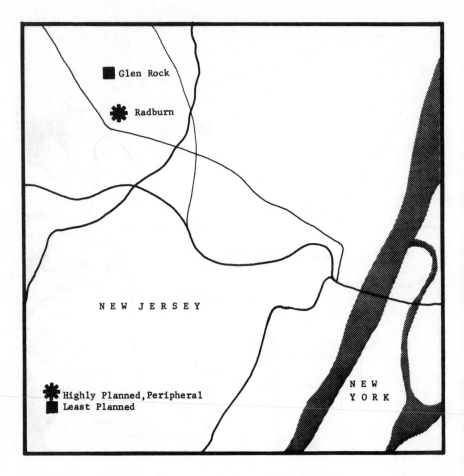

Map 2. Location of Communities in Northern New Jersey.

containing a central park area surrounded by houses located on cul-de-sacs accessible from the main streets forming the boundaries of the superblock.[5] No other older community seemed to have both an equal degree of planning and to have a population whose socioeconomic level was roughly comparable to that in Columbia and Reston.

In the selection of a section of Glen Rock as the matching community for Radburn, relevant information was assembled from the 1960 Census and from local informants. Glen Rock is the community north of Fairlawn where Radburn

---

[5]For a complete discussion of the planning of Radburn, see Clarence S. Stein, *Toward New Towns for America*, New York: Reinhold Publishing Corporation, 1957.

is located. Data from the 1960 Census indicate its comparability to Fairlawn. The following information seems most relevant:

	Total Population	Median Years School Completed	Median Family Income
Fairlawn	39,999	12.1	$ 8,346
Glen Rock	13,000	12.9	11,284

It should be noted that Radburn represents a higher educational and income level than Fairlawn as a whole and therefore was expected to be more in line with Glen Rock.

One section of Glen Rock was carefully checked to delineate an appropriate area for study. The area selected is characterized by single family homes built over a period of 30 years from 1925 to 1955. The average age of homes appeared to be between 25 and 35 years old. At the time of our site visits, houses were selling in the $30,000-$60,000 price range (some higher) with an average in the high 30's. Average family income (as judged by a local realtor) was $13,000-$16,000. Most families appeared to be in their 30's or early 40's and still raising children. (This impression proved to be inaccurate, as will be discussed below.)

Crofton has a different background. Recreation facilities (including an 18-hole golf course, tennis courts and swimming pool) were planned and put in, roads and underground utilities were laid out, a small shopping plaza was built, and sites were provided for schools. Many trees were retained in residential areas during construction. From the point of view of this study it is an advantage that some of the housing in Crofton was built by Levitt since the firm also developed Montpelier. We are interested in differences among communities other than differences in housing.

Montpelier is entirely a Levitt development. Recreation facilities (tennis courts and a swimming pool), roads and underground utilities were laid out, and school sites were provided. It is located near a developing shopping center. It seems reasonable to consider Montpelier moderately planned, though perhaps a shade lower on the continuum of degree of planning than Crofton.

Norbeck is located in Montgomery County, Maryland. The area selected is about one square mile in size and apparently includes six or more subdivisions whose street patterns are only minimally integrated, and then only at the subdivisions' edges. Few shopping facilities exist in the immediate area although brochures for new homes advertised shopping only "minutes away." With few exceptions recreation facilities within the area are limited to private or neighborhood clubs. Although direct access is restricted, the Rock Creek Regional Park is within two miles or less of residents in the Norbeck area.

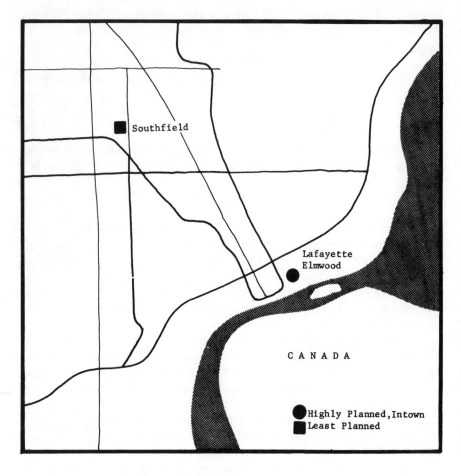

Map 3. Location of Communities in the Detroit Region.

Nowhere in the area is an effort made to separate different modes of travel. In most of the area utilities are overhead along the street. Although a few individual homeowners provide exceptions, it doesn't appear that extensive efforts were made to provide or preserve trees and integrate the natural environment with construction. Other than a small pre-existing business concern contiguous to the southeast corner of the area, no business or industry has been located in the area to complement the "bedroom" function of the suburb.

The part of Southfield, Michigan, selected for the study represents a comparatively unplanned community in the same metropolitan area as Lafayette-Elmwood. Without going into similar detail we may say simply that it, like Norbeck, is a suburban community which lacks most of the 15 characteristics that we regard as associated with a high degree of planning.

We feel reasonably confident of our judgments as to which of our communities are highly planned, which moderately planned, and which show the lowest level of planning. If there is a margin for disagreement it is as to the distinction between moderately planned and less planned, which might be shifted by someone who weighted particular features differently. For example, someone who took the absence of sidewalks especially seriously might rate Montpelier farther down the continuum. Although the distinction between moderately planned and least planned is not central to our study, there is certainly room for further development of methods for ranking communities on a continuum of degree of planning.

2

CHARACTERISTICS OF THE RESIDENTS

This chapter is concerned with the degree of success in the selection of communities to carry out the design of the study. Our central objective, as set forth in Chapter 1, was to select communities which differ in degree of planning but not in other respects. We shall examine, first, the success of the attempt to select communities comparable on four variables which could be estimated in advance of the interviewing: length of residence, type of dwelling, home ownership, and value of dwelling. We shall then turn to two types of characteristics of the residents about which only very limited information was available in advance, their demographic and socioeconomic characteristics, and their personal predispositions.

A. *Evaluating the Attempt to Select Comparable Communities*

Length of residence: The selection of suburban communities began with the new towns. As shown in Table 2, the residents of Columbia in the sample all moved in during the period 1967-1969. Reston is almost as new—8 out of 10 of the residents moved in during these years. Of the moderately planned communities, Montpelier is between Columbia and Reston in length of residence, with 93 percent who moved in during these years. Crofton is slightly older, with 7 out of 10 residents having moved in during 1967-1969.

Norbeck and Southfield, the least planned suburbs, are both older than we would have liked. About half the residents of Norbeck, and 35 percent of the residents of Southfield moved in before 1965. In comparing these communities with those which are more planned we shall have to keep in mind the possibility that this difference in how long the residents have lived there may influence our comparisons.

The two planned communities with central locations are comparatively new. In the Lafayette-Elmwood area two-thirds of the families moved in during

19

Table 2

Housing Characteristics of Sampled Communities
(percentage distributions)

Housing Characteristic	Columbia	Reston	Crofton	Montpelier	Norbeck	Southfield	Lafayette Elmwood	Southwest Washington	Radburn	Glen Rock
Year moved in										
1964 or before	-	*	2	-	52	35	22	-	77	76
1965	-	6	18	-	15	15	4	11	3	5
1966	-	14	10	7	10	24	8	11	8	7
1967	10	21	23	40	9	12	23	17	4	6
1968	48	35	31	39	10	10	27	37	6	5
1969	42	24	16	14	4	4	16	24	2	1
Total	100	100	100	100	100	100	100	100	100	100
Type of dwelling unit										
Single family	76	49	85	100	100	100	-	-	88	98
Townhouse[1]	24	51	15	-	-	-	100	100	12	2
Total	100	100	100	100	100	100	100	100	100	100
Home ownership										
Own	97	90	96	100	99	100	95	34	98	99
Rent	2	10	3	-	1	-	2	64	-	1
Other	1	*	1	-	-	-	3	2	2	-
Total	100	100	100	100	100	100	100	100	100	100
Number of families	216	203	98	105	99	110	106	107	103	106

Table 2 - continued

Housing Characteristic	Columbia	Reston	Crofton	Montpelier	Norbeck	Southfield	Lafayette Elmwood	Southwest Washington	Radburn	Glen Rock
Present value of home (homeowners only)										
Under $32,000	38	7	18	2	39	15	59	-	39	26
$32,000-$37,999	38	22	35	70	39	24	35	11	24	25
$38,000-$43,999	14	24	23	26	13	27	4	23	21	22
$44,000-$49,999	5	21	15	1	6	24	1	20	9	14
$50,000 and over	5	26	9	1	3	10	1	46	7	13
Total	100	100	100	100	100	100	100	100	100	100
Number of homeowners	198	182	94	104	98	110	99	35	101	105
Median home value	$33,900	$43,300	$39,800	$36,100	$33,700	$40,400	$30,900	$48,800	$34,800	$37,800
Rent per month										
Under $200		-						22		
$200-$249		10						19		
$250-$299		75						37		
$300 and over		15						22		
Total	a	100	a	a	a	a	a	100	a	a
Number of renters	4	20	3	0	1	0	2	68	0	1

*Less than one-half of one percent.

[1] Units connected only by a common garage wall as in Radburn are considered single family units here. Otherwise, the definition of townhouse included structures with two or more units having a common wall, separate outdoor entrances, and no dwellings above or below the sampled dwelling.

[a] Too few cases to percentagize.

In this and succeeding tables "-" indicates that no cases were recorded in this cell.

1967-1969 and in Southwest Washington, 78 percent moved in during that period. These two communities, then, are on the average newer than Norbeck and Southfield, but not so new as Columbia.

Radburn, of course, is an older community. Glen Rock turned out to be an excellent match for Radburn in terms of length of residence. In both, three out of four residents had moved in five years or more before the interviewing period. As anticipated, both are examples of suburban communities which not only are much older than the new towns but also are characterized by residents of many years standing.

Type of dwelling: It will be recalled that direct control was exercised over type of dwelling by the exclusion of apartments from consideration in this study. No serious problems arose in executing this decision.

No attempt was made to go one stage farther and locate moderately planned or least planned communities with the same mix of single family houses and townhouses as that found in Columbia and Reston. As it turned out, one housing unit in six in the sample in Crofton is a townhouse, compared to about one in four in Columbia and one in two in Reston. The housing units in the centrally located communities are all townhouses. (We may note parenthetically that there are in both these communities particularly large populations living in apartments which are not considered in this study.) We shall consider in Chapter 5 the reaction of respondents to their townhouses.

Home ownership: Since home owners are likely to respond to their community differently from renters, it is fortunate from a statistical point of view that in nine out of ten communities practically everyone owns his home. The only exception is Southwest Washington in which two out of three families are renters. We shall have to keep this fact in mind in the analysis.

Value of home: Since there are so few renters, economic level is largely a matter of the value of owner-occupied homes. We attempted to match the level of Columbia and Reston in the four other suburban communities. The median value proved to be about $34,000 in Columbia and $43,000 in Reston. The medians for the other four are all in the range from $34,000 to $40,000. We had hardly hoped to do as well.

Again Glen Rock proved a good match for Radburn. The medians are only about $3,000 apart.

The median value for owner-occupied homes in Lafayette-Elmwood, $31,000, is remarkably low, some $10,000 lower than in Southfield, the suburban community in the Detroit area. The prices in Southwest Washington for the small number of owner-occupied units seem particularly high, about $18,000 higher than in Lafayette-Elmwood. Comparisons between these two areas may be influenced by these economic differences. The distribution of the two combined, however, would be reasonably close to that for the other new communities.

We note that we are not dealing with poor communities in this study. In early 1968 the median value for all nonfarm owner-occupied homes in the country was $15,000.[1] Roughly speaking, we are considering communities of homes of two to three times that value.

B. Demographic and Socioeconomic Characteristics of Residents

No attempt was made or could be made in the selection of communities to control directly on the socioeconomic characteristics of the residents. We anticipated, however, that by selecting places of similar age, similar housing cost, and similar location on a central-suburban continuum we would in fact be selecting places inhabited by people with similar characteristics. We were especially interested in whether planned communities attract people with any special characteristics which might condition their responses to these environments. If a unique group of people have been attracted to Reston, for example, their responses to Reston may be different from those of people who are in some relevant sense different from them and who now live elsewhere. The extreme (and unlikely) possibility is that everybody who would like Reston is already there. We can check on these possibilities by examining the characteristics of the people who live in each of the ten communities. In this section we shall examine their income, education, age, stage in the family life cycle, and race. In the next section we shall examine some of their attitudes.

Income: The six suburban communities are roughly similar in income, as one would expect from the similarity in house value (Table 3). The median family income ranges from $17,000 to $20,000. The range, thus, is narrow, and it is noteworthy that the extremes are Columbia and Reston with the other four falling between them. We can make comparisons across these communities without being too greatly concerned about income differences, but we may note that there are considerably more "low" income people in Columbia than Reston if we define "low" income as below $15,000 a year! In the country as a whole median family income was about $7,940 in 1968 according to the 1969 Survey of Consumer Finances.[2]

In Radburn the median income is about $16,000, which is only slightly below the $17,000 for Columbia. We note that incomes in Radburn appear slightly depressed by the fact that there are more people over 65 there than in the new communities. A concentration at the other end of the age distribution explains what seems at first a remarkably low level of incomes in Southwest

---

[1]George Katona, William Dunkelberg, Jay Schmiedeskamp and Frank Stafford, *1968 Survey of Consumer Finances,* Institute for Social Research, The University of Michigan, Ann Arbor, Michigan, 1969.

[2]George Katona, William Dunkelberg, Gary Hendricks and Jay Schmiedeskamp, *1969 Survey of Consumer Finances,* Institute for Social Research, The University of Michigan, Ann Arbor, Michigan, 1970.

Table 3

Characteristics of Community Residents
(percentage distributions)

	Columbia	Reston	Crofton	Montpelier	Norbeck	Southfield	Lafayette Elmwood	Southwest Washington	Radburn	Glen Rock
Family Income										
Under $10,000	5	7	2	2	2	5	3	33	12	17
$10,000-$12,499	13	2	12	3	6	4	11	11	11	3
$12,500-$14,999	22	8	10	16	19	12	11	5	21	9
$15,000-$17,499	12	14	14	15	20	20	9	6	12	16
$17,500-$19,999	19	19	13	20	19	17	6	9	13	9
$20,000-$24,999	16	24	35	31	20	22	28	12	12	19
$25,000-$29,999	8	14	8	9	12	10	15	10	7	9
$30,000 and over	5	12	6	4	2	10	17	14	12	18
Total	100	100	100	100	100	100	100	100	100	100
Median family income	$17,100	$20,000	$19,800	$19,300	$17,900	$18,800	$21,800	$15,400	$16,300	$18,900
Number of families	212	198	96	102	90	107	102	104	98	98
Race of Respondent										
White	85	93	100	96	96	99	77	86	100	98
Black	14	6	-	1	1	-	21	14	-	1
Other	1	1	-	3	3	1	2	-	-	1
Total	100	100	100	100	100	100	100	100	100	100
Number of respondents	216	201	98	103	97	109	104	100	103	106

Table 3 - continued

Life Cycle of Head	Columbia	Reston	Crofton	Montpelier	Norbeck	Southfield	Lafayette Elmwood	Southwest Washington	Radburn	Glen Rock
Under 45; single; no children at home	6	2	1	3	-	1	16	42	-	1
Under 45; married; no children at home	10	9	6	10	2	8	12	8	2	-
Married; youngest child at home under 5	40	37	23	46	30	31	16	19	14	15
Married; youngest child at home 5-14	34	31	41	33	48	36	18	6	35	38
Married; youngest child at home 15 or over	2	5	8	1	8	9	2	2	11	9
45 or over; married; no children at home	5	10	17	3	7	7	23	12	25	25
45 or over; single; no children at home	2	2	2	-	3	6	8	9	7	10
Other (e.g., separated; children at home)	1	4	2	4	2	2	5	2	6	2
Total	100	100	100	100	100	100	100	100	100	100
Number of heads	215	200	98	105	99	110	106	107	103	106
Education of Married Couples										
Neither respondent nor spouse has B.A. degree; NA respondent and/or spouse education	16	11	28	16	43	40	18	12	33	37
Respondent only or spouse only has B.A. degree or more	43	46	48	48	40	40	37	27	41	39
Respondent and spouse have B.A. degree or more	41	43	24	36	17	20	45	61	26	24
Total	100	100	100	100	100	100	100	100	100	100
Number of married couples	200	185	93	100	94	101	76	51	91	92

Table 3 - continued

Age of Head	Columbia	Reston	Crofton	Montpelier	Norbeck	Southfield	Lafayette Elmwood	Southwest Washington	Radburn	Glen Rock
18-24	-	-	1	1	-	1	1	18	-	-
25-34	44	33	16	37	17	18	22	33	10	9
35-44	39	38	47	50	50	45	31	26	27	22
45-54	14	22	23	10	23	22	26	14	26	34
55-64	1	6	10	2	8	11	11	6	22	22
65-74	2	1	3	-	-	2	6	3	13	8
75 or over	*	-	-	-	2	1	3	-	2	5
Total	100	100	100	100	100	100	100	100	100	100
Number of respondents	214	200	98	105	98	110	106	107	103	106
Median age	36	39	42	37	41	41	43	34	50	50

*Less than one-half of one percent.

Washington. A number of housing units in that area proved to be occupied by groups of bachelors who share expenses. For example, several secretaries may live together. Each individual in such a group is a "family" in our system of definitions. Hence, it is not surprising that one family in three in that area has an income below $10,000. Income per capita in a single person family, of course, is likely to be high. Broadly speaking, the economic level of the people seems similarly high across all ten communities.

Education: Given the similarity in income, one would expect similarity in level of education. The facts are otherwise. In both Columbia and Reston the education level is remarkably high. In Columbia 41 percent and in Reston 43 percent of married couples *both* have a bachelor's degree or more. In the moderately planned communities, Crofton and Montpelier, these percentages are 24 and 36, respectively. In the less planned communities, Norbeck and Southfield, the figures are 17 and 20 percent. Averaging within types of community, the percentage of married couples both of whom have a B.A. degree is about 42 percent in the new towns, 30 percent in the moderately planned communities, and 18 percent in the less planned communities.[3]

These large differences in education level, incomes being similar, came as a surprise to the investigators. Such differences in education level are likely to lead to differences in many other social and psychological characteristics which would be noticeable to the people who live in them as well as to the people interested in studying different communities.

It is worth noting explicitly that high education levels among adults cannot possibly be a consequence of where they have lived in the last few years. People who already had high levels of education must have been attracted by the new towns more strongly than they were attracted by Norbeck and Southfield.

We also want to make clear that in our minds no evaluation of the communities is implied by this finding. Education surely is "a good thing" to us, as to most Americans. But it is also worth consideration that people in the other communities have achieved an equally high income without equal educational advantages.

In the two planned communities in the central locations the level of education of married couples is as high as in Columbia and Reston or higher. In both Radburn and Glen Rock, however, only one married couple in four reports that both members have a B.A. degree or more. We would have expected Radburn to score higher than Glen Rock in this respect despite the similarity between the two, since our major finding is a strong association between education and living in a more highly planned community.

---

[3]Of all heads of families in the United States in 1967, according to the Survey of Consumer Finances, only 15 percent had a college degree. By national standards all of the communities we are considering represent concentrations of well educated people.

Age: We expected to find people of about the same age level in the six new suburban communities. The exclusion of apartment dwellers was expected to reduce the variation across communities in the number of young and old people. The median age of the people interviewed is within the range from 36 to 42 years across the six areas. The median for Lafayette-Elmwood, 43 years, also is very close to this range. We have already noted the concentration of young single people in Southwest Washington, where 18 percent are under 25. Since Radburn and Glen Rock are older communities it is not too surprising that the median age iŝ older although our casual impression had been that people in Glen Rock were younger. It is another indication of how close a "match" Glen Rock is for Radburn that the median age is 50 years in both.

The age distributions are closely associated with the distribution by stage in the family life cycle, also shown in Table 3. For example, 42 percent of the "families" interviewed in Southwest Washington are young single people, a category rarely found in townhouses or single family homes in suburban communities. One point is made clear by the family life cycle tabulation but not by the age distribution of heads of families. While families with children over 5 years of age can be found in the inner city planned areas, they are much more common in the suburban communities. For example, in the Detroit area only 20 percent of the families in Lafayette-Elmwood are married couples whose youngest child is over 5, compared to 45 percent in Southfield.

Race: There is a tendency for the more planned communities to contain a higher proportion of black families. The inner city planned communities contain the highest percentage of blacks—21 percent and 14 percent for Lafayette-Elmwood and Southwest Washington, respectively. Columbia and Reston also contain black minorities of 14 and 6 percent, respectively. In the other communities there are very few blacks, 1 percent of the sample or less.

We interpret this result as a consequence partly of the difference in education levels. It has been shown in other research that attitudes toward racial integration are strongly influenced by attending college.[4] It is possible, of course, that other aspects of urban planning may appeal especially to blacks, but we believe that the racial attitudes of the white community are likely to be more important. We would also explain the concentration of blacks in the inner city communities partly as a result of the fact that there are large black populations nearby. The special combination of population groups living in the inner city planned communities seems to us a matter of interest from the point of view of race relations. These communities contain predominantly white families plus black minorities from the upper strata of income and, especially, of education,

---

[4]See Angus Campbell and Howard Schuman, *Racial Attitudes in Fifteen American Cities,* Institute for Social Research, The University of Michigan, Ann Arbor, Michigan, 1968.

living close to the centers of large cities and also close to large populations of low income blacks. From a social point of view it may be that these environments perform an important function by providing this kind of integrated community near the center of large cities.

C. *Social Psychological Predispositions of Residents*

We have considered already the question of whether people of certain demographic and socioeconomic characteristics are attracted to planned communities, and found that, indeed, they are. We now raise a further question: are there also social psychological characteristics of people which tend to predispose some to live in planned residential environments? Are the residents of the planned communities a small, select group unrepresentative of the population in terms of their social psychological predispositions? To this question it is not possible to give a conclusive negative answer since someone may in the future discover differences on dimensions which we have not considered. We have made only a limited attack on the question. Our main conclusion is that while we do find differences in attitudes between residents of planned and less planned areas, the differences we find are about what we would expect in view of the differences in education already presented.

Our results are summarized in Table 4. The correlations among some of our psychological variables and their relation to income and education are shown in Tables 5 and 5a.

Items (1), (2), and (3) were selected to form a scale which measures concern with social standing. As shown in Table 5, the replies to the three questions are correlated with one another, as they should be if all three are measures of one underlying variable. We would not go so far as to say that we have in these items a general measure of all aspects of concern with social position, but we do believe we have at least a crude measure of some dimensions of such a variable. Since the people in the less planned communities with comparatively high incomes for their education must have been working hard to get ahead, we expect them to score high on this measure. In Table 4 we show the sume of the percentages which agree with each of the first three items and the rank order of the communities on this measure. The less planned communities do rank high, and the planned, low.

We speculated that a preference for modern over colonial home architecture might be associated with a preference for a planned community (item 4). As it turns out, the people who agree with a statement expressing a preference for modern are the residents of Lafayette-Elmwood, Southwest Washington and Reston, which are in fact the communities which do contain homes built in the modern style. (The townhouses designed by Mies van der Rohe in Lafayette Park are well known to architectual historians.) The people in one highly planned community, Columbia, however, feel about modern architecture about the same

Table 4

Responses to Psychological Questions by Residents of Different Communities

Item and Summary Statistic	Columbia	Reston	Crofton	Montpelier	Norbeck	Southfield	Lafayette Elmwood	Southwest Washington	Radburn	Glen Rock
1) "The raising of one's social position is one of the most important goals in life."										
Percent of respondents who agree	31	28	48	29	35	43	36	38	30	31
2) "As a rule, you can tell quite a bit about a person by the way he dresses."										
Percent of respondents who agree	44	46	58	49	62	65	48	51	51	58
3) "It is worth considerable effort to assure one's self a good name with important people."										
Percent of respondents who agree	41	32	60	47	57	40	44	55	40	43
(1)+(2)+(3) Sum of Percent Who "Agree" to These Items	116	106	166	125	156	148	128	144	121	132
Rank order	9	10	1	7	2	3	6	4	8	5
4) "A modern style of architecture is more attractive for a new home than a colonial style."										
Percent of respondents who agree	48	64	24	39	43	46	64	62	31	17
5) "We need a lot more freeways in and around our big cities."										
Percent of respondents who agree	67	60	71	62	62	70	59	49	56	73

Table 4 - continued

Item and Summary Statistic	Columbia	Reston	Crofton	Montpelier	Norbeck	Southfield	Lafayette Elmwood	Southwest Washington	Radburn	Glen Rock
6) "As far as you're concerned, do you think it's a good idea for neighborhoods--and here again I'm thinking of clusters of five or six homes--to have people of different religious backgrounds or the same religious backgrounds, or doesn't it matter?"										
Percent of respondents who say good to have people of different religious backgrounds	50	46	28	41	35	40	42	44	46	34
7) "And as far as you're concerned, do you think it's a good idea for neighborhoods to have people of different racial backgrounds or the same racial background or doesn't it matter?"										
Percent of respondents who say good to have people of different racial backgrounds	56	57	17	32	22	26	67	53	26	22
8) "I would enjoy living a year or two in a foreign country."										
Percent of respondents who agree	84	90	81	83	73	72	85	88	74	74
Number of respondents	216	203	98	105	99	110	106	107	103	106

Table 5

Zero Order Correlation Coefficients for Selected Attitudes[1]

Variable	(1)	(2)	(3)	(4)	(5)	Family Income	Respondent's Education
(1) "The raising of one's social position is one of the most important goals in life."	-						
(2) "As a rule, you can tell quite a bit about a person by the way he dresses."	.26	-					
(3) "It is worth considerable effort to assure one's self a good name with important people."	.41	.25	-				
(4) "A modern style of architecture is more attractive for a new home than a colonial style."	.04	.00	-.01	-			
(5) "We need a lot more freeways in and around our big cities."	.20	.08	.20	-.08	-		
Family income	.04	-.02	.01	.00	-.08	-	
Respondent's education	.08	.06	.07	-.10	.08	.11	-

[1]The entries in the table are Pearson product moment correlation coefficients. The psychological variables were coded in the form of four point scales (see the questionnaire for the categories) and these scales were used in the calculations. Missing data were treated by omitting from the calculations those (few) respondents for whom information was incomplete on particular questions.

way as the people in Norbeck and Southfield, the least planned suburban communities.

Another speculation was that people who chose to live in planned communities would share the view of many urban planners that American cities do not need more freeways. As it turns out, the percent who agree with a favorable statement about urban freeways (item 5) is not very different from one type of community to another. Thy percent who are favorably disposed is about the same in, say, Southfield as in Columbia. About half to two-thirds or more of all those interviewed agree with the item.

Attitudes toward having people of different religious backgrounds in the same neighborhood (item 6) do not differ markedly across communities. Attitudes toward a mix of races do differ sharply, as we would expect in view both of the differences in education and actual percentages of black residents (item 7). The greater the degree of planning, the more favorable residents' feelings about having people of different races living in their neighborhood.

There undoubtedly are many other topics on which people's attitudes differ to some degree across communities. As far as we have ascertained,

Table 5a

Zero Order Correlation Coefficients between Selected Attitudes

and Respondent's Education and Family Income [1]

Variable	Correlation with Respondent's Education	Family Income
(6) "As far as you're concerned, do you think it's a good idea for neigh-borhoods -- and here again I'm thinking of clusters of five or six homes -- to have people of different religious backgrounds or the same religious backgrounds, or doesn't it matter?"	-.12	.00
(7) "And as far as you're concerned, do you think it's a good idea for neigh-borhoods to have people of different racial backgrounds or the same racial background or doesn't it matter?"	-.24	-.03
(8) "I would enjoy living a year or two in a foreign country."	-.25	.00

[1] The entries in the table are Pearson product moment correlation coefficients. Items (6) and (7) were coded on three point scales; item (8) on a four point scale (see the questionnaire for the categories). Missing data were treated by omitting from the calculations those (few) respondents for whom information was incomplete on particular questions.

however, these differences would result primarily from the differences in level of education. For example, most people in all ten communities like the idea of living in a foreign country for "a year or two" (item 8), with a liking for living abroad most often expressed in the more planned communities. As noted in Table 5a, feelings about living abroad are correlated with education.[5]

[5] This item was included in the questionnaire as one item for a scale of preference for new and different situations. The "scale" proved to consist of items uncorrelated with each other, and has been omitted from the analysis.

PART II

**PEOPLE'S RESPONSES
TO RESIDENTIAL ENVIRONMENTS**

3

RESIDENTS' OVERALL RESPONSES
TO THEIR COMMUNITIES

Part II of this report is directed at the first of the two project objectives: an assessment of people's overall responses to residential environments and their responses to particular features of these environments. Overall responses are reported in this chapter. Chapter 4 considers the effects of the availability of nearby recreation facilities on participation in seven forms of outdoor recreation. Chapter 5 investigates the effects of neighborhood density, site planning and social homogeneity on neighborhood satisfaction.

The present chapter first reports what people have to say about the appeal of the different communities when they were looking for a place to live. We then present our findings on the current levels of overall satisfaction reported by residents with their communities. We explore the topic of satisfaction with the communities not only by asking for the reasons for each respondent's overall community evaluation, but also by asking for evaluation of the community as a place for the retired, for teenagers, and for children under 12. Finally, to explore the possibility that residents in planned communities are generally happier with their lot in life, we conclude with a brief discussion of reported levels of overall life satisfaction in the communities.

A. *Community Appeal Prior to the Move*

Moving to a new home is a major event in people's lives, and people can recall the experience a few months or years later. The passage of time and the experience of living in the communities we are studying, however, have undoubtedly colored recollections of what was important to the respondents when they were deciding on a place to live. This study was timed so as to gauge with maximum accuracy the responses of people to environments they had

37

experienced, not their expectations before they moved in.[1] We are interested, however, in comparisons of expectations across communities characterized by different degrees of planning. Did people come to Columbia and Reston with different expectations from those that people had when they came to, say, Southfield?

The presence or absence of each of fourteen types of response was coded from answers to an open-ended question: "When you were looking for a place to live what especially appealed to you about coming here?" Note that the responses in Table 6 were stated by people in their own words in reply to a general question. We infer that frequently mentioned reasons allow us to identify the most salient community characteristics.

The general community plan or idea is cited as something that attracted 51 percent of the people in Columbia and 36 percent in Reston. The community concept is mentioned by smaller proportions in the moderately planned suburban areas (Crofton, 22 percent, and Montpelier, 7 percent), and by very few people (1 to 4 percent) in the least planned new suburban areas. Average length of residence is longer for Radburn and Glen Rock so recollections of reasons for moving should be treated cautiously, but 18 percent in Radburn and only 7 percent in Glen Rock mention the general idea of the community or its concept. It is, perhaps, more remarkable that in the highly planned in-town communities only 6 or 7 percent say that when they were looking for a place to live the plan or concept appealed to them. People may, of course, have been attracted by particular features of these planned environments.

One example of this tendency to comment on a particular feature occurs in Radburn. In talking about reasons for moving to Radburn some people mention the town's concept, but the most frequent appeal is the recreation facilities and playgrounds for children. Undoubtedly people are referring to the superblock arrangement with public open space in the center of the superblock.

In the in-town locations nearness to work, shopping and "downtown" are mentioned much more frequently than the community plan as sources of the area's appeal. In Lafayette-Elmwood, for example, 53 percent mention the nearness of work and 42 percent, nearness of shopping, entertainment, or, more generally, nearness of downtown Detroit. People in Southwest Washington speak of similar characteristics as having appealed to them when they were thinking of moving there. People seem very conscious of these locational advantages as

---

[1]Studies of residential behavior using a classic "before and after" design have been infrequent in large part because of the difficulty of selecting an appropriate "before" sample of persons who would be moving into the residential setting under investigation. Gans was able to collect data from a sample of the Levittown residents before their move, for example, with the cooperation of the developer who mailed a questionnaire to families who had bought but not yet moved in. See the appendix in Herbert J. Gans, *The Levittowners*, New York: Random House, 1967.

Table 6

"When you were looking for a place to live what especially appealed to you about coming here?"

(percentage of respondents giving different responses)

	Columbia	Reston	Crofton	Montpelier	Norbeck	Southfield	Lafayette Elmwood	Southwest Washington	Radburn	Glen Rock
Characteristics of the Community										
Liked the town's concept (plan, idea, image, philosophy)	51	36	22	7	1	4	7	6	18	7
Recreation facilities available for children; playgrounds	7	7	5	1	-	-	-	1	26	-
Good schools	11	2	-	4	23	26	8	5	7	44
Liked the (nice) type of people, neighbors	18	11	8	12	14	14	26	36	23	21
General or unspecified appeal of town, area	6	6	10	10	9	16	6	8	10	18
Characteristics of the Location										
Nearness of work	22	11	18	48	20	30	53	43	15	21
Nearness to shopping, entertainment, downtown	19	12	22	21	16	20	42	36	21	25
Nearness to country, outdoor recreation, "nature"	9	38	39	13	15	10	4	6	20	12
Desire for a small neighborhood; peace and quiet; no congestion	6	20	13	10	8	6	1	4	9	17
Characteristics of the Dwelling or Lot										
A good price on home (or lot)	11	8	17	37	23	16	4	6	12	8
Home (or lot) has enough space for activities, play, etc.	5	5	7	21	17	12	16	10	9	11
House (or lot) well planned; well laid out	2	8	7	18	12	14	8	6	4	8
Few(er) problems with maintenance	1	2	1	-	2	-	18	4	2	1
Contemporary style; architecture; newness of home	4	11	2	6	3	1	8	10	-	1
Number of respondents	216	203	98	105	99	110	106	107	103	106

reasons for selecting in-town planned communities as places to live.

In Montpelier, nearness to work was the attraction mentioned most often (48 percent), even though the mean distance (10.8 miles) and median time (43 minutes) for Montpelier journeys to work are not exceptionally short as will be discussed in Chapter 6. Montpelier people also mentioned aspects of the house and lot more frequently than community characteristics—"good price on home" (37 percent), "home has adequate space" (21 percent), and "home well planned" (18 percent).

This emphasis on features of the individual house or lot seems to characterize all three of the six new suburban communities located toward the less planned end of the continuum. People in Montpelier place unusual stress on the amount of house for the money, reflecting no doubt the reputation of the Levitt organization in the building field, but people also recall their reasons for moving in much more often in terms of the house or lot than do people in the planned communities. In the terms of Chapter 1, emphasis is on planning house and lot rather than neighborhood or community.

We can also read Table 6 to find for each community the rank order of reasons people give for coming there to live. The most frequently voiced reason for Reston's appeal was not its plan (36 percent), but its proximity to "nature," outdoor activities, and the countryside (38 percent). Indicative of the importance of this aspect of Reston are the additional responses (20 percent) which emphasized a desire for peace and quiet and a lack of urban congestion. Surprisingly, these latter responses for Reston are quite unlike those for Columbia and resemble what many people say about reasons for moving to Crofton.

In the context of the differences in education level across our communities noted in Chapter 2, it is also surprising to find that "good schools" were an attraction for residents in the less planned communities where the parents' education level is lowest and are seldom mentioned as a factor in the communities where the parents' education level is highest. We can only speculate on the reasons for this finding. It may be, first, that people in the communities with relatively lower education levels believe that, despite their own high incomes, education is the key to success for their children. Second, the people with more education in the highly planned areas may take for granted that the education facilities provided will be of high calibre. Third, "good schools" may be an euphemism for predominantly "white schools." We have shown earlier that the percentage of respondents who say it is a good idea for neighborhoods to have people of different racial backgrounds is relatively low in Glen Rock, Norbeck, and Southfield. People in these communities most often mention "good schools" as the reason for moving there. Finally, school facilities in the new, more planned communities were either non-existent or very new when most of our respondents moved in, so that it was hardly possible for the schools

Figure 1. The availability of Radburn parks, playgrounds and recreation facilities was mentioned most often as the reason for moving to Radburn. (Photograph by Robert W. Marans)

to have established a reputation.

We have included in Appendix E tables showing the rank order for each community of the factors most often cited as sources of its appeal. In brief, people give very different reasons for going to live in planned versus less planned suburban communities. For the new towns they stress the plan, idea, or concept of the community or nearness to the country or outdoor recreation. People in the less planned new suburban areas stress features of the individual house or lot and the schools. The same comparison holds between Radburn and Glen Rock: people chose Radburn because of the plan or the park or the recreation facilities; Glen Rock, because of the schools. People report that they selected the in-town planned areas either because of the advantages of closeness to urban facilities or because of the people who live there.

It seemed natural after a question about their expectations to ask people whether living in the area had worked out about as they expected, better than they expected, or not as well. This question, however, was asked only of those who had moved in during the five years before the interview, since it seemed difficult to ask longer term residents for initial reactions to the community when they moved in as distinct from their current evaluations. (We shall turn to current assessments in the next section.)

It turns out in Table 7 that most people who moved in after 1964 say they found things more or less as they expected them or better than expected. In the two most planned areas what worked out well may often be the plans or programs of the developer (16 percent in Columbia, 8 percent in Reston). There are also 9 to 10 percent who make negative comments about how these plans worked out in Columbia and Reston. In Crofton some 19 percent speak of plans not working out while only 1 percent comment favorably. There seems to be a greater sense of things not working out as planned among Crofton residents than among people in any other community studied.

In the other three new suburban communities few people comment favorably or otherwise on community plans. Their most frequent comments concern their neighbors. In all communities people speak of finding their neighbors friendly, helpful, or generally nice much more often than the reverse. If anything, references to the neighbors are more positive in the less planned than in the more planned suburban communities.

In the in-town communities the most frequent comments are about the location, which, it will be recalled, was also important in people's initial expectations. Few people report disappointments about the central city location.

In general, people's comments about how their expectations worked out more or less reflect the differences in the initial expectations with which they approached different communities. In the less planned areas they talk less about community plans and more about their individual homes; in central locations they discuss accessibility and, occasionally, crime and delinquency. There is a general tendency for people to report that their personal relations with their neighbors worked out as well as or better than expected.

B. *Community Satisfaction*

Obtaining a measure of people's current satisfaction with their communities which would be comparable for all our communities presented methodological problems. We wanted to be able to pose a question about satisfaction in the same way for all respondents and, within each community, have some assurance that respondents were reacting to the same area. A straightforward question asking the respondent to evaluate his community would obviously have meant different things to different people. Although in seven of the ten communities the area sampled more or less corresponded with the boundaries of a named area, in the less planned communities (Norbeck, Southfield and Glen Rock) our sample areas were only subsets of larger communities and these subsets, as far as we know, do not have single names in common use that could have been used in questions posed to our respondents. Even in the planned areas there are

Table 7

The Fate of Expectations about Moving to the Present Location

(percentage distributions of respondents who moved in after 1964)

	Columbia	Reston	Crofton	Montpelier	Norbeck	Southfield	Lafayette Elmwood	Southwest Washington	Radburn	Glen Rock
How Expectations Worked Out										
Better than expected	25	30	19	31	11	16	30	23	53	28
About as expected	57	43	64	62	74	76	66	61	42	68
Better in some ways, not in others	9	15	1	3	2	-	3	6	5	-
Not as well as expected	9	12	16	4	13	8	1	10	-	4
Total	100	100	100	100	100	100	100	100	100	100
Things Which Worked Out Well or Better Than Expected										
Plans, programs of developers working out	16	8	1	4	-	3	4	4	-	-
Convenience of location (job, shopping, friends, etc.)	9	15	19	23	5	17	37	34	32	20
Neighbors are friendly, helpful, nice	20	19	20	22	24	31	16	22	32	16
Quality of schools is excellent, good	4	2	1	1	9	15	-	-	5	16
Lack of crime, delinquency	1	-	-	-	-	-	-	6	5	-
House and/or lot worked out well	3	2	9	10	20	4	9	7	5	4
Peaceful, quiet, uncongested	2	5	4	1	4	-	4	2	5	4
Other mentions	7	12	4	6	4	3	12	3	11	8
No mention of things which worked out "well" or "better"	38	37	42	33	34	27	18	22	5	32
Total	100	100	100	100	100	100	100	100	100	100

Table 7 - continued

Things Which Worked Out Poorly or Less Well Than Expected	Columbia	Reston	Crofton	Montpelier	Norbeck	Southfield	Lafayette Elmwood	Southwest Washington	Radburn	Glen Rock
Plans, programs of developers not working out	9	10	19	2	-	3	3	-	-	-
Inconvenient location (job, shopping, friends, etc.)	5	9	10	4	11	1	1	3	-	4
Neighbors not friendly, helpful	2	5	2	1	5	4	-	2	5	-
Quality of schools is poor, not good	1	1	1	2	-	-	-	3	-	12
Area suffers from crime, delinquency	1	-	-	-	-	-	1	8	-	-
House and/or lot disappointing, hasn't worked out well	1	4	1	4	5	3	4	9	-	-
High cost of living	1	2	1	3	13	3	-	-	-	4
Polluted, noisy, congested	-	1	1	2	4	4	-	-	-	-
Other mentions	3	1	1	1	2	2	1	3	-	-
No mention of things which worked out "poorly" or "less well than expected"	77	67	64	81	60	80	90	72	95	80
Total	100	100	100	100	100	100	100	100	100	100
Number of respondents who moved in after 1964	215	201	96	105	45	71	83	105	19	25

problems. For some in Lafayette-Elmwood, for example, "community" might imply only Lafayette Park. Even more seriously, for others it might imply greater Detroit. We foresaw similar problems had we asked about the new towns by name. For persons living near Lake Anne, for example, "Reston" might include only the Lake Anne Village area, while for those in Hunters Woods it might imply only *their* village area.

The method we adopted was to define areas ourselves and show each respondent a map of an outlined area which we wished to have him evaluate as "a place to live." Details of the criteria used in preparing the "community" maps together with reduced copies used in the interviews are presented in Appendix B. The question used in conjunction with the maps was:

> I'd like to ask you how you feel about this area as a place to live—I mean the area outlined on the map (SHOW MAP). From your own personal point of view, would you rate this area as a place to live as excellent, good, average, below average, or poor?

Note that the word "community" does not appear in this question. While we might have hesitated to rely on people's ability to read a map if we had been interviewing a population with a low level of education, we felt reasonably confident that the people we were studying would understand us.

The overall evaluations appear in the first section of Table 8. Of the ten communities, Reston receives the highest evaluation with 61 percent of the respondents rating it "excellent." Three other planned communities also score high: Columbia with 52 percent excellent; Lafayette-Elmwood, 53 percent; and Radburn, 54 percent. We find a general tendency for degree of planning to be associated with high overall ratings. But there are exceptions. Particularly low overall ratings were received by moderately planned Montpelier (only 18 percent excellent) and highly planned Southwest Washington (only 26 percent excellent). The score for Glen Rock, 49 percent, is very close to the 54 percent for Radburn. Considering only this pair of communities a difference of about 16 percentage points would be needed for statistical reliability with our size of sample. We observe a difference of 5 percent—a difference in the predicted direction, it is true, but hardly an impressive difference from a statistical point of view. Possible reasons for these ratings will arise as additional data are discussed.

For households with members of the appropriate age, parallel questions were asked about the community as a place for the retired, for teenagers, and for children under 12. Although the number of observations rating the communities as places for retired persons is small, in only one community, Reston, is this rating as high as the overall rating. Lafayette-Elmwood also scores about as high for the retired as for people generally. We purposely excluded apartment dwellings to reduce the proportion of our sample at both early and late stages of

Table 8

Satisfaction with the Mapped Area Overall and for the Retired, the Teenagers, and the Children under 12

(percentages of all respondents and of those respondents living in households having someone 55 or more years old, 12-17 years old, and 0-11 years old, respectively)

	Columbia	Reston	Crofton	Montpelier	Norbeck	Southfield	Lafayette Elmwood	Southwest Washington	Radburn	Glen Rock
Mapped Area Rated Overall as:										
Excellent	52	61	42	18	41	36	53	26	54	49
Good	40	33	39	51	44	49	39	59	37	38
Average	6	4	13	22	13	12	6	10	7	9
Below average; poor	2	2	6	9	2	3	2	5	2	4
Total	100	100	100	100	100	100	100	100	100	100
Number of respondents	208	198	98	104	97	108	102	106	102	105
Mapped Area Rated for Retired as Excellent	44	61	24	-	36	21	50	12	33	22
Number of respondents living in households having someone 55 or more years old	16	18	17	6	14	19	20	8	36	37
Mapped Area Rated for Teenagers as Excellent	30	15	12	19	38	51	57	-	40	26
Number of respondents living in households having someone 12-17 years old	50	54	32	21	56	40	14	3	35	43
Mapped Area Rated for Children Under 12 as Excellent	77	79	54	35	37	50	42	9	87	42
Number of respondents living in households having someone under 12 years old	157	135	54	80	67	60	29	23	45	38

the life cycle. As a result our sample of households with persons age 55 or over is small and may not be representative of the opinions of many in this age bracket in our communities. Even with this limitation of our data, however, it appears that most of the communities we selected have not been completely effective in satisfying needs of the older citizen. It seems characteristic of the new areas to have a small proportion of households containing people aged 55 or over. Only in Radburn and Glen Rock do a third or more of households contain people in this age range. Between these two, Radburn rates better for the retired. There is evidence, however, that the planned communities rate better than the less planned, on the average, as places for retired people.

From the teenagers' point of view, as reported by their parents,[2] the planning that went into Reston (only 15 percent excellent), Crofton (12 percent) and Montpelier (14 percent) has not been a success. Columbia fares slightly better (30 percent), but the most congenial of the peripheral areas are less planned Norbeck (38 percent) and Southfield (51 percent). We shall return to the question of why the least planned suburban communities are rated best for teenagers, but we may suggest immediately that the problem rises from the comparative isolation of the planned areas. There are very few families with teenagers in the inner city communities so that the data are no more than suggestive, but the few people who do rate Lafayette-Elmwood rate it high. It is an interesting question why there are so few people with teenage children in the inner city areas. We did not attempt to interview people who have moved away. We can only offer the suggestion based on casual conversations with residents, that once children leave the local elementary school the inner city school system seems inadequate to parents of high socioeconomic status.

For children under 12, the highly planned communities outside the central cities definitely rate very highly. In Radburn, 87 percent of the respondents with young children rate the area excellent. Reston (79 percent) and Columbia (77 percent) were the communities with the next highest ratings. The highly planned centrally located communities do not rate highly for children under 12. Southwest Washington actually received the lowest rating (9 percent excellent) of all ten communities.

In considering the four sets of ratings jointly, we have found it natural to

---

[2]Interviewers were reminded to stress that we wanted the teenagers' viewpoint, not the parents'. Responses which were clearly the parents' viewpoints are omitted.

ask how closely the different ratings are related to each other. The entries in the table below are zero-order correlation coefficients.

Evaluation Variables Correlated	r	N (pairs)
Overall - Retired	.32	189
Overall - Teenagers	.32	338
Overall - Children 0-11	.30	671
Retired - Teenagers	-.02	39
Retired - Children 0-11	.36	31
Teenagers - Children 0-11	.23	210

The matrix provides no surprises. A moderately strong intercorrelation exists among the component evaluation measures and with the overall measure. Thus, people who rate a community high in general also rate it high for different subgroups of the population. There is one exception. Areas which are satisfying for teens are not satisfying for retired people. These results are consistent with our initial expectation that people of different ages have different needs. Respondents are able to distinguish among these needs and rate the same community differently for different age groups.

As we have seen, the planned suburban areas tend to be rated higher for people generally than the less planned areas. For children under 12 the planned suburban communities are rated very highly by parents. For teenagers these communities are not a spectacular success—the least planned communities are rated as well or better. For retired people it may be too early to judge the newer communities, but Radburn is rated better than Glen Rock. The inner city planned areas present a complex picture. Lafayette-Elmwood is rated well, overall, much higher than Southwest Washington. For young children the Southwest is rated very low indeed, and Lafayette-Elmwood only moderately high. There are few teenagers in either, virtually none in Southwest Washington, but those few families with teenagers in Lafayette-Elmwood seem satisfied with the area. There are also very few families with anyone over 55 in the Southwest. Those in Lafayette-Elmwood rate the area highly for retired people.

The reasons respondents gave for their overall evaluations of the community are summarized in Table 9. We have found it helpful to group these comments under three main headings which refer to the transportation system including considerations of location and accessibility; to environmental quality, including landscaping, architecture, and the like; and to other community and neighborhood characteristics. As with Table 6, it is helpful to scan both the columns (communities) and rows (reasons) of the table to grasp the relative impact of the factors mentioned in the different communities.

Table 9

Reasons for Evaluating the Mapped Area Overall Positively or Negatively

(percentage of respondents giving different responses)

	Columbia	Reston	Crofton	Montpelier	Norbeck	Southfield	Lafayette Elmwood	Southwest Washington	Radburn	Glen Rock
Positive Mentions										
Community and neighborhood reasons										
Physical facilities in the area are planned, provided for, accessible; town is planned	22	27	15	10	13	10	14	9	14	10
Good schools	9	3	1	15	24	27	4	3	8	19
Recreation facilities available for play, etc.	2	4	5	1	1	4	1	-	11	4
Neighbors are "friendly," "desirable," "nice"	8	12	9	10	23	24	33	17	25	22
Area is safe from crime; traffic	5	10	8	2	5	5	8	9	11	7
Area has good public services	1	1	1	2	3	4	2	-	1	13
General or unspecified appeal of the area	7	5	5	6	6	10	8	7	4	12
Transportation system reasons										
Accessibility of job, stores, downtown, etc.	47	28	48	49	48	56	63	58	53	44
Good bus service or other public transportation	2	2	2	4	3	1	12	6	19	17
Good access to freeways	5	3	3	10	8	20	13	5	8	2
Environmental quality reasons										
Area has trees, hills, lakes, etc.	13	24	7	8	3	3	2	2	4	7
Plenty of space, little or no congestion	12	23	14	9	7	7	7	2	7	5
Area is quiet; free of pollution	3	5	9	2	3	8	5	2	2	12
Attractive architecture	3	4	-	2	7	7	6	19	4	4
Property is well kept up	*	1	2	1	1	11	1	2	6	8
General beauty, attractiveness of the area	11	13	2	3	5	3	2	4	1	3
Negative Mentions										
Physical facilities not well planned, inadequate, etc.	5	4	6	20	-	5	4	5	2	1
Inconvenient or inaccessible to job, stores, etc.	6	18	10	10	8	2	2	2	6	1
Crowded, not much space available	1	2	-	14	5	3	-	1	4	5
Reference to crime; lack of traffic safety	-	*	1	4	2	-	5	17	2	5
Number of respondents	216	203	98	105	99	110	106	107	103	106

*Less than one-half of one percent.

In every community the reason most often cited for positive evaluation is good accessibility to job, shopping and other facilities. The emphasis on these considerations is interesting in itself. People do not think of themselves as living within the confines of our "communities," and our findings in later chapters about the frequency of weekend travel, miles driven per annum, and the like, show that they do move about a great deal. The relation of their area to the rest of the metropolitan region, accordingly, is a matter of concern to them.

Had our coding of positive "accessibility" responses been more sensitive (i.e., job and shopping accessibility treated separately) differences might have become apparent. Even with this coding scheme, however, something can be said about differences across communities. Positive mentions of accessibility are made by only about half as many Reston residents as anyone else. In addition, 18 percent of Reston's respondents made specific negative comments about accessibility, about twice as many as were made anywhere else. We will show in Part III that there is a firm basis for these responses. In brief, more than half (51 percent) of Reston's employed heads of household commute over 45 minutes to get to work, and almost two-thirds of the families (64 percent) must travel ten minutes or more to reach their most frequently used grocery store. (What remains to puzzle us after referring to Part III are the uncomplaining residents of Crofton, the only community less conveniently located on the average for both work and shopping than Reston!) Despite these problems with accessibility, however, Reston was the most highly rated overall of all the communities. Reston residents often mention the planned nature of the community (27 percent), various aspects of the physical environment, the surrounding trees, hills and lakes (24 percent), and the adequacy of space and lack of congestion (23 percent). In comparison with the responses in Table 6 it would appear that the characteristics of the area which appealed prior to moving into Reston have turned out to be bases of satisfaction as well, namely the appeal of being near "nature," the countryside, and "peace and quiet."

In Columbia, on the other hand, where 51 percent of the respondents mentioned the community's concept and plan as an appeal to moving in, less than half that number (22 percent) mention this plannedness as a source of satisfaction after living in the community. It is also of interest that fewer residents mentioned having "friendly" or "desirable" neighbors in Columbia than in any of the other communities. "Nice neighbors," was most often cited in Lafayette-Elmwood and was the second most frequently mentioned reason after "nearness to job, shopping and downtown" in that community.

In the less planned suburban communities the principal sources of satisfaction after accessibility were "friendly neighbors" and "good schools." It appears that the quest for good educational facilities which respondents mentioned as a reason for moving to these areas has been rewarded.

Several reasons for the low overall rating of Southwest Washington are

Figure 2. The quality of the physical environment in Reston contributed to the high overall rating by its residents. They often mentioned the trees, hills, and lakes in the surrounding environment. (Photograph by Robert W. Marans)

suggested in the table. First, roughly one-sixth of the respondents mention crime and safety as a cause for concern in the area. Second, and perhaps more important, is that, except for nearness to work and shopping, the only other frequently mentioned source of satisfaction is attractive architecture. Not much else seems to stand out in people's minds.

In addition to the tables summarizing the sources of each communities' appeal for the residents when looking for a place to live, we have included in Appendix E similar tables indicating which factors were most often cited as sources of community satisfaction once the residents had experienced the environment.

We proceed to brief discussions of the reasons volunteered for the evaluations of the communities as places to live for the different age groups. As Table 10 indicates, a key reason for the relatively low evaluation of our sampled communities for the retired is the cost of living these people must cope with. Among the communities studied, the more planned seem to be rated higher for the retired than the less planned. While the cost of living is generally a cause of dissatisfaction, the facilities and activities available as well as the adequacy of transportation to these facilities are apparently prime sources of satisfaction for some residents and of dissatisfaction for others in the same community. In Crofton, for example, transportation or accessibility is mentioned favorably by 26 percent of the residents questioned—and unfavorably by 26 percent as well. To clarify the impact of these items in the ten communities we include in the lowest third of Table 10 the *net* percent positive mentions referring to each of these factors.

On the basis of net positive mentions of facilities and available activities, the more planned communities are generally rated well for retired people. Radburn, however, seems unimpressive in this respect—there are about as many negative as positive comments about activities and facilities for older people. Comments about transportation facilities in the more planned communities were again more favorable. In Crofton, however, negative responses cancelled out the positive responses. In transportation facilities and activities planned communities have an advantage over less planned for retired people.

As we noted above, teenager satisfaction with the community is not related to plannedness. Respondent reports show more ambivalence than appeared in the evaluation for retired persons. In the planned communities both positive and negative comments are frequent about facilities and activities for this age group. The row, "Total Percent Net Positive Mentions," in Table 11 shows the absence of a relationship between highly planned communities and teenager satisfaction. We will disregard Southwest Washington here because of the small number of interviews with families with teenagers (although the small proportion of teenage children is itself an understandable source of teenager dissatisfaction). Apart from Southwest Washington, the community with the

Table 10

Reasons for Evaluating the Mapped Area for Retired Persons Positively or Negatively[1]

(percentage of respondents living in households having someone 55 years of age or older giving different responses)

	Columbia	Reston	Crofton	Montpelier	Norbeck	Southfield	Lafayette Elmwood	Southwest Washington	Radburn	Glen Rock
Positive Mentions										
Good transportation and accessibility to shopping, church, etc.	38	55	26	a	14	20	64	a	35	9
Facilities or activities available	31	55	32	a	-	5	32	a	12	9
Quietness, peacefulness	6	10	5	a	21	20	4	a	2	2
Nice neighbors or other people in community	12	15	5	a	21	20	18	a	20	11
Low or reasonable cost of living	-	-	5	a	7	5	4	a	5	-
Negative Mentions										
Inadequate transportation and accessibility	6	20	26	a	29	10	-	a	-	9
Lack of facilities or activities	6	15	10	a	7	5	-	a	10	7
Crime and safety of person and property	-	-	-	a	-	-	9	a	-	-
Lack of traffic safety	-	-	-	a	14	-	-	a	-	-
High cost of living	19	15	21	a	50	45	23	a	42	77
Net Percent Positive Mentions Referring to:										
Facilities or activities	25	40	22	a	-7	0	32	a	2	2
Transportation and accessibility	32	35	0	a	-15	10	64	a	35	0
Percent of households having someone 55 years of age or older	7	10	19	6	14	18	21	9	39	42
Number of households having someone 55 years of age or older	16	20	19	6	14	20	22	10	40	44

[1] The questions were: "For retired people how would you rate this area as a place to live? Would you say it was excellent, good, average, below average, or poor? In what ways?"

[a] Too few cases to percentagize.

Table 11

Reasons for Evaluating the Mapped Area for Teenagers Positively or Negatively[1]

(percentage of respondents living in households having someone 12-17 years of age giving different responses)

	Columbia	Reston	Crofton	Montpelier	Norbeck	Southfield	Lafayette Elmwood	Southwest Washington	Radburn	Glen Rock
Positive Mentions										
Facilities and activities	38	30	44	27	24	52	29	a	60	50
Transportation and accessibility	19	8	19	14	26	39	57	a	26	20
Companionship and friendship	12	13	31	27	22	39	64	a	34	26
Schools, teachers, coursework	6	3	6	23	14	34	7	a	-	15
General or unspecified positive responses	17	10	-	18	7	7	29	a	11	11
Negative Mentions										
Lack of facilities or activities	25	51	39	27	22	7	-	a	20	26
Lack of transportation or accessibility	15	28	28	14	21	7	-	a	11	2
Lack of companionship or friends	4	10	8	4	3	9	21	a	6	11
Dissatisfaction with schools, teachers, coursework	5	7	3	9	-	-	14	a	-	4
General or unspecified negative responses; indifference	10	10	-	4	3	-	-	a	11	9
Net Percent Positive Mentions Referring to:										
Facilities and activities	13	-21	5	0	2	45	29	a	40	24
Transportation and accessibility	4	-20	-9	0	5	32	57	a	15	18
Companionship and friendship	8	3	23	23	19	30	43	a	28	15
Schools, teachers, coursework	1	-4	3	14	14	34	-7	a	0	11
General or unspecified responses	7	0	0	14	4	7	29	a	0	2
Total percent net positive mentions	33	-42	22	51	44	148	151	a	83	70
Percent of households having someone 12-17 years of age	24	30	37	21	59	40	13	5	34	43
Number of households having someone 12-17 years of age	52	61	36	22	58	44	14	5	35	46

[a]Too few cases to percentagize.

lowest evaluation in Table 11 is, by a large margin, highly planned Reston. Columbia fares somewhat better, but the fact that Southfield and Lafayette-Elmwood are the most amenable communities for teens is the primary message of the table. The reasons which differentiate these areas of high satisfaction from the less amenable locations seem primarily related to the adequacy of nearby facilities and activities and to the availability of transportation to them. Friends and companions seem more easily accessible to teenagers in the less planned suburban communities than in the most highly planned.

The evaluations of the ten communities as places for children under 12 to live reported in Table 8 indicate that Radburn, Reston and Columbia received particularly high ratings while Southwest Washington received a particularly low evaluation. Our discussion of Table 12 will focus on these four areas to attempt to delineate the ways in which they differ markedly from our other communities and to explain the success of the first three as places for young children to live.

Southwest Washington differs from the other nine locations in a number of ways. Few respondents made positive references to the adequacy of facilities, programs, or activities for young children in the area. Traffic safety, schools and other children nearby to play with were favorably mentioned least often by the parents here. In fact, one-third made *negative* comments about school quality in the area, a proportion about 3 1/2 times greater than in any other community. In relative terms, Southwest Washington ranks "best" only for having its schools nearby—18 percent of the residents mention this as a positive factor. In all, it seems that negative feelings toward the schools available in Southwest Washington are not significantly offset by any positive aspects of the area—hence its low overall rating for children under 12.

Reasons for the high ratings of Radburn, Reston and Columbia are complex because several different aspects of a community may be considered important by parents and these places are not alike in all respects. In Columbia, for example, more residents with young children (38 percent) mention "good schools" as a source of satisfaction than any other factor, but schools are mentioned relatively seldom in Reston (15 percent) and Radburn (4 percent). Conversely, traffic safety is mentioned relatively seldom in Columbia (13 percent), but is the most frequent mention in Reston (31 percent) and frequently noted in Radburn as well (31 percent). Crofton, the community rated fourth highest for young children, had the largest proportion to mention traffic safety (37 percent). As for the general category of programs and activities, Radburn generally leads with the sum of the mentions of this type being 65 percent. Crofton and Columbia follow, however, with sums of 41 percent and 38 percent, respectively, while Reston ranks fourth with but 26 percent.

A similar summing of positive responses about facilities and play areas, however, does differentiate the three highly ranked communities from the other

Table 12

Reasons for Evaluating the Mapped Area for Children under 12 Positively or Negatively[1]

(percentage of respondents living in households having someone under 12 years of age giving different responses)

	Columbia	Reston	Crofton	Montpelier	Norbeck	Southfield	Lafayette Elmwood	Southwest Washington	Radburn	Glen Rock
Positive Mentions										
Facilities and play space										
Parks, playgrounds, pools are provided	27	22	7	22	3	18	22	15	38	13
Open fields, woods, etc. available	15	27	6	7	2	3	-	4	-	3
General positive reference to available play space	13	18	15	10	9	3	6	4	9	10
Programs and activities										
Social or cultural programs available	15	10	11	5	6	3	3	4	16	10
Athletic programs, teams available	5	6	15	4	6	3	-	-	13	8
General positive mention; "Kids have plenty to do."	18	10	15	10	4	5	-	-	36	3
Other characteristics of the area										
Safe from traffic	13	31	37	14	16	18	19	4	31	13
Good schools	38	15	6	35	34	40	28	-	4	33
Schools are nearby, within walking distance	16	5	20	9	24	18	6	18	9	8
Companionship, friends, nice children to associate with	24	29	26	43	27	53	47	18	24	33
Negative Mentions										
Lack of available play space	2	4	11	5	9	14	12	11	-	3
Lack of safety from traffic, crime	2	1	2	5	7	-	12	11	-	8
Negative reference to school quality	1	2	2	7	3	-	9	33	-	3
Percent of households having someone under 12	73	67	55	77	68	56	30	25	44	37
Number of households having someone under 12	157	136	54	81	67	62	32	27	45	39

[1]The question was: "As a place to raise children under 12 how would you rate this area - would you say it was excellent, good, average, below average, or poor?"

Figure 3. The attractive architecture was one reason why residents in Southwest Washington evaluated their area positively. Nevertheless, the community's overall rating and the rating of the area for children under 12 were relatively low. (Photograph by Robert W. Marans)

seven. In Reston the sum of responses for these items is 67 percent; in Columbia, 55 percent; and in Radburn, 47 percent. (The next community on this basis is Montpelier with a sum of 39 percent for the three responses.) It appears, therefore, that of the factors considered, the provision of easily accessible playgrounds, pools and other facilities, along with other less supervised play areas (fields, woods), contributes significantly to the positive evaluation of planned communities as places for young children to live.

C. Satisfaction With Life

Much of the rhetoric about community planning since the first new town advocate, Ebenezer Howard,[3] has implied that people living in a planned setting would be happier people more satisfied with their overall lives. We attempted to see, therefore, if people in the most planned areas of our sample are appreciably more satisfied with their lives than other residents. We were able to use but a single item to measure life satisfaction, but fortunately the item has demonstrated a degree of reliability and validity in past studies. The item used was:

In general, how satisfying do you find the way you're spending your life these days? Would you call it *completely* satisfying, *pretty* satisfying, *not very* satisfying, or *not at all* satisfying?

Results in two national surveys using this item,[4] after collapsing the least satisfied categories, yielded the following distributions:

	Completely Satisfied	Pretty Satisfied	Not Very or Not at All Satisfied	
1965 Study	24	65	11	= 100%
1968 Study	24	66	10	= 100%

Table 13 presents the results of this question for our communities. Except for Montpelier and Southwest Washington, it is interesting that our communities report smaller proportions of "completely" satisfied persons than the national

---

[3]Ebenezer Howard, *Garden Cities of To-Morrow, 1902.* Reprinted as an M.I.T. Press Paperback, Cambridge: M.I.T. Press, 1965.

[4]Reported in *Measures of Social Psychological Attitudes* by John P. Robinson and Phillip R. Shaver, Survey Research Center, The University of Michigan, Ann Arbor, Michigan, August 1969, Chapter 2.

Table 13

Satisfaction with Life

(percentage distribution of respondents)

"In general, how satisfying do you find the way you're spending your life these days? Would you call it..."	Columbia	Reston	Crofton	Montpelier	Norbeck	Southfield	Lafayette Elmwood	Southwest Washington	Radburn	Glen Rock
Completely satisfying	18	18	16	26	13	14	17	27	19	19
Pretty satisfying	74	76	79	72	78	75	70	63	72	74
Not very or not at all satisfying	8	6	5	2	9	11	13	10	9	7
Total	100	100	100	100	100	100	100	100	100	100
Net Life Satisfaction (percent "completely satisfying" minus percent "not very" or "not at all satisfying")	10	12	11	24	4	3	4	17	10	12
Number of respondents	214	199	97	104	98	110	104	106	102	106

samples.[5] Looking next at the Net Life Satisfaction, comparisons across the ten communities indicate that the less planned peripheral locations do, in fact, have lower levels of life satisfaction. Other differences do not appear systematic. The fact that Montpelier has easily the highest Net Life Satisfaction was a comparative surprise since, as we noted earlier, Montpelier residents were also the *least* satisfied with their community as a place to live. Contemplating these mixed results we are forced to the conclusion that level of life satisfaction is a complex subject. The simple view of the early enthusiasts that people who lived in new towns would be happy underestimates the many forces which impinge upon the lives of the highly educated, high income people who live in the environments we are studying.

---

[5]In the national studies the question was asked orally while in this study it was part of the self-administered questionnaire. This may account, in part, for the lower levels of life satisfaction reported in our study inasmuch as Sudman (*Reducing the Cost of Surveys,* Chicago: Aldine, 1970, p. 57) found, in investigating the effectiveness of self-administered questions in a 1964 NORC national study of Catholics, that "36 per cent of personally interviewed respondents, but only 23 per cent of respondents on the self-administered form, said that they were very happy when the question was asked, 'Taken altogether, how would you say things are these days—would you say that you are very happy, pretty happy, or not too happy?' "

4

OUTDOOR RECREATION

One characteristic of planned environments is the provision of facilities for outdoor recreation within close proximity to people's residences. We shall be concerned with four questions related to outdoor recreation facilities. First, we shall look at the basic relation between distance from facilities and participation in outdoor recreation. Second, we shall attempt to summarize the number, kinds, and location of recreation facilities which exist in the communities studied. Third, we shall attempt to trace the relation between community facilities and the frequency with which people participate in outdoor recreation in each community. Finally, we shall report some limited information on the frequency with which people who participate often in outdoor activities travel distances of two miles or more to arrive at the recreation facilities.

A. *Distance and Frequency of Participation*

Analysts of outdoor recreation customarily posit the existence of a relationship between distance to a facility and use of that facility in which distance plays the same part that price plays in demand curves for consumer goods. Distance is not exactly equivalent to price since it is a measure both of money cost for transportation and of time required to reach a facility. Nevertheless one would ordinarily expect use of a facility to decline with distance just as one expects purchases of a consumer good to decline as its price is increased. One can think of the slope of the curve of relationship in either context.

We may think not just of demand for individual facilities for outdoor recreation, but of demand for categories of facilities. One would prefer that the facilities be identical. It is then possible to think generally of the relationship between distances from people's homes to particular types of facilities and frequency of participation in the associated activities. For example, distance to the nearest tennis court may determine, other things being equal, how often a person plays tennis.

Knowledge of the shape of curves showing relationships of this type, if it could be relied upon, would have a variety of implications for the planning of recreation and related transportation facilities. For example, suppose the demand for swimming pools proved sensitive to distance to the nearest pool. It would follow that the total volume of usage of swimming pools in a community would depend on how close the pools are to the places where people live. Questions of this type arise in the next sections of this chapter.

We have estimated, using maps and site plans, the distance between each respondent's place of residence and the nearest public or semi-public facility for several types of outdoor recreation. The facilities considered are the nearest outdoor swimming pool, the nearest tennis court, the nearest golf course and the nearest marina or boat launching facility. Public facilities are those open to the public at large or to all residents of the community being studied. Facilities such as apartment swimming pools and golf courses associated with country clubs are considered to be semi-public if at least 10 percent of the population in the sample community who participate in that activity use them.

Distances between the center of the micro-neighborhood[1] where the respondent lives and the nearest facility are based on straight-line measurements up to one-eighth mile. Where the distance is more than one-eighth (.125) mile, the minimum road distance is used. These criteria are based on the assumption that, on the average, people living within one-eighth of a mile of a recreation facility will walk to that facility while beyond that distance people will drive.

For people who report that they do engage in an activity we have also estimated the distance to the place where they most often participate. This estimate cannot be made for people who do not participate at all. Yet it is a more satisfactory measure because we are quite certain that the person can use the facility, whereas for semi-public facilities there is some margin of doubt. We can examine the relationship between distance to the facility he uses and how often he reports he does use it.

Results are summarized in Graphs 1, 2, and 3, and in Tables 3 and 4 of Appendix *E*. We shall focus attention on the percentage who participate in each activity five or more times in a year. Graph 1 is based on Table 3 of Appendix *E* and reports the percentage of the total population who participate in different activities as a function of distance to the nearest facility. Graphs 2 and 3 are based on Table 4 of Appendix *E* and refer to the percentage of frequent users of

---

[1]Micro-neighborhood is defined as a cluster of four, five, or six dwellings which face one another on a street or common court. For a discussion of the use of the micro-neighborhood in the measurement of neighborhood satisfaction and in the sampling procedures, see Chapter 5 and Appendix A, respectively.

Graph 1

Percent of Population Who Participate Frequently by Distance to
Nearest Public or Semi-Public Facility

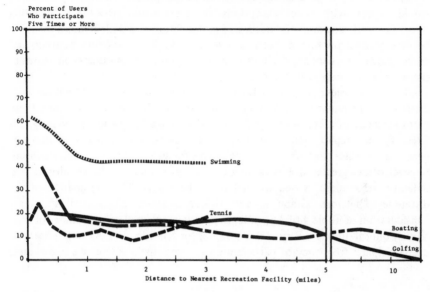

Graph 2

Percent of Users Who Participate Frequently by Distance to
Place Where Respondent Most Often Engaged in
Outdoor Swimming, Tennis, Golfing and Boating

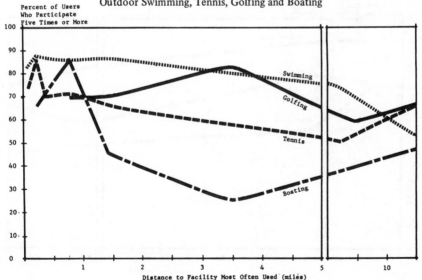

all users as a function of distance to the facility or place most often used.

The results are more easily grasped from the graphs than from a verbal presentation. In Graph 1 all the curves fall as one proceeds to the right, as one would expect, with minor exceptions which we would attribute to sampling error. For golf, however, the decline in participation rate with distance seems to be very gradual up to a distance of over 5 miles. For swimming, boating, and tennis, however, there are declines in participation rates as distance increases in the range up to roughly half a mile or a mile.

If we consider only users for these facilities, as in Graph 2, and measure distance to the facility actually used, results are broadly similar. As before, there is no evidence of a decline for golf up to five miles. Frequency of boating still falls off very rapidly with distance, but the curve now seems to flatten out nearer three miles than one mile. The curves for swimming and tennis also seem to level off at greater distances than before, somewhere in the vicinity of two miles or so, as close as one can tell from these data. The explanation of the differences between Graph 1 and Graph 2 seems apparent from closer consideration of Table 4 of Appendix *E*. A few people will go swimming (or play tennis) only if they are very close to a pool (or tennis court). Among those who do participate, frequency of participation is somewhat less sensitive to distance.

Graph 3

Percent of Users Who Participate Frequently by Distance to
Place Where Respondent Most Often Engaged in
Hiking or Walking, Bicycling and Picnicking

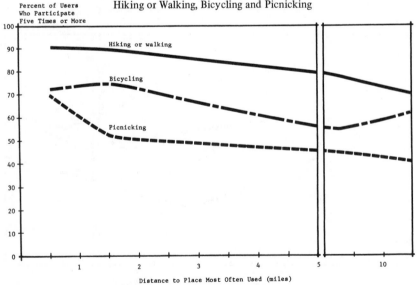

Distance to Place Most Often Used (miles)

In Graph 3 the percentage of people who hike or walk, bicycle, and picnic frequently decline gradually beyond two miles. For hiking and walking, the curve appears nearly level indicating a wide area up to five miles within which people walk at about the same frequency. The frequency of bicycling and picnicking also declines gradually as the distance to the place most often used increases.

B. *Inventory of Outdoor Recreation Facilities by Community*

As stated in Chapter 1, one characteristic of planned communities is the provision of facilities for outdoor recreation within close proximity to people's homes. We have prepared an inventory of facilities for each of our seven types of outdoor recreation by community.

This inventory was compiled from a number of sources. Where available, aerial photographs and illustrative site plans were used as a primary source. For the two communities in the Detroit area, information was gathered from site visits. However, the main source of information in each community was the respondents who use the facilities, and who reported what facilities they use. In addition, assistance was provided by local planners and engineers, representatives of park and recreation planning agencies, real estate people working in the communities, officers of neighborhood associations and former residents of the communities. Representatives of state golf associations and managers of golf courses provided the main source of information for golf courses. Where possible, information was verified by more than one source.

The inventory falls into two sections. The first section, presented in Table 14, provides data for each community. The table lists the number of facilities within one mile of the center of the sample population for swimming and tennis. For golf and boating, it notes the number and availability of facilities within ten miles of the center of the sample population. For hiking or walking and picnicking it notes the availability of facilities within one mile of the center of the sample population.

The one mile distance was used for activities which for the most part are engaged in within a person's community. All sample communities can be encompassed within this radius.[2] The ten mile distance was used for activities which people generally engage in beyond the limits of their immediate environment. The location where each respondent performed each activity was precisely recorded if it were within 10 miles. The selection of this exact distance for this purpose and for the inventory was arbitrary.

---

[2]The population of Reston is located in two neighborhoods approximately 2.5 miles apart. For these neighborhoods, Lake Anne and Hunters Woods, information is provided on facilities available within the specified distance of the center of the sample population. In subsequent analysis of Reston, however, the number of facilities for the two neighborhoods is combined. See Tables 19 through 24.

Table 14

Inventory of Recreation Facilities by Community - Fall, 1969

Activity	Columbia	Reston — Lake Anne	Reston — Hunters Woods	Crofton	Montpelier	Norbeck	Southfield	Lafayette Elmwood	Southwest Washington	Radburn	Glen Rock
Swimming											
Number of outdoor swimming pools within one mile of the center of the sample population[1]	5	4	1	1	1	3	1	2	10	2	1
Tennis											
Number of tennis courts within one mile of the center of the sample population	5	6	2	2	4	4	12	2	23	4	5
Number of locations within one mile of the center of the sample population	1	2	1	1	1	2	2	1	4	1	2
Golf											
Number of golf courses within ten miles of the center of the sample population											
Public and semi-public[2]	3	3	2	2	2	5	11	7	7	8	0
Private[3]	4	8	7	5	11	20	15	5	10	14	15
Total	7	11	9	7	13	25	26	12	17	22	24
Boating											
Availability of marinas or boat launching facilities within one mile of the center of the sample population	Yes	Yes	No	No	No	No	No	No	Yes	No	No
Availability of five or more marinas or boat launching facilities within ten miles of the center of the sample population	No	No	No	Yes	No	No	No	Yes	Yes	No	No

Table 14 - continued

Activity	Columbia	Reston Lake Anne	Reston Hunters Woods	Crofton	Montpelier	Norbeck	Southfield	Lafayette Elmwood	Southwest Washington	Radburn	Glen Rock
Hiking/walking and bicycling											
Availability of internal walkway system with walks that do not parallel streets	Yes	Yes	Yes	No	No	No	No	Yes	Yes	Yes	No
Picnicking											
Availability of picnic facilities within one mile of the center of the sample population[4]	Yes	Yes	a	Yes	No	No	No	Yes	Yes	Yes	Yes

[1]Does not include private pools associated with individual dwellings or pools associated with high-rise and garden apartments unless at least 10 percent of the swimmers in the sample community use the facility.

[2]Includes public and semi-public golf courses and private golf courses if 10 percent of the golfers from the sample community use that facility.

[3]Includes golf courses associated with universities, military installations and golf and country clubs unless at least 10 percent of the golfers from the sample community use the facility.

[4]A picnic facility is defined as a public park containing one or more picnic tables.

[a]Information not available.

The second part of the inventory, the results of which are shown in Tables 15 and 16, takes into account the distance from people's homes to outdoor recreation facilities. These tables show the proportion of the population of each area within different distances of each type of facility. As in the previous section we consider for everyone, users and non-users, distance to the nearest public or semi-public facility. We also estimate for users the distance to the facility they actually use.

We have prepared in Table 17 a set of summary scores by community on availability of outdoor recreation facilities. The total score is the sum of six individual scores, one for each type of facility, each of which can vary from zero to one. In addition, the average proportion of facilities available by community is presented by dividing the total score by the number of activities for which information on facilities is available. Facilities, thus, are assumed to be of equal importance. A more refined scoring system might include other facilities than our list of six, and might assign weights based on relative importance to the different activities. (It would be of interest to explore several systems of scoring developed from the point of view of different age groups using weights which could allow for the different relative importance of different activities for the young and the old.) Nevertheless, we think our system permits meaningful comparisons across communities for the population as a whole.

For the first four activities shown, the score is the proportion of the population who are within a specified distance of the appropriate facility for that activity. We use a half mile for swimming pools and tennis courts. For golf courses and boat launching facilities we use two miles. We do not have measures of distance from each cluster of dwellings to the internal pathway system—such a measure would be of uncertain meaning—the score is simply 1.00 or .00 depending on the presence or absence of such a system in the community. We also have treated public picnic facilities on a community level in the same manner.

We find that there is, as expected, a large difference in the average proportion of outdoor recreation facilities available between planned and less planned areas. The minimum possible value on our scale is .00, which is closely approximated by Southfield with .06, while the maximum possible score is 1.00, with Southwest Washington scoring 0.95.

C. *Frequency of Participation in Outdoor Recreation by Community*

Residents of planned communities might take the benefit from easier access to outdoor recreation facilities in either of two ways. They might increase their participation in outdoor recreation, just as people often increase their consumption of consumer goods if prices fall. Or they might continue to participate in outdoor recreation at about the same level as before, taking the benefit in the form of less time and money spent on getting to the place where

Table 15

Distance from Center of Micro-Neighborhood to the Nearest Public
or Semi-Public Recreational Facility[1,2]
(percentage distribution of respondents)

	Columbia	Reston	Crofton	Montpelier	Norbeck	Southfield	Lafayette Elmwood	Southwest Washington	Radburn	Glen Rock
Distance to Nearest Outdoor Swimming Pool										
Less than .125 miles	18	22	4	15	9	-	6	82	58	-
.125-.249 miles	14	11	-	12	-	-	4	18	9	-
.250-.49 miles	33	28	8	50	12	16	40	-	29	-
.50-.74 miles	18	16	25	23	24	10	50	-	4	7
.75-.99 miles	15	1	42	-	34	30	-	-	-	29
1.00-1.99 miles	2	13	21	-	21	44	-	-	-	64
2 miles or more	-	9	-	-	-	-	-	-	-	-
Total	100	100	100	100	100	100	100	100	100	100
Distance to Nearest Tennis Courts										
Less than .125 miles	-	13	4	15	5	-	-	3	10	-
.125-.249 miles	-	20	-	12	-	5	-	13	7	6
.25-.49 miles	18	12	8	50	19	17	34	53	69	48
.50-.74 miles	11	3	25	23	39	46	49	24	14	43
.75-.99 miles	19	20	42	-	22	16	17	7	-	3
1.00-1.99 miles	49	23	21	-	15	16	-	-	-	-
2 miles or more	3	9	-	-	-	-	-	-	-	-
Total	100	100	100	100	100	100	100	100	100	100

Table 15 - continued

	Columbia	Reston	Crofton	Montpelier	Norbeck	Southfield	Lafayette Elmwood	Southwest Washington	Radburn	Glen Rock
Distance to Nearest Golf Course[3]										
Less than 1.0 mile	49	39	79	-	-	-	-	4	-	-
1.0-1.9 miles	46	25	21	100	-	-	-	96	88	-
2.0-2.9 miles	5	-	-	-	32	3	100	-	12	100
3.0-3.9 miles	-	18	-	-	68	97	-	-	-	-
4.0-4.9 miles	-	9	-	-	-	-	-	-	-	-
5.0-9.9 miles	-	9	-	-	-	-	-	-	-	-
10 miles or more	-	-	-	-	-	-	-	-	-	-
Total	100	100	100	100	100	100	100	100	100	100
Distance to Nearest Marina or Boat Launching Facility										
Less than 1.0 mile	14	39	-	-	-	-	-	85	-	-
1.0-1.9 miles	39	25	-	-	-	-	100	15	-	-
2.0-2.9 miles	25	-	-	-	-	-	-	-	-	-
3.0-3.9 miles	22	19	-	-	7	-	-	-	-	-
4.0-4.9 miles	-	5	100	-	55	-	-	-	-	-
5.0-9.9 miles	-	12	-	-	38	100	-	-	-	-
10 miles or more	-	-	-	100	-	-	-	-	100	100
Total	100	100	100	100	100	100	100	100	100	100
Number of respondents	216	203	98	105	99	110	106	107	106	103

[1] Distance based on straight-line measurement between center of sample cluster and the nearest semi-public recreation facility. Where the distance is more than .125 miles, minimum road distance is used.

[2] Public facilities are those open to the public at large or to all residents of the community being studied. Facilities such as apartment swimming pools and country club golf courses are considered to be semi-public if at least 10 percent of the population in the sample community who participate in that activity use them.

[3] Measurement made from the center of the micro-neighborhood to the club house of the nearest golf course.

Table 16

Distance from Center of the Micro-Neighborhood to Place Where
Respondent Most Often Engaged in Recreation Activity[1]
(percentage distributions of respondents)

Place Where Respondent went Swimming[2]	Columbia	Reston	Crofton	Montpelier	Norbeck	Southfield	Lafayette Elmwood	Southwest Washington	Radburn	Glen Rock
Less than .125 miles	23	22	6	14	15	23	9	56	51	17
.125-.24 miles	10	8	-	14	-	-	-	24	5	-
.25-.49 miles	28	27	7	47	6	4	21	6	33	-
.50-.99 miles	27	16	51	20	33	21	24	-	6	29
1.00-1.99 miles	4	16	20	-	14	15	-	-	-	39
2.00-9.99 miles	3	6	2	-	17	21	12	4	-	-
10 miles or more	5	5	14	5	15	16	34	10	5	15
Total	100	100	100	100	100	100	100	100	100	100
Number of respondents	158	136	70	89	52	48	33	79	64	48
Place Where Respondent Played Tennis										
Less than .125 miles	-	9	5	24	-	-	33	-	25	-
.125-.249 miles	-	27	-	8	-	-	-	7	5	-
.25-.49 miles	5	11	5	44	37	25	5	17	65	17
.50-.99 miles	26	18	47	16	25	-	-	17	5	67
1.00-1.99 miles	42	31	24	-	13	67	5	28	-	8
2.00-9.99 miles	11	4	5	-	25	8	28	7	-	8
10 miles or more	16	-	14	8	-	-	29	24	-	-
Total	100	100	100	100	100	100	100	100	100	100
Number of respondents	38	45	21	25	8	12	21	29	20	12
Place Where Respondent Played Golf[3]										
Less than .50 miles	2	2	7	-	-	-	-	-	-	-
.50-.99 miles	-	23	48	-	-	-	-	11	-	7
1.00-1.99 miles	24	25	23	26	-	3	3	33	29	-
2.00-4.99 miles	49	25	-	-	72	14	16	6	-	7
5.00-9.99 miles	5	2	3	16	14	14	13	6	14	33
10 miles or more	20	23	19	58	14	69	68	44	57	53
Total	100	100	100	100	100	100	100	100	100	100
Number of respondents	41	44	31	19	14	42	31	18	20	15

Table 16 - continued

Place Where Respondent went Boating[4]	Columbia	Reston	Crofton	Montpelier	Norbeck	Southfield	Lafayette Elmwood	Southwest Washington	Radburn	Glen Rock
Less than .50 miles	6	43	-	-	-	-	-	-	-	-
.50-.99 miles	3	8	-	-	-	-	8	16	-	-
1.00-1.99 miles	35	7	-	-	-	-	4	4	-	-
2.00-4.99 miles	29	4	-	-	8	-	15	12	-	-
5.00-9.99 miles	-	-	8	-	4	8	-	-	-	5
10 miles or more	27	38	92	100	88	92	73	68	100	95
Total	100	100	100	100	100	100	100	100	100	100
Number of respondents	71	73	36	16	25	37	26	25	14	22
Place Where Respondent went Hiking or Walking										
Less than 1.00 miles	88	87	65	66	55	66	71	61	86	65
1.00-1.99 miles	3	3	-	-	-	2	6	10	3	-
2.00-9.99 miles	4	3	2	3	16	2	9	7	3	2
10 miles or more	5	7	33	31	29	30	14	22	8	33
Total	100	100	100	100	100	100	100	100	100	100
Number of respondents	156	170	65	58	67	58	56	59	67	52
Place Where Respondent went Bicycling										
Less than 1.00 miles	98	25	94	95	90	98	67	43	92	90
1.00-1.99 miles	-	74	-	-	5	-	4	14	3	-
2.00-9.99 miles	-	1	-	-	5	-	21	29	-	-
10 miles or more	2	-	6	5	5	2	8	14	5	10
Total	100	100	100	100	100	100	100	100	100	100
Number of respondents	67	84	36	42	20	55	24	21	36	20

Table 16 - continued

Place Where Respondent went Picnicking	Columbia	Reston	Crofton	Montpelier	Norbeck	Southfield	Lafayette Elmwood	Southwest Washington	Radburn	Glen Rock
Less than 1.00 miles	27	28	25	4	7	13	20	19	3	54
1.00-1.99 miles	26	28	2	-	-	2	10	2	38	2
2.00-9.99 miles	23	6	8	18	35	22	23	25	18	6
10 miles or more	24	38	65	78	58	63	47	54	41	38
Total	100	100	100	100	100	100	100	100	100	100
Number of respondents	136	103	48	68	55	63	40	57	39	61

[1]Distance is based on straight line measurement between the center of the micro-neighborhood and the facility most frequently used. Where the straight line distance is more than .125 miles, distance is based on a minimum road measurement.

[2]Outdoor swimming pool.

[3]Measurement made from the center of the micro-neighborhood to the club house of the golf course.

[4]Measurement made from the center of the micro-neighborhood to marina or boat launching facility. When the micro-neighborhood is within .125 miles of the edge of a lake, straight line distance is used.

they engage in these activities. Graphs 1 and 2 suggest that the latter is the more likely effect of being closer to some facilities, for example, golf courses. Frequency of participation in other activities, it will be recalled, is somewhat more sensitive to distance than playing golf. Even for an activity like tennis, however, participation rates seem to be insensitive to variations in distance in the range from half a mile to two miles or more. Other factors then may be important in the explanation of observed variations in participation rates across communities.

In Table 18 we have summarized participation rates in each of our seven activities by community. Comparative data from other studies are shown in Tables 5 and 6 of Appendix *E*. We shall discuss each of the activities in order, including for each activity a summary which brings together data from the previous section on availability of facilities in the community and participation rates. These summaries relating participation to facilities are presented in Tables 19 to 24.

Outdoor swimming at a pool:[3] Table 18 illustrates the differential rates of participation in swimming at a pool as reported by residents of our sample communities. The highest percentage of swimmers (85 percent) was found in Montpelier, a moderately planned residential environment. Southwest Washington ranked second with 77 percent of the respondents swimming in the past year followed closely by Columbia with 76 percent. Crofton and Reston ranked next with 71 percent and 69 percent, respectively, while Lafayette-Elmwood contained 38 percent or the lowest percentage of swimmers. Of the two older residents of Glen Rock swam at an outdoor pool in the past year. In the two new communities designated as less planned, 58 percent of the residents of Norbeck and 47 percent of the residents of Southfield reported swimming at an outdoor pool in the past year.

When we consider the proportion who are frequent swimmers, we find Montpelier again ranks first with 77 percent swimming five or more times. Residents of Southwest Washington are the second most frequent swimmers (67 percent) and are followed by residents of Columbia and Reston, with 61 percent and 59 percent, respectively. The percentage who swim five times or more is lowest in Lafayette-Elmwood and Southfield with 26 and 33 percent, respectively.

Data on participation in swimming from three additional studies of

---

[3]While most recreation demand studies consider swimming at beaches and at a pool, this study considers only use of outdoor swimming pools since it is the type of swimming facility most commonly associated with residential environments.

Table 17

Summary Scores on Availability of Selected Facilities for Outdoor Recreation by Community

	Columbia	Reston	Crofton	Montpelier	Norbeck	Southfield	Lafayette Elmwood	Southwest Washington	Radburn	Glen Rock
Proportion who have a pool within one-half mile	.65	.61	.12	.72	.21	.16	.51	1.00	.96	.00
Proportion who have a tennis court within one-half mile	.18	.45	.12	.77	.24	.22	.34	.69	.86	.54
Proportion who have a golf course within two miles	.49	.39	1.00	1.00	.00	.00	.00	1.00	.88	.00
Proportion who have a marina or boat launching facility within two miles	.53	.64	.00	.00	.00	.00	1.00	1.00	.00	.00
Availability of internal pathway system[1]	1.00	1.00	.00	.00	.00	.00	1.00	1.00	1.00	.00
Availability of picnic facilities[1]	1.00	1.00	1.00	.00	1.00	.00	1.00	1.00	1.00	1.00
Total score	3.85	4.09	2.24	2.49	1.45	.38	3.85	5.69	4.70	1.54
Average proportion of facilities available	.64	.68	.37	.42	.24	.06	.64	.95	.78	.26

[1] These scores refer to the presence or absence of the facility indicated in the community as a unit.

[a] Based on information for the Lake Anne area.

Table 18

Comparative Participation Rates in Seven Outdoor Recreation Activities

(percentage distribution)

	Columbia	Reston	Crofton	Montpelier	Norbeck	Southfield	Lafayette Elmwood	Southwest Washington	Radburn	Glen Rock
Outdoor Swimming at a Pool										
Did not participate	24	31	29	15	42	53	62	23	37	49
Participated	76	69	71	85	58	47	38	77	63	51
once or twice	7	2	9	2	5	7	2	3	6	2
three to four times	8	8	9	6	6	7	10	7	3	5
five to ten times	17	12	13	13	15	13	8	10	9	18
more often	44	47	40	64	32	20	18	57	45	26
Total	100	100	100	100	100	100	100	100	100	100
Tennis										
Did not participate	81	76	79	74	90	88	80	68	79	87
Participated	19	24	21	26	10	12	20	32	21	13
once or twice	3	1	6	8	3	1	2	-	2	2
three to four times	5	2	4	5	-	7	3	7	1	3
five to ten times	4	6	5	7	4	4	6	9	4	3
more often	7	15	6	6	3	-	9	16	14	5
Total	100	100	100	100	100	100	100	100	100	100
Golfing										
Did not participate	82	78	66	81	84	61	71	80	85	86
Participated	18	22	34	19	16	39	29	20	15	14
once or twice	4	2	2	4	1	9	4	4	2	4
three to four times	1	1	7	4	3	5	5	5	1	-
five to ten times	5	6	3	7	3	10	5	6	5	5
more often	8	13	22	4	9	15	15	5	7	5
Total	100	100	100	100	100	100	100	100	100	100

Table 18 - continued

	Columbia	Reston	Crofton	Montpelier	Norbeck	Southfield	Lafayette Elmwood	Southwest Washington	Radburn	Glen Rock
Boating										
Did not participate	61	64	64	83	73	66	74	64	85	78
Participated	39	36	36	17	27	34	26	36	15	22
once or twice	9	8	10	2	14	11	6	10	3	5
three to four times	12	5	7	6	4	9	6	11	6	7
five to ten times	10	9	5	5	7	4	7	10	2	5
more often	8	14	14	4	2	10	7	5	4	5
Total	100	100	100	100	100	100	100	100	100	100
Hiking or Walking										
Did not participate	28	14	34	42	40	40	47	40	32	48
Participated	72	86	66	58	60	60	53	60	68	52
once or twice	2	2	2	-	8	3	4	4	1	2
three to four times	5	9	4	4	7	10	1	7	2	6
five to ten times	20	14	6	13	10	9	12	8	4	11
more often	45	61	54	41	35	38	36	41	61	33
Total	100	100	100	100	100	100	100	100	100	100
Bicycling										
Did not participate	69	56	61	62	78	49	76	79	63	80
Participated	31	44	39	38	22	51	24	21	37	20
once or twice	3	5	4	5	4	4	3	6	3	6
three to four times	7	7	3	5	1	6	6	1	6	2
five to ten times	6	9	8	10	5	13	4	7	8	4
more often	15	23	24	18	12	28	11	7	20	8
Total	100	100	100	100	100	100	100	100	100	100
Picnicking										
Did not participate	35	49	50	35	42	43	59	41	60	40
Participated	65	51	50	65	58	57	41	59	40	60
once or twice	16	8	14	9	7	18	9	14	8	5
three to four times	19	13	19	21	14	19	17	21	13	10
five to ten times	19	13	9	27	21	12	8	11	14	21
more often	11	17	8	8	16	8	7	13	5	24
Total	100	100	100	100	100	100	100	100	100	100
Number of interviews	216	203	98	105	99	110	106	107	103	106

outdoor recreation are presented in Table 5 of Appendix E.[4] These studies consider participation in outdoor swimming everywhere and do not attempt to limit participation to use of swimming pools. These rates would be lower if beach swimming were excluded. The ORRRC study by Mueller-Gurin was a national survey conducted in 1959-1960. A more recent national survey of outdoor recreation was conducted in 1964-1965 by the Bureau of the Census.[5] Data from this survey primarily covered participation during the summer months. A summary of annual rates presented for selected activities is shown in Table 6 of Appendix E. The 1966 study by Lansing and Henricks had as its universe persons living in the seven counties of southeastern Michigan. One of the suburban counties, Oakland, was the focus of the Ladd-Dub study conducted in 1968. The community of Southfield is located in Oakland County.

As indicated earlier, we attempted to control for income in the selection of our ten sample communities. Median family income in our population is approximately $18,700. In the ORRRC national sample ten years earlier, the highest income group was $10,000 and over, whereas the highest income group in the southeastern Michigan and Oakland County studies was $15,000 and over.

The ORRRC national survey found that 67 percent of those with an income of $10,000 and over engaged in outdoor swimming in 1959-1960. In the 1964-1965 national survey, 73 percent of those with family incomes between $15,000 and $25,000 went swimming outdoors: these figures are comparable to the percent who participated in swimming in Columbia (76 percent), Reston (69 percent), Crofton (71 percent), Montpelier (85 percent) and Southwest Washington (75 percent), but above the percent in the remaining five communities. It should be noted that these communities are located in the Baltimore and Washington regions and are designated as highly or moderately planned with swimming pools provided as an integral part of the environment.

Considering all income groups, 45 percent of the 1959-1960 national survey engaged in outdoor swimming in the preceding year. Of the ten communities in our study, a lower percentage of swimmers was found only in Lafayette-Elmwood, a community which does not provide pools for its townhouse residents.

The study of the Detroit region in 1965 indicates that 53 percent

---

[4]Eva Mueller and Gerald Gurin, *Participation in Outdoor Recreation,* ORRRC Study Report 20, Washington, D.C., 1969; John B. Lansing and Gary Hendricks, *Living Patterns and Attitudes in the Detroit Region,* a report of TALUS, the Detroit Regional Transportation and Land Use Study, Detroit, Michigan, January, 1967; and William M. Ladd and Oleh Dub, *Leisure Time Activity in Oakland County,* a report prepared for the Oakland County Planning Commission and the Oakland County Parks and Recreation Commission, January, 1969.

[5]Bureau of Outdoor Recreation, U.S. Department of the Interior, *The 1965 Survey of Outdoor Recreation Activities,* October, 1967, mimeographed.

of those with incomes of $15,000 and over participated in outdoor swimming during the preceding year. This figure is below all sample communities except Glen Rock (51 percent), Southfield (47 percent) and Lafayette-Elmwood (38 percent). Considering all income groups, 45 percent of the sample from the Detroit region participated in outdoor swimming.

Finally, the 1968 Oakland County study reveals that 71 percent of those residents with incomes of $15,000 or more participated in outdoor swimming in the preceding year. By contrast only 47 percent in Southfield went swimming in an outdoor pool. Again, participation in swimming is higher in five of the six communities in the Baltimore and Washington regions despite the fact that Oakland County contains numerous fresh water lakes amenable to swimming. The warmer climate seems to be the most likely explanation for the higher participation rates in the Baltimore-Washington area.

The number of days of warm weather, mean temperature and precipitation during a given period undoubtedly influence the length of the swimming season and consequently the length of time a swimming pool remains open. As indicated in the following table, the total number of cooling degree days during 1969 was over 100 percent greater in the Washington area than in Detroit. The number of total annual cooling degree days is defined as the sum of the differences between the mean daily temperatures over 65 degrees and 65 degrees that occur in any year.

Total Cooling Degree Days by Region during 1969[a]

Region[b]	Total Cooling Degree Days
Detroit	741
New York	1234
Baltimore	1371
Washington	1580

[a]These figures are based on the United States Weather Bureau Monthly Summaries from Washington National Airport, Friendship International Airport, Detroit Metropolitan Airport and the New York Central Park Observatory.

[b]The Detroit region includes Lafayette-Elmwood and Southfield; New York includes Radburn and Glen Rock, New Jersey; Baltimore includes Columbia, Crofton and Montpelier; and Washington includes Reston, Norbeck and Southwest Washington.

The rates we find for participation in swimming seem similar to what one would expect for the people we are studying on the basis of the other studies.

Table 19

Relationship between Accessibility of Outdoor Swimming Pools
and Frequency of Swimming

Community (in order of number of outdoor swimming pools within one mile of the sample population)	Number of Outdoor Swimming Pools within One Mile of the Sample Population	Percent of All Adults Who Went Swimming Five or More Times in the Last Year
Southwest Washington	10	67
Columbia	5	61
Reston	5	59
Norbeck	3	47
Radburn	2	54
Lafayette-Elmwood	2	26
Montpelier	1	77
Crofton	1	53
Glen Rock	1	44
Southfield	1	23

Community (in order of percent of adults who have an outdoor swimming pool within one-half mile)	Percent of All Adults Who Have an Outdoor Swimming Pool within One-Half Mile	Percent of All Adults Who Went Swimming Five or More Times in the Last Year
Southwest Washington	100	67
Radburn	96	54
Montpelier	72	77
Columbia	65	61
Reston	61	59
Lafayette-Elmwood	51	26
Norbeck	21	47
Southfield	16	23
Crofton	12	53
Glen Rock	-	44

While the relationship is weak, the number of outdoor swimming pools within one mile of the center of the sample population does influence the percentage of the population who swim frequently (five or more times a year). Table 19 indicates that this percentage increases as number of available pools increases, the two exceptions appearing in Lafayette-Elmwood and Montpelier. As we indicated earlier, the Lafayette-Elmwood pools are associated with apartments and are included in the inventory because at least 10 percent of the 40 respondents who reported swimming used them.[6] The lone pool in Montpelier is used exclusively by residents of our sample area and is situated in the approximate center of population. The importance of this factor can be seen in the second half of the table where Montpelier ranks as the third highest community with 72 percent of its population within one-half mile of the pool.

When we compare communities ranked by the percent of respondents who have a pool within one-half mile with their rank in percent of population who are frequent swimmers, there is again evidence of relationship. Communities

---

[6] Fourteen out of 40 people who reported swimming used the two pools.

Figure 4. Frequency of participation in swimming is influenced by the distance between homes and swimming pools and to a lesser extent, the number of pools available to community residents. In Columbia over two-thirds of the residents have a swimming pool within one-half mile of their homes. (Photograph by Robert C. Lautman)

with high rates of frequent participation appear at the top of the list, the exception being Crofton. We conclude from this analysis that frequent participation in swimming is influenced by the availability of outdoor swimming pools. Other factors such as climate and the availability of natural bodies of water suitable for swimming no doubt are also important.

Tennis: As indicated in Table 18 the highest percentage playing tennis at all in the past year was found in Southwest Washington (32 percent). Montpelier ranked second with 26 percent, followed by Reston with 24 percent and Crofton and Radburn with 21 percent. The lowest percentage of tennis players was reported in the three less planned communities, Glen Rock (13 percent), Southfield (12 percent), and Norbeck (10 percent). If we consider those who participated in tennis five or more times in the past year, the highest percentage was reported in Southwest Washington with 25 percent, followed by Reston with 21 percent, Radburn with 18 percent, and Lafayette-Elmwood with 15 percent. Montpelier and Crofton, which rank second and fourth in percentage of those who participated in tennis, rank fifth and sixth in percentage who reported playing tennis five or more times with 13 percent and 11 percent respectively. Columbia also has 11 percent who report playing tennis five or more times, followed by the three less planned communities.

Table 20

Relationship between Accessibility of Tennis Courts and Frequency of Playing Tennis

Community (in order of number of tennis courts within one mile of the sample population)	Number of Tennis Courts within One Mile of the Sample Population	Percent of All Adults Who Played Tennis Five or More Times in the Last Year
Southwest Washington	23	25
Southfield	12	4
Reston	8	21
Glen Rock	5	8
Columbia	5	11
Montpelier	4	13
Norbeck	4	7
Radburn	4	18
Crofton	2	11
Lafayette-Elmwood	2	15

Community (in order of percent of adults who have a tennis court within one-half mile)	Percent of All Adults Who Have a Tennis Court within One-Half Mile	Percent of All Adults Who Played Tennis Five or More Times in the Last Year
Radburn	86	18
Montpelier	77	13
Southwest Washington	69	25
Glen Rock	54	8
Reston	45	21
Lafayette-Elmwood	34	15
Norbeck	24	7
Southfield	22	4
Columbia	18	11
Crofton	12	11

Of the studies selected for comparing participation rates in outdoor recreation activities, only the Oakland County study reports participation rates on tennis. For those in the county with incomes of $15,000 and over, 14 percent report playing tennis during 1967-1968. This figure is below all our sample communities except Glen Rock (13 percent), Norbeck (10 percent), and Southfield (12 percent). Of those living in Oakland County with an income of $15,000 or more, 10 percent played five times or more as compared to 4 percent in Southfield who played tennis that amount. It is difficult to come to any definite conclusions, however, as to how our results on frequency of tennis playing would compare with those for the nation.

Southwest Washington and Reston both have large numbers of tennis courts and high proportions of the population who are frequent players. Southwest Washington has 23 tennis courts, and Reston, 8. Southfield, however, has 12 courts and a small proportion of frequent players (Table 20). There appears to be only a weak relationship between the number of tennis courts within one mile of the center of the sample population and the percent of respondents who play tennis five or more times. Participation is more likely to be influenced by the proportion of population within one-half mile of the nearest tennis court.[7] With some exceptions the communities ranking high in percent of respondents who have a tennis court within one-half mile also have a relatively high percent of respondents who play tennis frequently.

Golfing: As indicated in Table 18, the highest percentage of golfers (39 percent) was found in Southfield followed by Crofton with 34 percent and Lafayette-Elmwood with 29 percent. Reston and Columbia ranked fourth and seventh with 22 percent and 18 percent respectively. Nineteen percent of the respondents in Montpelier and 20 percent in Southwest Washington played golf during the past year. The two New Jersey communities ranked lowest with 15 percent in Radburn and 14 percent in Glen Rock.

If we consider frequent golfers, Crofton and Southfield ranked first with 25 percent each. While the rankings of Lafayette-Elmwood and Reston remain the same, the rank order for the remaining six communities changes considerably. Columbia, Norbeck, and Radburn increase in their rankings while Montpelier and Southwest Washington decrease. In the first group of communities there are a higher proportion of golfers who played five or more times than in Montpelier and Southwest Washington.

Comparable data are not available for the national studies. In the Detroit regional study, however, 24 percent of the residents with an income of $15,000 or more played golf in the preceding year. Of the ten sample communities, only Southfield, Lafayette-Elmwood and Crofton have higher rates of participation. Within Oakland County 38 percent of the residents with incomes of $15,000 and over played golf in the preceding year. Southfield, which is located within Oakland County, had the highest rate of participation, 39 percent, a rate which seems typical for high income people in that county.

Table 21 indicates little relationship between the number of public and semi-public golf courses within ten miles and the percent of respondents who play golf frequently. Southfield, however, does show a high percentage of respondents who play golf frequently (25 percent) and it is located within ten miles of no less than 11 public and semi-public golf courses. Crofton, on the other hand, does not have many courses in the vicinity, but all of the residents are within two miles of a course, and 25 percent are frequent players. In general, however, the number of golf courses and the distance to the nearest one are not important factors influencing participation rates for golf. This result is consistent with our general finding that, within the range we are considering, distance to the golf course is not related to whether people play golf.

Boating: In this study questions were asked about "boating," which presumably includes canoeing, power boating, rowing and sailing. In the three

---

[7]While it was shown in Graph 2 that participation in tennis is lower beyond one-quarter of a mile, the variation among communities in the percent of respondents who have a tennis court within this distance was too small for the present analysis.

Table 21

Relationship between Accessibility of Golf Courses and Frequency of Playing Golf

Community (in order of number of public and semi-public golf courses within ten miles of the sample population)	Number of Public and Semi-Public Golf Courses within Ten Miles of the Sample Population	Percent of All Adults Who Played Golf Five or More Times in the Last Year
Southfield	11	25
Glen Rock	9	10
Radburn	8	12
Southwest Washington	7	11
Lafayette-Elmwood	7	20
Reston	5	19
Norbeck	5	12
Columbia	3	13
Crofton	2	25
Montpelier	2	11

Community (in order of percent of adults who have a golf course within two miles)	Percent of All Adults Who Have a Golf Course within Two Miles	Percent of All Adults Who Played Golf Five or More Times in the Last Year
Crofton	100	25
Montpelier	100	11
Southwest Washington	100	11
Radburn	88	12
Columbia	49	13
Reston	39	19
Southfield	-	25
Lafayette-Elmwood	-	20
Norbeck	-	12
Glen Rock	-	10

comparative studies the activity is defined as "boating and canoeing." The extent to which the respondents in these studies excluded any of the above forms of boating is difficult to determine. In the same way, it is difficult to know if the response to our questions included all types of boating.[8]

As indicated in Table 18, the highest rate of participation is found in Columbia, 39 percent. Reston, Crofton and Southwest Washington report 36 percent of the respondents boating in the past year, while Southfield reports 34 percent. The lowest rates of participation are in Glen Rock with 22 percent, Montpelier with 17 percent, and Radburn with 15 percent. We note immediately that there are no bodies of water within 10 miles of these communities which are suitable for navigation under normal conditions of recreational boating.

If we consider respondents who participated in boating five or more times, the four communities with the highest percentage of boaters continue to rank ahead of the other communities although the exact rank order changes. Whereas Reston and Crofton ranked second and fourth in overall participation, they now

---

[8]An attempt to deal with this problem is presented in the more recent report of the Bureau of Outdoor Recreation which distinguishes between participating in boating, canoeing, and sailing. Bureau of Outdoor Recreation, *op. cit.*, 1965.

Table 22

Relationship between Accessibility of Marinas or Boat Launching
Facilities and Frequency of Boating

Marinas or Boat Launching Facilities Available within One Mile of the Sample Population	Percent of All Adults Who Went Boating Five or More Times in the Last Year	Community (in order of percent of adults who have a marina or boat launching facility within two miles)	Percent of All Adults Who Have a Marina or Boat Launching Facility within Two Miles	Percent of All Adults Who Went Boating Five or More Times in the Last Year
Reston	23	Southwest Washington	100	14
Columbia	17	Lafayette-Elmwood	100	13
Southwest Washington	14	Reston	64	23
Marinas or Boat Launching Facilities Not Available within One Mile of the Sample Population				
Crofton	20	Columbia	53	17
Southfield	14	Crofton	-	20
Lafayette-Elmwood	13	Southfield	-	14
Glen Rock	10	Glen Rock	-	10
Montpelier	9	Montpelier	-	9
Norbeck	9	Norbeck	-	9
Radburn	6	Radburn	-	6

rank first and second indicating a higher proportion of boaters who participate frequently as compared to Columbia and Southwest Washington. The communities lacking navigable water bodies within 10 miles contain the lowest percentage of frequent boaters.

Data from the ORRRC national study indicate that 45 percent of the population with an income of $10,000 and over went boating or canoeing in the preceding year, which is a higher proportion of boaters than found in any of our ten communities. In southeastern Michigan participation in boating for the population with an income of $15,000 and over is 38 percent while the Oakland County study indicates that 43 percent of the population in this income group went boating in the preceding year. The large number of navigable water bodies easily accessible to all parts of the region and the high concentration of lakes in the non-urbanized sections of Oakland County contribute to these relatively high rates of participation in boating.

As indicated in Table 22, the availability of marinas or boat launching facilities within one mile of the sample population appears to influence frequent participation in boating. If we consider communities with five or more marinas within 10 miles (Crofton and Lafayette-Elmwood) in addition to those with boating facilities within one mile, a relatively high percentage of respondents who went boating five or more times in the last year is found in them. For those communities with a proportion of their population living within 2 miles of a marina or boat launching facility, frequent participation rates are relatively high. Two exceptions are Crofton and Southfield. Having facilities within 10 miles seems to be important, as already noted. Of the residents of the three communities with no such facilities roughly 18 percent went boating, whereas of the residents of the communities best served by facilities roughly 36 percent went boating at least once during the year.

We conclude that participation in boating is influenced by the availability of nearby boating facilities as well as by having at least five marinas or other boat launching facilities within 10 miles.[9] We would suggest that further research should distinguish more carefully among different types of boats. Facilities adequate for canoes, such as the artificial lakes in the new towns, may be wholly inappropriate for larger pleasure boats.

Hiking or walking: For purposes of this study hiking and walking are combined as one activity. These activities were also combined in the southeastern Michigan and Oakland County studies, but the ORRRC survey gathered data on hiking and nature or bird walks as separate activities. Subsequent studies of participation by the Bureau of Outdoor Recreation distinguish among hiking, nature walks, and walking for pleasure. Our classification was intended to include all three forms of activity.

As indicated in Table 18 the highest percentage who hiked or walked in the past year was reported in Reston (86 percent). Columbia ranked second with 72 percent followed by Radburn and Crofton with 68 and 66 percent respectively. Sixty percent of the respondents in Norbeck, Southwest Washington, and Southfield and 58 percent of those in Montpelier reported hiking or walking. The lowest percentages were reported in Lafayette-Elmwood (53 percent) and Glen Rock (52 percent). If we consider those who hiked or walked five or more times in the past year, the highly planned out-town communities again had the highest rates of participation. Reston ranked first with 75 percent, followed by Columbia and Radburn with 65 percent each. Crofton and Montpelier, the moderately planned communities, ranked fifth and sixth with 60 percent and 54 percent respectively. Although Lafayette-Elmwood ranked ninth in overall participation, a higher proportion of frequent hikers and walkers were found in this community than in the less planned environments of Southfield, Norbeck and Montpelier.

The 1960 ORRRC study reports participation in hiking as a separate activity. While 19 percent of all respondents engaged in this activity in the preceding 12 months, 23 percent was reported for those with incomes of $10,000 and over. Of those respondents in this income group 10 percent hiked five or more times. The rates in the 1964-1965 national study for those with

---

[9] A relationship undoubtedly exists between the number of boating facilities within 10 miles of the community and the length of shoreline within that area. Preliminary study in our communities indicates that Southwest Washington, Lafayette-Elmwood and Crofton have the greatest lengths of shoreline on navigable waters. A precise measurement was not attempted.

Figure 5. Participation on boating is influenced by the availability of boating facilities near housing. In Reston where 64 percent of the population live near water nearly one out of four adults went boating five or more times. (Photograph by William A. Graham)

incomes between $15,000-$25,000 are lower. These rates are substantially lower than hiking-walking rates found in our communities.[10]

Among those with incomes of $15,000 and over, 56 percent in southeastern Michigan and 49 percent in Oakland County walked or hiked during the preceding year. Compared to the Detroit region, only Glen Rock and Southwest Washington have fewer hikers and walkers. Participation rates for Oakland County are lower than those in the ten sample communities.

Internal walkway systems are characteristic of our five highly planned communities (Table 23). With the exception of the inner city areas, Lafayette-Elmwood and Southwest Washington, the percentage of adults who went hiking or walking five times or more is high in the communities with walkway systems. In Reston, Columbia, and Radburn the percentage of frequent walkers is 65 to 75

[10]Walking for pleasure seems to have become a major form of outdoor recreation. According to the national report prepared for the Bureau of Outdoor Recreation, the number of individuals participating in hiking during the summer months increased from 6 to 7 percent between 1960 and 1965. For the same period, the number who walked for pleasure during the summer increased from 33 to 48 percent. Bureau of Outdoor Recreation, *Outdoor Recreation Trends,* Washington, D.C., April 1967.

Table 23

Relationship between Availability of Internal Walkway System and
Frequency of Hiking or Walking and Bicycling

	Percent of All Adults Who Went Hiking or Walking Five Times or More in the Last Year	Percent of Adults Who Went Hiking or Walking Who Did So within Two Miles	Percent of All Adults Who Went Bicycling Five Times or More in the Last Year	Percent of Adults Who Went Bicycling Who Did So within Two Miles
Internal Walkway System Available				
Reston	75	90	32	99
Columbia	65	91	21	98
Radburn	65	89	28	95
Lafayette-Elmwood	48	77	15	71
Southwest Washington	49	71	14	57
Internal Walkway System Not Available				
Crofton	60	65	32	94
Montpelier	54	66	28	95
Southfield	47	68	42	98
Norbeck	44	66	17	90
Glen Rock	44	65	12	90

percent of the adult population, roughly 68 percent on an average across the three areas. In Montpelier, Southfield, and Norbeck the range is 44 to 54 percent, roughly 47 percent on an average. Crofton occupies an intermediate position both in the provision made for walking and in the proportion who say they walk five times or more, which is 60 percent.

The two in-town communities include 48 to 49 percent who say they walk frequently, which is almost exactly the same proportion as that for the suburban communities without internal walkways. We suggest that there must be other aspects of the in-town location which offset the effects of the walkway system on frequency of walking. The extent of the system is a factor. Lafayette-Elmwood, for example, is much more compact than, say, Reston, so that there are differences in how far one can walk on the pathways.

The percentage of those who went hiking or walking who did so within two miles also seems influenced by the walkway systems. In places with no walkway system about 66 percent of the walkers stayed within two miles compared to 89 to 91 percent of walkers in suburban communities which do have a walkway system.

Bicycling: Table 18 illustrates differential rates of participation in bicycling across our sample communities. The community with the highest proportion of bicyclists is least planned, Southfield, with 51 percent. The highly planned community of Reston is the second highest with 44 percent followed by the two moderately planned communities, Crofton and Montpelier, with 39 and 38 percent, respectively. The other highly planned community, Columbia, had a

Figure 6. Participation rates in walking or hiking and bicycling in in-town communities such as Lafayette-Elmwood are relatively low despite the availability of an internal walkway system. In suburban communities with internal walkway systems participation rates are high. Differences in rates of walking or hiking and bicycling suggest that other aspects of the in-town location may offset the effects of internal walking systems on participation in these activities. (Photograph by Robert W. Marans.)

somewhat smaller proportion of adults who bicycle (31 percent). In the two New Jersey communities 37 percent of the population in Radburn and 20 percent in Glen Rock reported bicycling in the past year. The two in-town communities of Lafayette-Elmwood and Southwest Washington had rates of 24 and 21 percent.

If we consider frequency of bicycling, the proportion who participated five or more times in the past year was again highest in Southfield with 42 percent, followed by Reston and Crofton, 32 percent each. In the older communities, 28 percent in Radburn and only 12 percent in Glen Rock engaged in bicycling five or more times. The two in-town communities also had low percentages of frequent bicyclists with 15 percent in Lafayette-Elmwood and 14 percent in Southwest Washington.

The three comparative studies do not have participation rates for bicycling.

As indicated in Table 23, the influence of an internal walkway system on frequent bicycling is not as great as it appears to be on frequent hiking or walking. Southfield, Crofton and Montpelier, which lack internal walkway systems, have a relatively high proportion of their population who went bicycling five or more times. The streets in these communities, as opposed to those in Norbeck and Glen Rock have little through traffic. Portions of the walkway systems in Southwest Washington and Lafayette-Elmwood are inter-

Table 24

Relationship between Availability of Picnic Facilities
and Frequency of Picnicking

Picnic Facilities Available within One Mile of the Sample Population	Percent of All Adults Who Went Picnicking Five Times or More in the Last Year	Percent of Those Who Went Picnicking within Two Miles
Glen Rock	45	56
Reston	30	56
Columbia	30	53
Southwest Washington	24	21
Radburn	19	41
Crofton	17	27
Lafayette-Elmwood	15	20
Picnic Facilities Not Available within One Mile of the Sample Population		
Norbeck	37	7
Montpelier	35	4
Southfield	20	15

rupted by streets carrying through traffic.[11] These characteristics of the system may explain the relatively low rates of frequent participation and low proportion of population who went bicycling within two miles. None of the communities studied contains a system designed exclusively for bicycles.

Picnicking: Table 24 illustrates the differential rates of participation in picnicking reported by residents of the sample communities. Sixty-five percent of the respondents in both Montpelier (moderately planned) and Columbia (highly planned) went picnicking in the last year. Glen Rock (least planned) leads the next group with 60 percent followed by Southwest Washington with 59 percent, Norbeck with 58 percent and Southfield with 57 percent. Reston and Crofton report 51 percent and 50 percent while Lafayette-Elmwood reports 41 percent and Radburn reports 40 percent.

If we consider communities where respondents report picnicking five or more times, three less planned communities rank high. Glen Rock ranks first with 45 percent, followed by Norbeck with 37 percent, and Montpelier with 35 percent. Columbia and Reston are next with 30 percent each. While Norbeck improved its ranking, Southwest Washington and Southfield scored lower indicating a smaller proportion of frequent picnickers. Lafayette-Elmwood residents report the lowest percentage of frequent picnickers, 15 percent.

The ORRRC national survey in 1960 indicated that 72 percent of the

[11]The internal walkway system within Elmwood Park was not developed completely at the time of the study.

population with incomes of $10,000 and over engaged in picnicking in the past year. This figure is higher than the participation rate found in any of our sample communities which average approximately 56 percent. In the 1964-1965 national survey, however, 62 percent of the population with a family income between $15,000-$25,000 engaged in picnicking.[12]

Rates of participation in picnicking are considerably lower in the southeastern Michigan study and the Oakland County study. Among those with incomes of $15,000 or more, 56 percent and 48 percent of the respondents in the Detroit region and in Oakland County, respectively, went picnicking during the preceding year. Comparing these rates with our sample communities, we find that all six suburban communities are in the range 51 to 65 percent, which is close to the 56 percent observed for high income people in the Detroit area.

Since seven of our communities have picnic facilities within one mile of the center of the sample population, it is difficult to distinguish among them simply by noting the availability of this facility. Table 24 indicates that frequent participation is not influenced by whether or not picnic facilities exist within one mile. The three communities with no picnic facilities do not seem to differ from the other seven in proportion of frequent picnickers. The proportion of population who went picnicking and did so within two miles from their micro-neighborhood does seem influenced by availability.

Summary: We have shown that participation in each of the seven outdoor recreation activities varies considerably across our ten sample communities. Table 25 indicates the total number of activities participated in by adult residents of each community. The mean number of activities is shown for each place. The two highly planned peripheral places have relatively high rankings, with means of 3.2 and 3.4 activities, while the moderately planned peripheral communities, with means of 3.2 and 3.1, rank higher than the peripheral less planned communities, 2.5 and 3.0. Generalization, however, is hazardous. The differences are small. The mean for Lafayette-Elmwood is lower than that for Southwest Washington, yet we think of both of them as planned communities. In the two New Jersey communities the average number of activities is low, 2.6 in Radburn and 2.3 in Glen Rock.

The bottom row of Table 25 repeats the summary score on availability of facilities by community. It is at best weakly correlated with the mean number of activities per person. As was suggested at the beginning of this section, people do participate somewhat more in outdoor recreation if facilities are close at hand, but most of the benefit seems to be taken in less time and money spent reaching the facilities.

We have assumed in this discussion that the variations across communities

---

[12]Bureau of Outdoor Recreation, U.S. Department of Interior, *The 1965 Survey of Outdoor Recreation Activities,* October 1967, mimeographed.

Table 25

Participation in Leisure Time Activities: Number of Outdoor Activities

Participated in at Any Time in the Last Twelve Months

(percentage distributions)

Number of Outdoor Recreation Activities Participated in	Columbia	Reston	Crofton	Montpelier	Norbeck	Southfield	Lafayette Elmwood	Southwest Washington	Radburn	Glen Rock
None	5	2	3	4	12	13	19	8	13	21
One	11	9	11	14	13	8	22	13	17	16
Two	16	18	18	16	31	16	12	20	21	14
Three	24	22	33	22	18	20	23	17	18	19
Four	22	27	16	26	13	21	12	19	14	22
Five	14	17	10	15	9	14	6	14	12	5
Six	6	4	8	1	4	6	4	6	4	3
Seven	2	1	1	2	-	2	2	3	1	-
Total	100	100	100	100	100	100	100	100	100	100
Number of respondents	216	203	98	105	99	110	106	107	103	106
Mean number of activities	3.2	3.4	3.2	3.1	2.5	3.0	2.3	3.1	2.6	2.3
Average proportion of facilities available	0.64	0.68	0.37	0.42	0.24	0.06	0.64	0.95	0.74	0.26

in participation in outdoor recreation may be attributed, at least in large part, to the accessibility of facilities. It is always possible that socioeconomic and psychological characteristics of community residents and other environmental factors will be discovered which both vary across communities and make a difference in outdoor recreation. We are aware of two such considerations, neither of which seems likely to change our main conclusions.

It is well known that age is negatively related to participation in outdoor recreation. We also know that people in Glen Rock and Radburn are older—it will be recalled that the median age of those interviewed was 50 years in these two places and about 40 in the six suburban communities. We have here a reason why people in these two places score lower on average number of activities.

It remains possible, however, to compare Glen Rock and Radburn, and we observe a small difference in mean number of activities per person (2.6 versus 2.3) even though there is a large difference in the summary score on average proportion of facilities available (0.78 versus 0.26). Thus, data from this pair of communities fit our main conclusion that facilities make a difference but not a large difference.

In the six suburban areas, people are a bit younger in Columbia and Reston (median age about 38) than in the other four (medians range from 37 to 42 but only Montpelier has a median below 41). Any adjustment would reduce the mean activity scores for Columbia and Reston slightly, thereby bringing their participation rates even closer to the average for the other four places. The main result is still that the mean number of activities is little influenced by the summary score on availability of facilities.

The quality of facilities, as well as their availability, undoubtedly makes a difference. We have not been able to develop measures of quality. We have no reason to suppose in general that quality varies systematically across communities. To the extent that it does, we would expect quality to be better in the more planned communities where access is also better. If anything, then, we would expect any adjustment to further reduce the apparent importance of access. It seems unlikely, however, that the inclusion of measures of quality would change very much the relations between distance and use of facilities shown above in Graphs 1, 2, and 3.

D. Distance Travelled to Recreation Facilities by Community

In this section we will consider the relationship between the distance travelled to engage in outdoor recreation activities and type of community. "Frequent participators" for our purposes are people who engage in an activity five or more times in a year. The extent to which these people travel to places outside their communities for recreation can influence transportation planning. Limited opportunities for recreation within a community will force people to seek different uses of their leisure time within their home or community environment or travel to recreation facilities throughout the metropolitan area. The latter alternative increases use of both the recreation facilities and the roads linking the residential to recreation areas. On the other hand, provision of recreation facilities within a community should reduce travel outside the community for recreation purposes. Table 26 shows the relationship between frequent participation and where the activity takes place. We consider participation in activities within two miles of a person's place of residence as taking place within the community.

Outdoor swimming in a pool: As indicated in Table 26 the percent of swimmers who do their swimming within two miles is higher in the highly planned and moderately planned communities than in the less planned communities. The exception is Lafayette-Elmwood but there the swimming pools available to the sample population are limited in number. In the four newly planned suburban communities over 90 percent of the people who swim did so within two miles compared to 68 percent of the swimmers in the less planned suburban communities.

Tennis: People who frequently play tennis play more often in the highly and moderately planned suburban communities than in Norbeck. In Southfield and Glen Rock, the total number of people who play tennis five or more times is small and consequently, the high percent who play tennis frequently within two miles is not meaningful.

Golfing: As indicated in Table 26, the percent of golfers who play golf within two miles of their place of residence is highest in Crofton (71 percent) and Reston (51 percent), communities which have golf courses in the geographic center of the population. In the less planned suburban communities and the in-town communities, over 82 percent of the people who play golf frequently do so more than two miles away from home.

Boating: In Columbia and Reston, 65 percent and 35 percent of the people who boat frequently do so beyond two miles as compared to 100 percent in the remaining peripheral communities. It is possible to go boating within two miles only in Columbia and Reston of the six suburban areas. In the in-town locations one out of every five people who boat frequently use the river facilities within two miles.

Hiking or walking: The percentage of hikers and walkers who find a place for the activity within two miles is highest in the peripheral communities with internal walkway systems. The percentage is also high in Crofton where the main boulevard can serve as a promenade. People who hike or walk frequently are five times as likely to do so two or more miles away if they live in one of the three less planned communities rather than in Columbia, Reston, or Crofton.

Bicycling: Outside of the inner city areas over 90 percent of the people who bicycle frequently do so within two miles regardless of the level of planning. In Lafayette-Elmwood and Southwest Washington, however, the

Table 26

Distance to Place Where Respondent Most Often Engaged in Outdoor Recreation for Frequent Participators Only

(percentage distribution of respondents who engaged in each activity five or more times)

Usual Location	Columbia	Reston	Crofton	Montpelier	Norbeck	Southfield	Lafayette Elmwood	Southwest Washington	Radburn	Glen Rock	Total
Swimming											
Within two miles	92	88	90	95	68	68	46	85	95	76	81
Two miles or more	8	12	10	5	32	32	54	15	5	24	19
Total	100	100	100	100	100	100	100	100	100	100	100
Number of people who swim five or more times a year	131	119	52	81	47	34	26	67	56	42	655
Tennis											
Within two miles	70	90	91	77	28	100	47	58	89	100	72
Two miles or more	30	10	9	23	72	-	53	42	11	-	28
Total	100	100	100	100	100	100	100	100	100	100	100
Number of people who play tennis five or more times a year	23	41	11	13	18	4	15	26	18	8	177
Golf											
Within two miles	24	51	71	33	-	4	-	18	25	9	28
Two miles or more	76	49	29	67	100	96	100	82	75	91	72
Total	100	100	100	100	100	100	100	100	100	100	100
Number of people who play golf five or more times a year	29	37	24	12	12	26	22	11	12	11	196
Boating											
Within two miles	35	65	-	-	-	-	21	20	-	-	28
Two miles or more	65	35	100	100	100	100	79	80	100	100	72
Total	100	100	100	100	100	100	100	100	100	100	100
Number of people who participate in boating five or more times a year	37	46	18	9	9	15	14	15	6	9	178

Table 26 - continued

Usual Location	Columbia	Reston	Crofton	Montpelier	Norbeck	Southfield	Lafayette Elmwood	Southwest Washington	Radburn	Glen Rock	Total
Hiking or walking											
Within two miles	91	94	93	64	66	73	77	69	88	65	82
Two miles or more	9	6	7	36	34	27	23	31	12	35	18
Total	100	100	100	100	100	100	100	100	100	100	100
Number of people who hike or walk five or more times a year	140	147	58	56	44	49	48	45	66	46	699
Bicycling											
Within two miles	96	94	90	93	94	100	79	40	93	77	90
Two miles or more	4	6	10	7	6	-	21	60	7	23	10
Total	100	100	100	100	100	100	100	100	100	100	100
Number of people who participate in bicycling five or more times a year	46	63	30	30	17	44	14	15	29	13	301
Picnicking											
Within two miles	59	68	35	13	8	27	53	25	40	63	46
Two miles or more	41	32	65	87	92	73	47	75	60	37	54
Total	100	100	100	100	100	100	100	100	100	100	100
Number of people who participate in picnicking five or more times a year	64	59	17	15	37	22	15	24	20	43	316

percentages who go bicycling within that distance are lower, 79 percent and 40 percent, respectively.

Picnicking: The percentage of people who picnic frequently within two miles is highest in Reston (68 percent), Glen Rock (63 percent), Columbia (59 percent) and Lafayette-Elmwood (53 percent), while an average of 26 percent picnic frequently within that distance for the remaining communities.

Summary: People who live in planned communities and participate in recreation activities are more likely to find a place to do so within two miles than people who live in less planned communities. The presence of facilities near people's homes, as we have seen earlier, does have a tendency to lead them to participate more in some outdoor recreation activities, but the magnitudes of the effects we have observed are small. There is no doubt, however, that people in planned communities who participate in outdoor recreation activities can frequently do so comparatively close to home. We would expect, therefore, that there should be some resulting reduction in measures of total travel, such as miles driven per year, for people in planned communities. As we shall see in Chapter 6 there seem to be other, offsetting factors working in the opposite direction.

5

RESIDENTS' RESPONSES
TO THEIR IMMEDIATE ENVIRONMENT*

The question of whether one residential environment is not only different, but more or less preferable to another environment, has not been a matter of only recent discussion. In this chapter we will review previous research in which attempts have been made to identify determinants of satisfaction with the residential neighborhood. Several of the most promising factors noted in other studies will be considered in relation to reported satisfaction in our sample. Specifically, we will investigate the impact of variables which are amenable to manipulation by planner-developers—dwelling unit density, dwelling unit type and neighborhood site arrangement—on responses to, and satisfaction with, the neighborhoods in our sample.

The emphasis on dwelling unit density derives in part from the fact that residential densities have been shown to have widespread effects upon patterns of transportation and land use in metropolitan areas.[1] In addition, although increasing land and transportation costs in urban areas are encouraging developers to turn to higher density development, it is not clear whether higher density residential areas are likely to gain very wide acceptance in a country known to prefer detached single family homes. In this context we will be interested in the effect of different densities on responses to the neighborhood pertaining, for example, to perceived privacy, noisiness, and rates of casual interaction with nearby neighbors.

---

*This chapter draws extensively from parts of "Satisfaction With Neighborhoods: The Effects of Social Compatibility, Residential Density, and Site Planning," by Robert B. Zehner, unpublished Ph.D. dissertation, The University of Michigan, 1970.

[1]See the discussion in Chapter 1 and the references cited there.

We will then consider an aspect of the neighborhood setting viewed as particularly relevant for satisfaction by many social scientists—the social compatibility of the neighbors. Although compatibility is less subject to the influence of the planner, we will attempt to determine, first, which factors are most associated with the perception of neighbors as compatible, and second, what effect perceived compatibility has on the evaluation of the neighborhood.

In the next section the influence on satisfaction of several other factors (including characteristics of the resident's home and the accessibility of shopping and the head's place of work) will be treated briefly as well. Finally, a pair of multiple regression analyses will be presented for both higher and lower density environments to assess the relative importance of the predictors of satisfaction considered in the chapter.

A. *Previous Research*

An early attempt to quantify the effect of physical aspects of the immediate neighborhood environment on residents' behavior was carried out by Festinger, *et al.* in a study of married students' housing.[2] They found that the proximity of dwelling unit entrances was directly related to the frequency of casual interaction and subsequent growth of friendships. Residents who were physically more isolated (with a dwelling unit nearer the edges of the development, for instance) tended to develop fewer friendships within the neighborhood and reported less of an attachment to the residential area.

A parallel study of housing reported by Caplow and Forman also found that high interaction rates were heavily influenced by physical accessibility and were associated with "high morale and a high measure of reported satisfaction."[3] While stressing the effect of propinquity in their findings, however, Caplow and Forman also emphasized that the population they studied (as well as the one studied by Festinger, *et al.*) was exceptionally homogeneous. All residents, for example, were married, most had children, the heads of virtually all the families were students, and the physical dwelling units of the families were of basically identical design.

Drawing on these findings in addition to work of his own, Gans concluded that propinquity is less important than homogeneity in fostering interaction.[4] He expected the factors likely to be most relevant in the

---

[2]Leon Festinger, Stanley Schachter and Kurt Back, *Social Pressures in Informal Groups,* New York: Harper and Brothers, 1950.

[3]Theodore Caplow and Robert Forman, "Neighborhood Interaction in a Homogeneous Community," *American Sociological Review,* Vol. 15, No. 3 (June 1950), pp. 357-366.

[4]Herbert J. Gans, "Urbanism and Suburbanism as Ways of Life: A Re-evaluation of Definitions," Chapter 4 in *People and Plans,* New York: Basic Books, 1968.

neighborhood were life cycle stage, and social class as reflected in education, income and race. His subsequent work in Levittown tended to support these expectations and also indicated that shared attitudes about child rearing and life style, for example, and generalized "compatibility" were important as well for interaction and satisfaction in the neighborhood.[5]

In another study, Lansing and Hendricks report a multiple regression analysis which indicated for a Detroit region sample that an evaluation of neighbors as "friendly" is a better predictor of neighborhood satisfaction than is the frequency of the respondents' interaction with those neighbors.[6] These findings are of particular interest because most studies conceptualize compatibility primarily as a catalyst to social interaction which, in turn, leads to neighborhood satisfaction rather than conceptualizing compatibility or homogeneity as having a strong independent effect on reported satisfaction.

Parallel findings were reported by Keller[7] and by Michelson[8] who also suggested that sociability and perceived similarities with neighbors are central to neighborhood interaction and satisfaction, particularly among those whose socioeconomic level permits a measure of independence from neighbors in times of need.

Although the research cited to this point emphasizes the impact of the social setting on neighborhood satisfaction, the effect of the physical setting has underlying importance. According to many researchers, for instance, propinquity makes an important contribution to social interaction in homogeneous neighborhoods which may then lead to neighborhood satisfaction. On the other hand, the regressions reported by Lansing and Hendricks suggest that *lower* dwelling unit density (and hence *less* propinquity) is significantly associated with neighborhood satisfaction because it is usually related to greater privacy and less noise. This, together with their finding that compatible neighbors are more important than frequent neighborhood interaction for satisfaction, this suggests that site arrangements which preserve privacy by reducing density and increasing insulation from undesired intrusions are likely to be highly valued. Finally, in addition to density considerations, Lansing and Hendricks indicated that respondents who evaluated their neighborhoods as "well kept up" also tend to be satisfied with the neighborhood.

---

[5] Herbert J. Gans, *The Levittowners,* New York: Random House, 1967, pp. 153-184.

[6] John B. Lansing and Gary Hendricks, *Living Patterns and Attitudes in the Detroit Region,* Detroit Regional Transportation and Land Use Study, Detroit, Michigan, 1967.

[7] Suzanne Keller, *The Urban Neighborhood: A Sociological Perspective,* New York: Random House, 1968, pp. 106-123, 149-164.

[8] William Michelson, *Man and His Urban Environment: A Sociological Approach,* Reading: Addison-Wesley, 1970, pp. 168-190.

To summarize, earlier studies have established or implied the importance of privacy, social interaction, compatibility, the maintenance level, and several other factors for neighborhood evaluations. The relative importance of these variables for satisfaction in the neighborhoods we studied, however, remains to be established. These relationsihps will be explored after we describe, first, the operationalization of "neighborhood satisfaction" in our study, and second, a brief comparison of levels of satisfaction across communities.

B. *The Measurement of Neighborhood Satisfaction*

The concept of "neighborhood" has various connotations ranging from the residential dwelling and its immediate environs to the census tract to the elementary school district. Rather than allow residents to respond to questions about their neighborhood by considering "whatever it means to you," a stricter definition was selected for this study. It was operationally defined in the questionnaire by the following:

> By neighborhood we mean just what you can see from your front door, that is, the five or six homes nearest to yours around here.

The decision to focus on the micro-neighborhood, as it will be called, rather than on more inclusive residential units into which communities might have been divided was based on several factors. First, the micro-neighborhood is an area with which most residents—even commuters—have day to day experience. It is the area where children are raised, where interaction with close neighbors occurs, where leisure interests may be pursued, and where homeowners often have a sizeable investment. For all these reasons, it is an area with which residents are likely to be familiar and in which they are likely to have more than a passing interest. Accordingly, the sampling technique used in this study was designed to obtain the desired number of interviews in each community by selecting clusters of four to six (on the average) contiguous dwelling units. Such clusters can be analyzed as micro-neighborhoods. Finally, the exigencies of questionnaire construction which limited the length of the interview precluded the exploration in depth of responses to other scales of "neighborhood."

While it is possible operationally to define approximate boundaries of the micro-neighborhood—the five or six homes nearest to yours—the measurement of satisfaction is less straightforward, primarily because of the number of neighborhood characteristics upon which it depends. To try to capture the multi-dimensional nature of satisfaction, we constructed a satisfaction variable based on four general, evaluative questions posed to the respondent about his neighborhood. The items enabled the respondent to rate his micro-neighborhood on three semantic differential type dimensions (attractive-unattractive, pleasant-unpleasant, very good place to live-very poor place to live) and on an agree-disagree item,

"When I go outside and look around me at the street and the neighbors' homes I like what I see."

The zero order correlations of the items with the scale and with each other suggest that the items are, in fact, measures of a single dimension.[9]

	Scale	A	B	C	D
A. Attractive-unattractive	.77				
B. Pleasant-unpleasant	.71	.39			
C. Good place-poor place	.74	.42	.48		
D. Like what I see	.75	.46	.34	.38	

Much of the analysis which follows, therefore, will be based on the scale obtained by adding together the results of these four items.

Neighborhood satisfaction by community: Differences among communities are small as seen in Table 27. More respondents rated their neighborhood very highly in Reston (61 percent) than in any of the other communities. Southwest Washington neighborhoods, on the other hand, were least favorably evaluated; only 34 percent rated their immediate environments very highly.

In general, we had expected to find that the neighborhoods in the planned communities would have higher scores than the less planned. Across the six new suburban communities it is true that neighborhood satisfaction is lowest in the two least planned areas. In Norbeck and Southfield combined, about 39 percent score their neighborhood as high as 20 or 19 on the scale, compared to about 58 percent combined in Columbia and Reston. A similar average for Crofton and Montpelier works out to 53 percent, close to the two highly planned areas, and also very close to both Radburn and Glen Rock. We expected people in Radburn to like their micro-neighborhoods better than Glen Rock residents like theirs. It is not so much that the scores in Radburn look unfavorable (the distribution of ratings is almost identical with that for, say, Columbia), but that the scores for Glen Rock are surprisingly good too. Lafayette-Elmwood scores high, but neighborhoods in Southwest Washington, as we noted, are not very satisfactory in the view of the residents. The relative lack of satisfaction in Southwest Washington compared to Lafayette-Elmwood, in fact, is very evident in each part of the index as well as the total scale.

The components of the index also indicate some differences across the seven communities with similar overall scores. Crofton neighborhoods, for example, although clearly evaluated as the most "attractive," rank fifth or lower in the proportion of most favorable responses on the other three items.

---

[9]See Zehner, *op. cit.,* Chapter II, for a further discussion of the scale's validity.

Table 27

Neighborhood Satisfaction Scale and Items, by Community

(percentage distributions of respondents)

	Columbia	Reston	Crofton	Montpelier	Norbeck	Southfield	Lafayette Elmwood	Southwest Washington	Radburn	Glen Rock
A. Neighborhood Satisfaction Scale Scores										
20-19 (high satisfaction)	54	61	54	52	36	42	58	34	53	54
18-17	23	22	30	28	27	25	18	28	24	21
16-15	14	9	13	16	29	23	14	23	14	20
14-13	5	4	2	4	7	6	8	8	6	3
12 or less (low satisfaction)	4	4	1	-	1	4	2	7	3	2
Total	100	100	100	100	100	100	100	100	100	100
Mean satisfaction score	17.9	18.2	18.3	18.2	17.3	17.4	18.2	16.9	18.0	18.1
B. Neighborhood Satisfaction Scale Items[1] (score for scale construction in parentheses)										
Attractive (5)	53	58	74	55	38	51	62	43	57	54
(4)	30	33	21	36	43	27	22	37	26	27
(3)	14	7	4	8	16	19	12	16	14	19
(2)	2	2	1	1	2	3	1	3	2	-
Unattractive (1)	1	-	-	-	1	-	3	1	1	-
Total	100	100	100	100	100	100	100	100	100	100
Pleasant (5)	71	74	66	71	56	57	76	47	65	72
(4)	23	17	31	24	37	34	16	36	24	21
(3)	4	7	3	4	7	8	8	13	9	5
(2)	1	1	-	1	-	-	-	3	2	2
Unpleasant (1)	1	1	-	-	-	1	-	1	-	-
Total	100	100	100	100	100	100	100	100	100	100

Table 27 - continued

		Columbia	Reston	Crofton	Montpelier	Norbeck	Southfield	Lafayette Elmwood	Southwest Washington	Radburn	Glen Rock
Very good place to live	(5)	70	71	60	65	40	49	71	41	73	66
	(4)	22	21	33	29	44	34	21	43	17	26
	(3)	6	4	6	6	15	16	4	13	10	7
	(2)	1	2	1	-	-	1	3	3	-	-
Very poor place to live	(1)	1	2	-	-	1	-	1	-	1	1
Total		100	100	100	100	100	100	100	100	100	100
"When I go outside and look around me at the street and the neighbors' homes I like what I see."											
Agree strongly	(5)	49	67	58	58	48	50	63	42	59	64
Agree somewhat	(4)	40	26	36	39	46	42	29	47	32	29
Disagree somewhat	(2)	10	4	4	3	6	5	8	8	9	7
Disagree strongly	(1)	1	3	2	-	-	3	-	3	-	-
Total		100	100	100	100	100	100	100	100	100	100
Number of respondents		216	203	98	105	99	110	106	107	103	106

[1] The first three components used to construct the scale were five-point semantic differential type items. The question was: "Here are some words and phrases which we would like you to use to describe this neighborhood as it seems to you. By neighborhood we mean just what you can see from your front door, that is, the five or six homes nearest to yours around here. For example, if you think the neighborhood is 'noisy,' please put a check right next to the word 'noisy.' If you think it is 'quiet,' please put a check right next to the work 'quiet,' and if you think it is somewhere in between, please put a check where you think it belongs."

Generally, however, neighborhoods in communities (Reston, Montpelier and Lafayette-Elmwood) whose neighborhoods were highly rated overall tended to be rated highly across all four items. At the low end of the scale, neighborhoods in Norbeck, Southfield and Southwest Washington were generally given the least favorable responses on all the items.

It is important to note that, despite these differences across communities in neighborhood satisfaction, more than three-fourths of the residents in each community selected one of the two most favorable response categories for all four component items. In Wilson's study of Greensboro and Durham, North Carolina, 84 percent and 81 percent, respectively, reported being "satisfied" or "very much satisfied" with their neighborhood.[10] Similarly, Lansing found, using a less differentiated scale, in a study of residents in metropolitan areas (exclusive of New York), that 92 percent liked their neighborhood "moderately well" or "very much."[11] Strictly comparable data are lacking, but it appears on the basis of these studies that the generally high degree of satisfaction found in our communities is not atypical.[12]

C. Residential Density and Neighborhood Site Arrangement

We turn now to neighborhood characteristics related to satisfaction. Of particular interest to planners and developers (as well as social scientists) are the responses of residents to varying dwelling unit densities. As indicated in the first part of this chapter, density has been related in the literature to rates of interaction and to neighborhood satisfaction. Perhaps more germane from a transportation planner's or developer's point of view, however, is that rising land costs have put increasing pressure on the land developer to build more dwelling units per acre, which in turn can put increasing pressure on an area's transportation facilities. It becomes important, therefore, to gauge the relative appeal and effects of residential environments with a range of densities to determine if more dense environments are likely to satisfy an increasing proportion of the housing market.

The first part of this section will deal with the effects of dwelling unit density on responses to the neighborhood, followed by an exploration of the effects of neighborhood site arrangement on the same responses. The relation-

---

[10]Robert L. Wilson, "Livability of the City: Attitudes and Urban Development," Chapter II in *Urban Growth Dynamics,* F. Stuart Chapin, Jr. and Shirley F. Weiss (eds.), New York: Wiley and Sons, 1962, p. 371.

[11]John B. Lansing, *Residential Location and Urban Mobility: The Second Wave of Interviews,* Institute for Social Research, The University of Michigan, Ann Arbor, Michigan, 1966, p. 48.

[12]See Zehner, *op. cit.,* Chapter VII for a further consideration of community differences in our sample.

ship of these responses to neighborhood satisfaction will then be considered. We will conclude by looking at dwelling unit preferences of townhouse residents and their reasons for these preferences.

Residential density: Although a need to limit family life cycle variability among residents in our sample led to the exclusion of apartment dwellers, the micro-neighborhood densities in the communities selected range from 2.7 dwelling units per acre in Montpelier to 14.1 dwelling units per acre in Southwest Washington[13] (Table 28). It is obvious from the table, however, that there is a significant amount of variation within some of the communities which the means disguise.[14] While 90 percent of the densities tabulated in Montpelier fall into the same category, for example, Crofton encompasses all six levels of density, and Reston and Columbia have more than 20 percent of their tabulated densities in three different categories.

As was expected, the lowest average densities occur in the three communities in which only single family units fall in the sample. Conversely, the highest average densities occur in Lafayette-Elmwood and Southwest Washington where only townhouses were included in the sample.

The effect of density on responses to aspects of the neighborhood is indicated in the several parts of Table 29. At densities of 4.50 dwelling units per acre or higher, for example, residents are increasingly likely to report hearing their neighbors. It is of interest that people in higher density neighborhoods who are most likely to hear their neighbors are also slightly more likely to indicate that they "don't care." As expected, there is also a regular decrease in the "noisiness" of one's neighborhood as density decreases.

The feeling that one has privacy in one's yard, on the other hand, does not

---

[13]Our procedure in calculating the dwelling unit density of the micro-neighborhoods was to use a transparent grid consisting of 2 acre squares to determine the number of sample dwellings or single family lots falling in a single square. For each community a grid was prepared according to the scale of available maps or aerial photos.
Guidelines followed include:
   1) Placing the grid over the sample micro-neighborhood such that the center of a square coincided with the approximate center of micro-neighborhood dwellings (or lots when dwellings could not be identified).
   2) Placing the grid over the sample micro-neighborhood such that an edge of the square paralleled the street on which the majority of the sample dwellings were situated.
   3) Counting the sample dwellings or sample dwelling lots which fell in the square. If 50 percent or more of the area of a dwelling or lot fell within the square, it was included in the count.
For the sake of clarity we have simplified the density count to dwellings per acre in the report.
[14]That this is, in fact, the case is indicated by the following:
Total sum of squares = 80830
Between community means sum of squares = 47637
Within communities sum of squares = 33193

Table 28

Residential Density and Dwelling Unit Type, by Community

(percentage distributions)

	Columbia	Reston	Crofton	Montpelier	Norbeck	Southfield	Lafayette Elmwood	Southwest Washington	Radburn	Glen Rock
A. Residential Density (percentage distribution of respondent's neighborhood densities)[1]										
2.49 or less dwellings/acre	4	21	8	10	4	4	-	-	-	12
2.50-3.49	46	24	50	90	23	74	-	2	-	28
3.50-4.49	26	4	27	-	68	22	5	-	23	44
4.50-8.49	-	44	4	-	5	-	31	10	73	16
8.50-12.49	24	7	6	-	-	-	64	34	4	-
12.50-25 dwellings/acre	-	-	5	-	-	-	-	54	-	-
Total	100	100	100	100	100	100	100	100	100	100
Mean dwellings per acre	4.8	4.7	4.1	2.7	3.5	3.0	8.8	14.1	5.6	3.3
Standard deviation	3.0	2.6	2.8	0.4	0.6	0.5	2.2	5.6	1.5	0.8
B. Dwelling Unit Type (percentage distribution of respondent's dwelling units)										
Single family[2]	76	45	85	100	100	100	-	-	88	98
Townhouse	24	55	15	-	-	-	100	100	12	2
Total	100	100	100	100	100	100	100	100	100	100
Number of dwellings	216	203	98	105	99	110	106	107	103	106

[1] Neighborhood densities were obtained for each sample cluster using a two acre grid and plot maps or aerial photographs of the communities. Densities exclude apartment units in Southwest Washington which fell within the neighborhood area as defined on the grid.

[2] Units connected only by a common garage wall as in Radburn are considered single family units here. Otherwise, the definition of townhouse included structures with two or more units having a common wall, separate outdoor entrances, and no dwellings above or below the sampled dwelling.

decrease with increasing density until a density of 12.5 to 25 dwellings per acre is reached, at which point a sharp drop in feelings of privacy occurs. At that level of density more people also indicate that they have too little outdoor space near home for family activities. Roughly two-thirds or more of the respondents with children under twelve in their families rated places for their children to play outdoors near home as "good" or "excellent" at every density level, but there seems to be some decline in the percentage who say "excellent" at the high densities. A tabulation of the proportion of families in our sample with children under twelve by density, however, indicates a more regular inverse relationship.

	Dwelling Units per Acre					
	2.49 or less	2.50-3.49	3.50-4.49	4.50-8.49	8.50-12.49	12.50-25.00
Percent of households having one or more children under 12	63	65	60	46	36	27

In other words, families with young children tend to choose less dense neighborhoods although not, apparently, because of any differences in the quality of outdoor play space near the house.

There is a striking relationship between density and knowing one's neighbors by name. Particularly in the more dense neighborhoods, the closer one lives to neighbors, the *fewer* are known by name. In fact, only 8 percent of the residents living in the densest neighborhoods felt they knew all the adults in the "half dozen families" living nearest to them by name, compared to almost two-thirds of the residents in the least dense neighborhoods. To a much lesser degree this relationship is reflected in rates of neighborhood interaction. In the densest neighborhoods residents are somewhat less likely to interact daily or several times a week, and one-sixth of the respondents report casual interaction with neighbors only once a month or less. It is apparent, however, that interaction rates are less reduced by density than is simply knowing one's neighbors.

While the extent of anonymity in denser areas is striking, we did not ask about the absolute number of people known or interacted with within a defined area, say two square acres. Had we done so, perhaps we could have shown that people in high density areas are in fact less isolated than those in lower density "neighborhoods."

It may be, however, that the state of anonymity in the denser micro-neighborhoods reflects a desire for insulation from one's neighbors which, because of the propinquity of the neighbors one does know, can be maintained only imperfectly. An indication of this is provided in Southwest

Table 29

Neighborhood Responses Related to Density, by Dwelling Unit Density

(percentage distribution of respondents)

	Dwelling Units per Acre					
	2.49 or less	2.50- 3.49	3.50- 4.49	4.50- 8.49	8.50- 12.49	12.50- 25.00
A. Frequency of Hearing Neighbors						
Very often	-	1	1	6	8	10
Occasionally	11	6	10	20	33	40
Almost never	89	93	89	74	59	50
Total	100	100	100	100	100	100
B. Caring about Hearing Neighbors						
Care a great deal	35	51	42	36	40	23
Somewhat	35	23	23	22	26	33
Don't care	30	26	35	42	34	44
Total	100	100	100	100	100	100
C. Noise Level in Neighborhood						
Noisy	2	2	3	4	3	2
	2	4	4	4	8	5
	5	15	18	17	16	28
	31	26	26	29	26	30
Quiet	60	53	49	46	47	35
Total	100	100	100	100	100	100
D. Privacy in Yard from Neighbors						
Yes	57	53	49	53	54	40
No	43	47	51	47	46	60
Total	100	100	100	100	100	100
E. Adequate Outdoor Space for Family's Activities						
More than needed	14	14	7	16	13	16
Right amount	76	70	67	70	71	54
Too little	10	16	26	14	16	30
Total	100	100	100	100	100	100

Washington, the densest community, by responses to our agree-disagree item: "Most people around here would like to spend more time with their neighbors." More of the residents in Southwest Washington (60 percent) disagreed with this statement than in any other community. In Montpelier, the least dense community, on the other hand, only about 44 percent of the respondents disagreed with the item.

To summarize, dwelling unit density has a variable effect. Reporting a "noisy" neighborhood and "hearing neighbors" increases fairly regularly with density. On the other hand, variation in density under 12.5 dwellings per acre appears to have little systematic effect on private yard space for outdoor activities, or the adequacy of children's play areas near home. Finally, residents in neighborhoods with the highest densities are much less likely to know their neighbors by name although their rates of casual interaction are not significantly lower than rates in less dense areas. Since a majority of respondents in Southwest Washington, the densest community, indicated that most people around them would *not* like to spend more time with their neighbors, the

Table 29 - continued

	Dwelling Units per Acre					
	2.49 or less	2.50-3.49	3.50-4.49	4.50-8.49	8.50-12.49	12.50-25.00
F. Rating of Places Near Home for Children to Play						
Excellent	50	44	37	57	42	17
Good	30	28	27	22	27	59
Average	13	16	18	12	18	12
Below average	5	5	8	3	5	6
Poor	2	7	10	6	8	6
Total	100	100	100	100	100	100
Number of respondents in households having one or more children under 12	56	279	155	108	66	17
Percent of households having one or more children under 12	63	65	60	46	36	27
G. Proportion of Neighbors Known by Name						
All	65	59	60	57	43	8
Nearly all	17	25	25	22	23	11
Half of them	11	9	7	9	12	25
Just a few; none	7	7	8	12	22	56
Total	100	100	100	100	100	100
H. Frequency of Casual Interaction with Neighbors						
Every day	17	16	26	24	21	11
Several times a week	45	40	40	41	35	37
Once a week	16	23	19	16	17	24
Two or three times a month	11	11	11	7	13	11
Once a month or less	11	10	4	12	14	17
Total	100	100	100	100	100	100
Number of respondents	89	427	258	234	182	63

relative anonymity typifying the densest neighborhoods is apparently a desirable aspect of these settings.

Neighborhood site plan: As we noted in the first section of this chapter, previous studies of neighborhood satisfaction led us to expect that neighborhood site arrangements which limited or excluded public pedestrian and vehicular through traffic would result in fewer undesired instrusions and greater neighborhood satisfaction, particularly at the high socioeconomic level found in our communities. To be able to determine if site plans do, in fact, make a difference in responses to the neighborhood it was first necessary to develop guidelines for categorizing neighborhood settings. Working with aerial photographs and plat maps of the communities, a code was established to enable us to distinguish among five types of single family and townhouse micro-neighborhoods. In single family areas, neighborhoods located at the end of cul-de-sacs or dead-end roads are coded as having a *"cul-de-sac"* site arrangement. Other single family micro-neighborhoods, like those on one or both sides of a through street, are coded as having a *"linear"* arrangement. In townhouse areas, micro-neighborhoods that included only one structure, often facing on a thoroughfare, are

Figure 7. Average dwelling unit density is higher in Southwest Washington than in any of the other communities sampled. Dense neighborhoods are associated with more noise, less privacy, and lower levels of neighborhood satisfaction. (Photograph by Robert B. Zehner)

coded as "*single structure, linear*." Townhouse neighborhoods consisting of more than one structure whose entrances faced on a common area not open to public through traffic are coded as "*multiple structure, enclosed*." A cul-de-sac of townhouse units is the clearest example of this type of arrangement. The third category of townhouse neighborhood, "*multiple structure, open*," indicates two or more propinquitous structures in the micro-neighborhood with entrances opening into different public spaces. This is exemplified by an arrangement of linear townhouse structures at one corner of a street intersection whose entrances open onto different spaces or streets rather than onto a common "enclosed" area.

Applying the coding scheme to the micro-neighborhoods in our communities resulted in the distribution of respondents' neighborhood site plans shown in Table 30. Not surprisingly, the single family neighborhoods were easily coded. The townhouse areas, on the other hand, were frequently difficult to categorize with the maps and photographs we had available in part because of the difficulty in determining the orientation of townhouse entrances. Reduced N's in Table 30 are due primarily to this problem.

Table 30

Neighborhood Site Plan, by Community

(percentage distribution of respondent's neighborhood plans)

	Columbia	Reston	Crofton	Montpelier	Norbeck	Southfield	Lafayette Elmwood	Southwest Washington	Radburn	Glen Rock
Single family[1]										
Cul-de-sac	24	17	4	7	8	4	-	-	16	-
Linear	52	31	81	93	92	96	-	-	72	100
Townhouse										
Single structure, linear	2	16	3	-	-	-	36	31	-	-
Multiple structure, enclosed (cul-de-sac)	17	31	12	-	-	-	33	52	12	-
Multiple structure, open	5	4	-	-	-	-	31	17	-	-
Total	100	100	100	100	100	100	100	100	100	100
Number of respondents[2]	214	200	98	105	99	110	103	48	103	104

[1]Units connected only by a common garage wall as in Radburn are considered single family units here. Otherwise, the definition of townhouse included structures with two or more units having a common wall, separate outdoor entrances, and no dwellings above or below the sampled dwelling.

[2]Reduced N's (particularly in Southwest Washington) are a consequence of insufficient detail on maps or aerial photographs to permit estimating the type of neighborhood site arrangement.

Only Columbia and Reston contain each of the five types of micro-neighborhood plan. At the other extreme, all of the Glen Rock neighborhoods which we were able to categorize had a single family, linear arrangement. Nearly as homogeneous in this respect were Montpelier, Norbeck and Southfield where most respondents also live in single family, linear neighborhoods.

As with dwelling unit density, we have tabulated the series of responses to the neighborhood by neighborhood site plan. The results appear in Table 31. As expected, hearing one's neighbors is a more frequent consequence of townhouse living than of single family unit living. In single family areas site arrangement makes virtually no difference in this respect. Cul-de-sac or "enclosed" townhouse neighborhoods are apparently least susceptible of the townhouse arrangements to residents hearing their neighbors.

There is little variation across types of sites in the proportion who "don't care" about hearing neighbors except in the "multiple structure, open" townhouse neighborhood. There, where residents most often report that they hear their neighbors, a majority of the residents say that they "don't care."

The single family cul-de-sac was rated as the most quiet type of siting with the least quiet being the single structure, linear townhouse neighborhood. It is of interest that, particularly in the townhouse neighborhoods, residents in neighborhoods where neighbors are most often heard do not necessarily rate the neighborhood as "noisy."[15]

It is noteworthy that all townhouse residents with the exception of those in single structure, linear neighborhoods indicate that they have as much or more privacy in their yards as families living in single family homes. This exception may be due to the fact that many residents in that type of neighborhood in our sample were usually facing on a public street.

No differences appear across types of sites in the adequacy of outdoor space for family activities. Differences arise again, however, when the places near the home for children to play are evaluated. Cul-de-sac neighborhoods, where there is less traffic, are evaluated much more favorably among single family areas than neighborhoods on through streets. It is less clear why townhouse neighborhoods based on a similar cul-de-sac principle are evaluated lower than townhouse neighborhoods likely to be facing on a through street. The N for the highly evaluated townhouse neighborhood types is smaller than desirable, but these site arrangements are clearly more associated with excellent play areas for children than is the conventional linear single family neighborhood. The presence of "tot lots" and similar facilities may explain the high evaluations of two of the townhouse arrangements.

---

[15]The zero-order correlation between the two variables for the entire sample is only .23. Undoubtedly traffic noise, for example, which we did not ask about, also enters into the evaluation of a neighborhood as "noisy" or "quiet."

Table 31

Neighborhood Responses Related to Density, by Neighborhood Site Plan

(percentage distribution of respondents)

| | Single Family | | Townhouse | | |
| | | | Single Structure | Multiple Structure | |
	Cul-de-sac	Linear	Linear	Enclosed	Open
A. Frequency of Hearing Neighbors					
Very often	-	2	11	5	12
Occasionally	9	8	30	29	41
Almost never	91	90	59	66	47
Total	100	100	100	100	100
B. Caring about Hearing Neighbors					
Care a great deal	45	43	51	39	31
Somewhat	25	24	20	34	16
Don't care	30	33	29	27	53
Total	100	100	100	100	100
C. Noise Level in Neighborhood					
Noisy	2	3	4	1	2
	3	3	7	8	3
	15	15	23	15	9
	22	28	23	29	37
Quiet	58	51	43	47	49
Total	100	100	100	100	100
D. Privacy in Yard from Neighbors					
Yes	56	51	40	58	59
No	44	49	60	42	41
Total	100	100	100	100	100
E. Adequate Outdoor Space for Family's Activities					
More than needed	15	11	12	16	21
Right amount	70	70	76	65	70
Too little	15	19	12	19	9
Total	100	100	100	100	100
F. Rating of Places Near Home for Children to Play					
Excellent	67	39	62	42	62
Good	26	28	21	31	19
Average	3	19	3	15	19
Below average	1	7	7	3	-
Poor	3	7	7	9	-
Total	100	100	100	100	100
Number of respondents in households having one or more children under 12	93	441	29	75	21

Table 31 - continued

	Single Family		Townhouse		
			Single Structure	Multiple Structure	
	Cul-de-sac	Linear	Linear	Enclosed	Open
G. Proportion of Neighbors Known by Name					
All	71	59	47	44	48
Nearly all	22	23	24	27	14
Half of them	3	10	11	9	17
Just a few; none	4	8	18	20	21
Total	100	100	100	100	100
H. Frequency of Casual Interaction with Neighbors					
Every day	30	18	19	25	17
Several times a week	45	41	41	34	31
Once a week	15	21	16	20	21
Two or three times a month	5	11	13	10	12
Once a month or less	5	9	11	11	19
Total	100	100	100	100	100
Number of respondents	137	731	92	168	58

Residents of single family neighborhoods are more likely to know all of their half-dozen closest neighbors by name than townhouse residents. The type of townhouse site plan apparently has little effect on this aspect of neighborhood life. Single family neighborhoods based on the cul-de-sac, however, are more conducive to knowing neighbors than the linear single family plan.

Within the townhouse and single family categories the enclosed or cul-de-sac neighborhoods result in more daily casual social interaction than the linear or open settings. Overall, the single family cul-de-sac plan fosters the highest rates of interaction, while the open multiple structure townhouse plan leads to the least.

As with dwelling unit density, the effects of neighborhood site plans vary depending on the response being considered. In cases such as hearing or knowing one's neighbors, the most important differences arise between the single family areas on the one hand and the townhouse areas on the other. Responses to the adequacy of outdoor space for family activities, however, indicate that the site plans we considered had little effect. Responses about other aspects of neighborhood life, however, brought out areas in which specific types of plans had distinctive effects.

The single structure, linear townhouse plan, for example, which usually faced on a public thoroughfare in our communities was rated least quiet and most lacking in privacy. The single family cul-de-sac, on the other hand, was most quiet, had nearby children's play areas rated most highly, and had the highest rates of knowing and interacting with neighbors. Next, the enclosed or cul-de-sac townhouse neighborhoods and the linear single family areas were rated

Table 32

Neighborhood Satisfaction for Different Dwelling Unit

Densities and Neighborhood Site Plans

(percentage of respondents giving neighborhood highest ratings)[1]

	Percent Giving Area Highest Rating on Neighborhood Satisfaction Scale	N (base of percentages)
A. Dwelling Unit Density (in dwelling units per acre)		
2.49 or less	70	89
2.50-3.49	53	427
3.50-4.49	49	258
4.50-8.49	53	234
8.50-12.49	45	182
12.50-25	33	63
B. Neighborhood Site Plan		
Single family		
Cul-de-sac	63	137
Linear	51	731
Townhouse		
Single structure linear	52	92
Multiple structure enclosed (cul-de-sac)	46	168
Multiple structure open	50	58
Total sample	51	1253

---

[1]Respondents giving neighborhood highest ratings include those who rated the neighborhood most positively on all four scale items or most positively on three items and only one category less positively on the fourth.

least favorably in relation to nearby children's play areas. Finally, it should be noted that, as would be expected, differences in responses to neighborhood site plans which largely reflected differences between single family and townhouse areas parallel the differences found in the comparison of low and high dwelling unit densities.

Density, site plan and responses to the neighborhood related to neighborhood satisfaction: Having considered in some detail differences in response to the micro-neighborhood occasioned by variation in density and site planning, we will now focus on the effect of these factors on neighborhood satisfaction. Table 32 indicates that, within the range of densities we are studying, densities from 2.5 to 8.49 dwellings per acre have little effect on satisfaction. In the least dense category (under 2.50 dwellings per acre), however, satisfaction is noticeably higher while it is noticeably lower in the most dense neighborhoods (12.5-25 dwellings per acre). It is apparent that the site plan of neighborhoods has less effect on reported satisfaction than density. Of the site arrangements considered only the single family cul-de-sac is rated very differently from the overall average.

Table 33 presents the relation between the responses to the neighborhood and neighborhood satisfaction. Results tend to be systematic and in the expected direction. Residents who hear their neighbors often or report having a "noisy" neighborhood evaluate their neighborhoods least favorably while those in "quiet" neighborhoods who "almost never" hear their neighbors evaluate their neighborhood most favorably. Similarly, people with yard privacy are more likely to evaluate their neighborhood highly (57 percent) than those who lack such privacy (44 percent).

The adequacy of outdoor space for family activities is a factor in neighborhood satisfaction only if residents feel they have too little space available. In that case, only 35 percent of the residents rated their neighborhood at the highest level. The quality of outdoor play space near the home for children has a more striking effect on neighborhood satisfaction. Only 17 percent of residents who rated their neighborhood's play space poor rated the neighborhood highly. Residents rating the play area and facilities excellent were much more likely to rate the neighborhood highly (63 percent).

Less striking, but still in the direction suggested by the work of Festinger, et al., Gans, and others, is the fact that knowing and interacting with one's neighbors is positively related to neighborhood satisfaction. Fifty-six percent of those who know all their neighbors gave the neighborhood the highest ratings as did 58 percent of those who interact daily with their neighbors on a casual basis. At the other extreme, only 40 percent of those who know "none" or "just a few" of their neighbors, and 42 percent of those interacting with neighbors once a month or less gave their neighborhoods the highest ratings.

To summarize, on the basis of the factors considered thus far, the proportion of residents most satisfied with their neighborhoods is highest if the density is under 2.50 dwellings per acre (70 percent), if the neighborhood is "quiet" (67 percent), and if there are "excellent" play facilities nearby for children (63 percent). The proportions of residents who reported the least satisfaction with their neighborhoods are found when the nearby play facilities for children are "poor" (17 percent), when the neighborhood is relatively "noisy" (21 percent for the two lowest categories combined), when there is too little space for family activities (35 percent), and when neighbors are heard "very often" (36 percent). It is apparent that we are dealing with a set of factors which are related to each other as well as to neighborhood satisfaction. In the last part of this chapter we attempt to deal simultaneously with several predictors of neighborhood satisfaction.

Dwelling unit preferences of townhouse dwellers: To conclude this section on density and site arrangement we will focus on the residential preferences of those in our sample who are presently living in townhouses. Although townhouse dwellers are relatively rare in the general population at the income level of our sample,[16] 32 percent of the dwellings selected in our communities fell into this category. Recent figures indicate that townhouses do not account for much of the housing market of those at the $15,000 and over income level since roughly 99 percent of the new homes occupied by such families are either single family homes (65 percent) or apartments (34 percent).[17] We had an opportunity to determine the desirability of these dwelling units by asking residents who were living in a townhouse about their dwelling unit preferences.

Our results suggest that a market for these units does exist. Only about a third of those living in a townhouse indicate that they would prefer a single family dwelling while 60 percent indicate that a townhouse was, in fact, what they wanted.

Dwelling Unit Preference[18]

(for those living in townhouses)

Single family	36%
Townhouse	60
Apartment	4
	100%
Number of respondents	397

This degree of support for townhouses is substantial but not overwhelming in view of people's tendency to like what they have. Most of the people in the sample, it will be recalled, have moved into newly constructed units within the last few years so that one might expect a fairly high level of satisfaction with their living arrangements. In earlier national studies over 90 percent of those

---

[16]In a survey of residents in metropolitan areas exclusive of New York, Lansing reported the following distribution of housing type for those with $15,000 and over family income:

Single family house	90%
Two family house	6
Three-four family house	2
Apartment building (5 or more units)	2
Other (row house, apartment in commercial structure)	*
	100%

*Less than .5%.

Lansing, 1966, *op. cit.,* p. 7.

[17]These figures come from a 1966 survey of residents of all SMSA's with populations over 200,000 in central cities. John B. Lansing, Charles Wade Clifton, and James N. Morgan, *New Homes and Poor People,* Survey Research Center, The University of Michigan, 1969, p. 120.

[18]The question was: "If you could do as you pleased, would you prefer to live in a single family house, a townhouse, or an apartment?"

Table 33

Neighborhood Satisfaction for Responses Related to Density

(percentage of respondents giving neighborhood highest ratings)[1]

	Percent Giving Area Highest Rating on Neighborhood Satisfaction Scale	N (base of percentages)
A. Frequency of Hearing Neighbors		
Very often	36	44
Occasionally	41	191
Almost never	54	1013
B. Caring about Hearing Neighbors		
Care a great deal	50	523
Somewhat	46	304
Don't care	56	408
C. Noise Level in Neighborhood		
Noisy	23	31
	20	54
	34	198
	37	337
Quiet	67	615
D. Privacy in Yard from Neighbors		
Yes	57	646
No	44	602
E. Adequate Outdoor Space for Family's Activities		
More than needed	54	158
Right amount	54	861
Too little	35	224
F. Rating of Places near Home for Children to Play		
Excellent	63	300
Good	48	190
Average	42	107
Below average	41	37
Poor	17	47
G. Proportion of Neighbors Known by Name		
All	56	683
Nearly all	50	283
Half of them	42	127
Just a few; none	40	160
H. Frequency of Casual Interaction with Neighbors		
Every day	58	244
Several times a week	54	488
Once a week	44	241
Two to three times a month	45	128
Once a month or less	42	125
Total sample	51	1253

[1]Respondents giving neighborhood highest ratings include those who rated the neighborhood most positively on all four scale items or most positively on three items and only one category less positively on the fourth.

Figure 8. Sixty percent of the townhouse residents indicated that they would prefer to live in a townhouse rather than a single family or apartment dwelling. The primary reason for preferring a townhouse such as these in Lafayette-Elmwood was the need for minimal maintenance on the part of the resident. (Photograph by Robert W. Marans)

living in single family houses have said they prefer them to apartments or other types of homes, while of those living in apartments or other multiple family dwellings about 60 percent would prefer to switch to a single family house if they could do as they pleased.[19]

We asked respondents to explain their preferred dwelling unit choice. The reasons stated are summarized in Tables 34 and 35. Townhouse residents who would prefer single family dwellings desire more privacy and space than the townhouses provide. The overriding reason for preferring a townhouse, on the other hand, is the reduced need for maintenance. It is of interest, however, that a townhouse is often preferred because of the privacy and space residents feel it provides. Similarly, the proximity of neighbors in townhouse areas apparently provides some people a sense of companionship and social support.

In summary we find a tendency for low density site plans and types of dwelling unit to be preferred to high density, but the connnections are indirect and there are situations in which people like higher as well as lower density

---

[19]Lansing and Hendricks, *Automobile Ownership and Residential Density, op. cit.,* p. 104.

Table 34

Reasons for Preferring a Single Family House

(percentage distribution of those now living in townhouses
who would prefer a single family house)

	Percent
Privacy; fewer intrusions from neighbors	46
Space; less congested indoors and/or outdoors	34
Autonomy; ability to do what you want in the way of maintenance, activities; no townhouse cooperation to worry about	8
General, unspecified preference; "we've always wanted one"	6
Other specific reasons	4
Economic; better investment	2
Total	100
Number of respondents	137

arrangements. More people in single family cul-de-sac neighborhoods like their neighborhood than in single family linear neighborhoods, even though density is slightly greater in the cul-de-sac arrangement. People who live in townhouses state that they prefer them to single family homes in a ratio of slightly over three to two, yet there are roughly twice as many families per acre in townhouse as in single family neighborhoods. The preference for low density seems to arise out of needs for privacy, quiet, and outdoor space, needs which are met in varying degrees by different site arrangements.

D. *Neighborhood Compatibility*

Previous research has placed particular emphasis on the importance of compatibility of neighbors and homogeneity in the residential neighborhood. Despite what has been said about the importance of neighborhood homogeneity, however, Gans notes in his discussion of the topic that:

> I have been stressing the importance of resident characteristics without defining the terms *homogeneity* and *heterogeneity*. This omission has been intentional, for little is known about what characteristics must be shared before people feel themselves to be compatible with others. We do not know for certain if they must have common backgrounds, or similar interests, or shared values, or combinations of these. Nor do we know precisely which background characteristics, behavior patterns, and interests are most and least important or about what issues values must be shared.[20]

---

[20]Herbert J. Gans, "Planning and Social Life: Friendship and Neighbor Relations in Suburban Communities," *Journal of the American Institute of Planners,* Vol. 27, No. 2 (May 1961), pp. 134-140. (Reprinted as Chapter 12 in *People and Plans,* 1968.) Gutman raises virtually the same questions in a more recent article: "Site Planning and Social Behavior," *Journal of Social Issues,* Vol. 22, No. 4 (October 1966), pp. 103-115, especially, p. 110.

Table 35

Reasons for Preferring a Townhouse

(percentage distribution of those now living in townhouses
who prefer that type of dwelling unit)

	Percent
Maintenance; less worry and work with upkeep	49
Privacy; fewer intrusions from neighbors	11
General, unspecified preference; "we just like this kind of home"	10
Social support; friends are nearby when needed	10
Other specific reasons	6
Space; plenty of room for family, activities	6
Convenience; desire to live near stores, city center, etc.	5
Economic; best housing for the price, good investment	3
Total	100
Number of respondents	252

This part of the chapter will attempt to suggest which characteristics of those we can measure in this study need to be most homogeneous in a neighborhood for a resident to indicate that his neighbors are compatible. In this analysis we will look at two indicators of compatibility, both of the type referred to earlier in Table 27 in which people place their replies on a line representing a continuum. The distribution of responses for these items was as follows:

Friendly people	52%		People similar to me	24%
↓	28		↓	25
	16			35
	3			10
Unfriendly people	1		People dissimilar to me	6
	100%			100%

Although both distributions are skewed, residents are clearly more likely to consider a neighbor "friendly" than "similar." We will present below results which indicate which of these components of compatibility is most related to neighborhood satisfaction. First, however, we will briefly discuss measures of socioeconomic, demographic, and attitudinal homogeneity and the relation of these measures to residents' perceiving their neighbors as "friendly" or "similar."[21]

Measuring neighborhood homogeneity: For each micro-neighborhood it is

---

[21]A more detailed treatment of these topics including alternative homogeneity measures, the derivation of the homogeneity measure presented here, and a multivariate analysis of predictors of compatibility is presented in Zehner, *op. cit.,* Chapters II and III.

Table 36

Zero-Order Correlations of Fifteen Aspects of Micro-Neighborhood Homogeneity
to Measures of Neighborhood Compatibility, by Sex of Respondent

Type of Neighborhood Homogeneity	"Friendly people"		"People similar to me"	
	Male	Female	Male	Female
A. Demographic and socio-economic				
Age of male heads of household	-.02	-.06	-.02	.02
Age of wives; female heads	-.05	-.08	-.02	-.00
Education of male heads of household	-.01	.02	.01	-.02
Education of wives; female heads	-.09	-.06	.02	.05
Family income	.02	-.10	.09	-.01
Year moved into present home	.05	.11	.03	.05
Race	-.13	-.02	-.01	.00
B. Neighborhood attitudes				
Noisy-quiet	.10	.10	.04	.07
Poorly kept up-well kept up	.15	.13	.07	.16
Pleasant-unpleasant	.23	.29	.11	.18
Good place-poor place	.15	.21	.07	.17
Attractive-unattractive	.06	.11	.02	.14
Like what I see	.10	.02	.06	.06
C. Other attitudes				
People in community care	.13	.10	.10	.10
Satisfaction with community	.02	.14	.04	.12
Number of respondents	594	659	594	659

possible to determine what proportion of the residents have the same ages, family incomes, educations, attitudes about the neighborhood, and so forth. In this context, the higher the proportion of residents that are coded the same for a given variable, the greater the neighborhood homogeneity with regard to that variable. Using this rationale homogeneity computations for a number of possible bases of compatibility were made for the neighborhood clusters in our sample. The computations for a given neighborhood might indicate, for example, that four of five respondents reported the same family incomes. This proportion, .80, could then be assigned to all five of the respondents in that neighborhood to indicate the level of income homogeneity present in their neighborhood.

Following from Gans we would expect that respondents in neighborhoods with high levels of homogeneity would be more likely to judge their neighbors as compatible—"friendly" or "similar." Zero-order correlations of measures of neighborhood homogeneity for fifteen possible bases of compatibility with the respondents' ratings of neighbors as "friendly" and "similar" are shown in Table 36. Since men and women might have different perspectives as to which characteristics need to be shared to lead to compatibility, the correlations are presented separately by the sex of the respondent.

The results are hardly what we expected. In fact, when the respondent's ratings of his neighbors as "friendly" are correlated with measures of socioeconomic and demographic homogeneity in the neighborhood, most of the correlations are *opposite* in direction to what we expected. In other words, living in a neighborhood where characteristics of this type are homogeneous does *not* lead the respondents to perceive neighbors as "friendly." The association of the socioeconomic and demographic homogeneity measures with perceived similarity of neighbors is only slightly less surprising. In this case the proportion of people who match on a given trait is sometimes correlated in the predicted direction, sometimes not.

The largest single correlation in panel A of the table is, perhaps, the most interesting as well. It indicates that, at least in this particular sample, the male respondents are more likely to judge neighbors "friendly" if the neighborhood is racially *heterogeneous*. In sum, however, we must conclude that none of the measures of socioeconomic and demographic homogeneity considered here show consistently strong relationships to either perceived friendliness or similarity.

For people in our sample it appears that shared attitudes and evaluations concerning the neighborhood and community are most salient in defining neighbors as both "friendly" and "similar." Correlations in panels B and C of Table 36 are all in the expected direction and are generally the highest correlations presented. In other words, when consensus (homogeneity) exists among neighbors about qualities of the residential environment, the neighbors themselves tend to be more positively evaluated. If attitude factors are most important for compatibility, as our results suggest, future neighborhood research would do well to consider the impact of additional factors of this type. Gans suggested, for example, that views on child rearing, politics, and life style might be of particular importance for compatibility in the neighborhood setting.

Table 37 presents the relationship of the two compatibility items to the neighborhood satisfaction scale. It is clear that the perception of neighbors as compatible is highly associated with neighborhood satisfaction. The relationship of similarity to satisfaction is the strongest we have encountered in the analysis. Eighty-one percent of the persons who considered their neighbors most "similar" also rated the neighborhood most highly. In a parallel fashion the presence of "friendly" neighbors is associated with high satisfaction for 70 percent of the residents.

E. *Responses Related to Accessibility and Other Factors*

Although the primary concerns of this·chapter have been neighborhood density, site planning and social homogeneity, several other factors could be suggested as contributing to neighborhood satisfaction as well. To broaden the scope of the present investigation beyond that of most previous studies, we will present tabulations showing the relationship of a number of other variables to the neighborhood satisfaction scale.

Four indicators of accessibility were drawn from the data and are shown in

Table 37

Neighborhood Satisfaction as Related to Neighborhood Compatibility
(percentages of respondents giving neighborhood highest rating)[1]

The Neighbors are:	Percent Giving Area Highest Rating on Neighborhood Satisfaction Scale	N (base of percentages)
A. Friendly people	70	640
	37	343
	21	206
	27	33
Unfriendly people	9	11
B. People similar to me	81	298
	43	306
	46	433
	24	119
People dissimilar to me	29	68

[1]Respondents giving neighborhood highest ratings include those who rated the neighborhood most positively on all four scale items or most positively on these items and only one category less positively on the fourth.

the first four panels of Table 38. They indicate that having a grocery store, bus stop, or swimming pool nearby does not increase neighborhood satisfaction nor does living near the head's place of work—unless it is less than ten minutes away. It appears, in fact, that people who live nearest to a pool tend to value their neighborhoods less.

The next factors, family income, the respondent's education, and the head's occupation, do not suggest a significant effect upon the dependent variable although there is an indication that respondents with at least a college education tend to evaluate their micro-neighborhoods more critically.

It is of interest that while the respondent's family income is not related to satisfaction, the value of the home is. Each of the four items associated with housing cost (H, I, J and L) indicate that residents in more expensive housing are more satisfied with their neighborhood.

The rationale for tabulating the relative standing of the respondent (and of his neighborhood) was the expectation that a person's satisfaction with his immediate neighborhood is associated with his position in that neighborhood and with the neighborhood's standing in the community. A home or neighborhood which is appreciably more expensive than others, for example, might confer a certain status upon its owner which would lead that resident to value his neighborhood more than his less fortunate neighbors. As the data show, however, the results vary depending upon the particular measure being investigated.

Item N in the table, the neighborhood maintenance level, is clearly related to satisfaction in our sample and was found to be the single best predictor of

Table 38

Neighborhood Satisfaction for Responses Related to

Accessibility and Other Factors

(percentage of respondents giving neighborhood highest rating)[1]

	Percent Giving Area Highest Rating on Neighborhood Satisfaction Scale	N (base of percentages)
A. Distance to Grocery Store in Minutes		
Less than 5 minutes	50	493
5-9 minutes	51	344
10-14 minutes	50	236
15-19 minutes	58	78
20 minutes or more	52	90
B. Length of Head's Journey to Work in Minutes		
Less than 10 minutes	59	53
10-14 minutes	53	98
15-19 minutes	50	138
20-29 minutes	46	163
30-44 minutes	51	287
45-59 minutes	51	199
60 minutes or more	49	164
C. Distance to Nearest Outdoor Swimming Pool		
Up to 1/4 mile	45	365
1/4 to 1 mile	53	681
1 mile or more	53	207
D. Presence of a Bus Stop within a Ten Minute Walk		
Yes	51	962
No	55	247
E. Family Income		
Under $12,500	49	189
$12,500-$14,999	49	162
$15,000-$17,499	52	163
$17,500-$19,999	54	182
$20,000-$24,999	49	260
$25,000-$29,999	57	126
$30,000 and over	49	119

neighborhood evaluation in the multivariate analyses reported by Lansing and Hendricks.[22] The next item, the length of residence in the neighborhood, however, shows little relationship to satisfaction in these communities. We had expected that the longer residents lived in an area the more they might become attached to, and satisfied with, the immediate neighborhood.

Finally, given the presumed importance of privacy in residential neighborhoods we expected that there might be a point at which people felt that they saw quite enough of their neighbors and would prefer to see less of them to maintain their privacy. The last item in Table 38 was designed to allow

---

[22]*Living Patterns and Attitudes*, pp. 181-191. The authors also suggested that the upkeep of structures (rather than grounds) was the key component of the general "maintenance level." (p. 75)

Table 38 - continued

	Percent Giving Area Highest Rating on Neighborhood Satisfaction Scale	N (base of percentages)
F. Respondent's Education		
High school graduate or less	56	253
Some college	56	293
College graduate (B.A.)	47	323
Graduate training	48	381
G. Duncan Socio-Economic Decile of Head's Occupation		
9th decile	49	802
8th decile	55	273
7th or lower decile	55	133
H. Home Value		
Under $26,000	43	58
$26,000-$31,999	38	231
$32,000-$37,999	51	379
$38,000-$43,999	53	220
$44,000-$49,999	55	129
$50,000 and over	66	119
I. Rating of Home as Financial Investment		
Better than other homes considered	57	801
Same as other homes considered	44	233
Worse than other homes considered	25	45
J. Relative Standing in Micro-Neighborhood on Housing Cost[2]		
Very low	48	58
Low	56	176
Middle	48	701
High	54	201
Very high	61	67
K. Relating Standing in Micro-Neighborhood on Family Income[3]		
Very low	58	198
Low	55	132
Middle	50	549
High	49	128
Very high	42	193

respondents to indicate whether the "too neighborly" threshold had been reached in their neighborhoods. The tabulations indicate that, for roughly half the respondents, the threshold may have been reached and that this does lead to a devaluation of the neighborhood setting.

Summary: From the collection of variables considered in this section a few may be singled out as more important. Specifically, the residents whose rating of their neighborhood is highest are those who rate the neighborhood as "well kept up" (71 percent); who think their neighbors would like to see more of each other (70 percent); and whose homes are valued at $50,000 or over (66 percent). The least satisfied residents, on the other hand, are those who feel that their home was a relatively bad investment (only 25 percent highly satisfied); who feel strongly that people don't want to spend more time with their neighbors (39 percent); and who feel that the neighborhood is not "well kept up" (24 percent

Table 38 - continued

	Percent Giving Area Highest Rating on Neighborhood Satisfaction Scale	N (base of percentages)
L. Relative Standing of Average Housing Cost of Respondent's Neighborhood in Relation to Community Mean Housing Cost[4]		
Very low	44	129
Low	45	531
High	57	463
Very high	63	122
M. Relative Standing of Average Family Income of Respondent's Neighborhood in Relation to Community Mean Family Income[4]		
Very low	44	66
Low	48	534
High	54	590
Very high	56	62
N. Neighborhood Maintenance Level		
Well kept up	71	705
	28	398
	12	97
	4	24
Poorly kept up	18	11
O. Year Moved into Present Home		
1969	52	224
1968	54	344
1965-67	50	408
1964 or earlier	49	276
P. People Would Like to Spend More Time with Neighbors		
Agree strongly	70	83
Agree somewhat	56	537
Disagree somewhat	45	480
Disagree strongly	39	93
Total	51	1253

[1]Respondents giving neighborhood highest ratings include those who rated the neighborhood most positively on all four scale items or most positively on these items and only one category less positively on the fourth.

[2]Within each neighborhood sample cluster owners were compared with owners and renters with renters. Respondents who were the only owner or renter in the

for the four lowest categories combined). The relative impact of each of the factors considered in this section together with the factors included earlier is evaluated in the section which follows.

F. *Predicting Neighborhood Satisfaction*

The preceeding sections of this chapter introduced a number of potential predictors of neighborhood satisfaction related to dwelling unit density and site planning, social compatibility, accessibility, and other aspects of the residential environment. In this section we will first present simple bivariate correlations of these variables with the neighborhood satisfaction scale. Since we conceptualize

Table 38 - continued

cluster, therefore, are not included in this table. The code categories used to establish a resident's standing are those precoded in the questionnaire for questions 53a and 54. The classifications in this table indicate:

1. Very low - no one ranks below R in cluster and over half of the remaining respondents rank two or more code categories above R.

2. Low - no one ranks below R in cluster and over half of the remaining respondents rank one or more code categories above R.

3. Middle - R cannot be coded in categories 0, 1, 2, 4 or 5.

4. High - no one ranks above R in cluster and over half of the remaining respondents rank one or more code categories below R.

5. Very high - no one ranks above R in cluster and over half of the remaining respondents rank two or more code categories below R.

0. No rating - R is only respondent (owner, renter) in cluster; R's housing cost as owner or renter not ascertained.

[3]The same procedure was followed here as with housing cost. The basic code categories are those shown in the questionnaire for question 66.

[4]For both housing cost and family income neighborhoods were coded according to the code below. Too few cases matched the community means to include that category in the table. Average rental figures were used only when average home values were unavailable for a neighborhood.

1. Very low - average housing cost (family income) of neighborhood is 1 or more standard deviations below community mean.

2. Low - average housing cost (family income) of neighborhood is up to .99 standard deviations below community mean.

3. Middle - average housing cost (family income) of neighborhood is the same as the community mean.

4. High - average housing cost (family income) of neighborhood is up to .99 standard deviations above community mean.

5. Very high - average housing cost (family income) of neighborhood is 1 or more standard deviations above community mean.

density as the underlying factor for many of the items considered (e.g., hearing one's neighbors, privacy in the yard) and hence only indirectly affecting neighborhood satisfaction, the analysis in this section will control for this underlying effect by presenting parallel regression analyses for low density neighborhoods (up to 4.5 dwellings per acre) and for high density neighborhoods (4.5 or more dwellings per acre).[23] It will then be possible not only to determine which factors are most important for neighborhood satisfaction, but also to determine if different factors are important in neighborhoods of different densities.

The correlation and multiple regression analyses: The correlations of the neighborhood satisfaction scale with the potential predictors are shown in Table 39. They indicate that the factors most associated with satisfaction are the neighborhood's maintenance level, the friendliness and the similarity of the neighbors, and the neighborhood noise level.

---

[23]Partitioning the sample at this point means that 99 percent of the lower density dwellings are single family units and, from another perspective, 97 percent of the townhouse dwellings are located in the higher density settings.

Table 39

Summary of Variables under Consideration for Multivariate Analysis

Ordered by Zero-Order Correlation with the

Neighborhood Satisfaction Scale

Variable	Correlation with Neighborhood Satisfaction Scale
Poorly kept up-well kept up	.56
Unfriendly-friendly	.44
Similar-dissimilar	.36
Noisy-quiet	.34
Rating of places near home for children to play	.27
Investment quality of home	.19
People would like to spend more time with neighbors	.18
Standing of neighborhood in community-housing cost	.16
Frequency of hearing neighbors	.16
Proportion of neighbors known by name	.15
Frequency of casual interaction with neighbors	.15
Privacy in yard from neighbors	.14
Adequate outdoor space for family activities	.14
Home value	.11
Respondent's standing in neighborhood-income	-.09
Distance to nearest outdoor swimming pool	.09
Education of respondent	-.09
Standing of neighborhood in community-income	.08
Duncan decile of head's occupation	-.07
Distance in time to grocery store	.03
Caring if neighbors are heard	.03
Length of residence	.02
Presence of nearby bus stop	.02
Family income	.02
Distance in time to head's workplace	.00
Respondent's standing in neighborhood-housing cost	.00
Number of respondents	1253

Through a several step process of elimination it was possible to reduce the number of predictors to those included in the regressions reported in Table 40.[24] The rating of areas near home for young children to play was omitted because it was asked of only about half of the respondents.[25] The investment

_____

[24]This process is reviewed in detail in Zehner, *op. cit.*, Chapter VI. It was based on the statistical significance of the bivariate and multivariate relationships of the predictors to the neighborhood satisfaction scale. In addition to investigating differences in satisfaction by density level as reported here, *Satisfaction With Neighborhoods* also considers differences in neighborhood evaluation by the sex of the respondent. In general it was found that men and women use simliar criteria to rate their neighborhoods.

[25]When parallel regressions were run for only those people who were asked to rate play areas (respondents with children under 12 in their household), the quality of the children's play areas added about 3 percent to the explained variance in both high and low density areas.

quality of the home variable was entered in the equation as a set of dummy variables.[26] Note that the group of residents who rent are not included as part of any of the dummy variable set. In effect, persons who rent become the standard to which the homeowners are compared.

As we might expect on the basis of the bivariate correlations, by far the best predictor of neighborhood satisfaction reported in Table 40 is the maintenance level of the neighborhood which alone explains 27 percent and 33 percent of the variance. At both density levels the compatibility measures and the neighborhood noise level also contribute significantly to the explanation of variation in the neighborhood satisfaction responses. Beyond this point differences between density levels emerge. In the high density areas, for example, the adequacy of outdoor space for family activities becomes important—the more space available, the higher the neighborhood rating.

In the low density areas, on the other hand, owning a home which has turned out to be a worse investment than others considered at the time of purchase contributes markedly to dissatisfaction with the neighborhood. Of greater interest, however, is that for people living in low density areas the effect of home ownership (whether a better, same or worse investment) did not add to a favorable neighborhood evaluation. The residents who provide the basis of comparison for these homeowners (i.e., those not coded "1" on any one of the three dummy variables) rated neighborhoods more highly than the homeowners who answered the investment quality question.[27]

---

[26]For each respondent we coded, first, if he rated his home as a "better" investment" (coded 1) or not (coded 0); second, if he rated it as the "same" quality investment (coded 1) or not (coded 0); and third, if he rated it a "worse investment" (coded 1) or not (coded 0).

[27]Since in our sample as a whole renters rate neighborhoods much lower than homeowners, it is apparent that the plan to have only non-homeowners (mainly renters) as the omitted category in the home investment dummy variables may not have worked as expected. This proved to be the case since, of the 40 respondents who had not indicated that their home was either better, the same, or worse as an investment, only 10 were not homeowners. The other 30 were homeowners who had been unable or unwilling to answer the investment quality question.

Curiously enough, however, when these 40 cases were checked to determine what effect the 30 homeowners had on the mean satisfaction for the dummy comparison group, it turned out that both parts of the comparison group had the same mean. Specifically, in the low density sample the average satisfaction score for the 10 renters was 14.3; for the 30 homeowners who hadn't answered the investment question it was also 14.3; for the homeowners with a "better" investment it was 14.2; for those with the "same" investment, 13.8; and for those with a "worse" investment, 11.1.

In effect, in other words, while the 10 non-owners in the sample were given added weight by the 30 non-responding homeowners, the results of Table 40 are accurate in indicating that non-owners in the low density areas of our communities do tend to evaluate their neighborhoods more highly than homeowners—even those who feel their home is a particularly good investment.

Table 40

Multiple Regression Analysis of Neighborhood Satisfaction,
by Density of Neighborhood

Predictors	Low Density			High Density		
	Percent Added to Variance Explained	Standardized Regression Coefficient[1]	t-ratio	Percent Added to Variance Explained	Standardized Regression Coefficient[1]	t-ratio
Poorly kept up-well kept up	27.1%	.37	12.9	33.9%	.40	10.4
Unfriendly-friendly	7.9	.17	5.5	8.6	.26	6.6
Noisy-quiet	4.9	.21	7.6	1.2	.11	3.0
Similar-dissimilar	2.3	.14	5.0	1.7	.13	3.5
Adequate space near home	.4	.05	1.9	2.1	.14	4.0
Respondent's standing in neighborhood-Income	.5	-.06	2.4	.2	-.07	1.9
Neighborhood's standing in community-Housing	.9	.11	4.1	.0	.03	.9
Like more time with neighbors	.6	.09	3.2	.0	.01	.3
Duncan decile of head's occupation	.6	-.07	2.6	.2	.03	1.0
DV Home better investment	2.0	-.06	1.1	.9	.07	1.8
DV Home same investment		-.10	1.9		.05	1.3
DV Home worse investment		-.16	4.7		-.05	1.3
Total percent of variance explained	47.2%			48.8%		
Residual degrees of freedom[2]	748			457		
Constant term	12.03			10.13		

[1] This coefficient indicates in standard deviation units the amount of change in the dependent variable which is associated with a change of one standard deviation in the predictor variable.

[2] This quantity equals the number of respondents minus the number of predictors minus one. The number of respondents was defined for the regression as the average number of valid cases among the predictor variables. For the regression for low density, N=761; for high density, N=470.

Several other aspects of Table 40 should be noted. First, although all but one of the ten predictors attained t-ratios of 2.0 or above (.05 significance level relationships) in the low density areas, only five factors contributed more than one percent to the explanation of variance. In the high density areas, on the other hand, all five factors which were significant contributed at least one percent to the explained variance.

At both density levels the combination of the neighborhood maintenance factor plus the two social compatibility items clearly account for most of the explained variance. We will conclude this chapter with a brief assessment of the pertinence of these findings for persons concerned with the planning or development of residential environments.

Summary and conclusions: The analysis presented in this chapter suggests that several of the factors which are important for neighborhood satisfaction are amenable to design considerations. Of overriding importance for satisfaction in both high and low density areas was the general maintenance level of the neighborhood. To the extent, therefore, that a planner-developer either designs neighborhoods to favor ease of maintenance and/or provides for upkeep of the buildings and grounds, he can influence, if not fully determine, the residents' subsequent reports of satisfaction.

While the second most important factor was the compatibility of neighbors, a variable we assume planners cannot influence significantly, several other aspects of the neighborhood which proved salient are within the scope of a planner's designs. In higher density neighborhoods, for instance, residents indicate that adequate outdoor space for family activities is important. In these areas people who felt that they had too little space had several needs in mind including, primarily, space for children to play, but also space for family cookouts, small scale recreation (e.g., badminton), pets, and various hobbies. In addition, the evaluation of the neighborhood on the noisy-quiet dimension contributed appreciably to the explanation of variation in neighborhood satisfaction responses in both high and low density areas.

Of central concern to the transportation planner are people's preferences for environments of different levels of density. The analysis in this chapter leads to the general conclusion that while people on the average tend to prefer low density to high density environments, their level of satisfaction with the residential neighborhood depends on a complex set of variables. We have shown several of these variables to be related to density, but we have also found that these relationships are complex, and can best be understood in a multivariate context.

Finally, we must note that the communities and the respondents included in our study are hardly representative of the range of residential environments and residents existing in the country today. The applicability of our findings to other settings and other respondents can best be established empirically in subsequent research.

PART III

**TRAVEL BEHAVIOR OF PEOPLE
IN DIFFERENT TYPES
OF RESIDENTIAL ENVIRONMENTS**

6

CAR OWNERSHIP, ANNUAL MILEAGE, AND THE JOURNEY TO WORK

In Part III of this report we consider the effects of the type of residential environment in which people live upon their travel behavior. The residential environments we are studying range in location from the heart of the central city to new peripheral sites beyond the area of continuous surburban development. Such large differences in location must produce differences in travel behavior: we shall consider the nature of the differences. The residential environments also range from a high to a low level of planning. One feature of the more highly planned areas is special emphasis on provision of public transportation. We shall be interested in tracing as far as we can the effects of these facilities. It is also characteristic of the planned communities that they provide more public facilities, such as outdoor recreation facilities as discussed in Chapter 4, and that shopping and other facilities found in all communities may be arranged differently. We shall be interested in the effect on travel behavior of both differences in the facilities provided and of any differences in how they are arranged.

The first chapter in Part III is concerned with car ownership, annual mileage, and the journey to work. Car ownership and annual mileage are the most reliable guides we have to overall travel behavior in this study. The second chapter is concerned with reports of trips in the 24 hours prior to interview based on questions similar to those asked in home interviews in typical metropolitan transportation studies. We shall be especially concerned with a methodological problem in the accuracy of these reports related to who is reporting trip data for the family. Chapter 8 considers weekend travel in detail. Three important categories of local transportation about which special questions were asked, shopping trips, bus transportation, and walking and bicycle riding are dealt with in Chapter 9. In each of these chapters the theme will be the effects of the differences among the communities in the study on different aspects of travel behavior.

A. *Car Ownership*

In considering the level of car ownership in the communities we are studying we may use as a point of departure the level of car ownership in the nation as a whole. According to the 1969 Survey of Consumer Finances of all families in the nation 79 percent owned at least one car and 27 percent owned two or more cars in the winter of 1969. We know, however, that people in the communities we are studying are in the upper income groups. Table 41 shows the proportion of families in each income group who own at least one car, and who own two or more cars, also from the Survey of Consumer Finances. The first row of Table 42 repeats the statistics on median family income by community—it will be recalled that the medians range from $15,000 upwards.

Virtually every family in 9 of the 10 communities owns at least one car. In Southwest Washington, 14 percent own no car, but it will be recalled that this community contains a number of young single people sharing bachelor quarters. Also, since it is possible for people in Southwest Washington to walk or take a short bus ride to their placed of employment, it is not surprising that not every member of such a group owns a car. Elsewhere, ownership is very close to universal.

There are interesting differences, however, in the level of multiple ownership. Across the six suburban communities the proportion of families owning two or more cars does turn out to be related to the level of planning. It is 66 and 63 percent, respectively, in the two most highly planned communities, 72 and 76 in the moderately planned, and 86 and 82 in the least planned. That is, multiple ownership is about 20 percentage points higher in the least planned than the most highly planned communities.

We can place these findings in national perspective by further use of the data from the Survey of Consumer Finances. We know the income distribution for our 10 communities and we also know, from Table 41, the national level of ownership at each income level. We can estimate for each income class in each community what the ownership level would be if the national average applied, and, by combining these estimates, derive an expected level of ownership for the community. These predicted levels as well as the observed levels of ownership are shown in Table 43.

It turns out that the level of multiple ownership is about the same in the highly planned peripheral communities as expected but higher than expected in the less planned communities.

The centrally located communities show much lower levels of multiple ownership than would be predicted on the basis of the incomes of the people

Table 41

Vehicle[1] Ownership - within Family Income Groups in the United States

(percentage distribution of families)

Annual Family Income	Number of Vehicles Owned						Total
	None		One		Two or More		
	1966	1968	1966	1968	1966	1968	
Less than $5,000	43	46	44	43	13	11	100
$5,000-$7,499	14	13	55	56	31	31	100
$7,500-$9,999	6	6	50	50	44	44	100
$10,000-$14,999	4	4	36	36	60	60	100
$15,000 or more	7	3	22	27	71	70	100
All families	20	18	44	42	36	40	100

[1]Includes cars, trucks, pick-ups, vans, and jeep-type vehicles.

Source: 1969 Survey of Consumer Finances conducted by the Survey Research Center.

who live there. In Southwest Washington, indeed, only one family in ten owns two cars; on the basis of their incomes we would expect over half of the families to own two cars.

The two older communities, Radburn and Glen Rock, show slightly lower levels of multiple ownership than the income level of the people who live there would suggest. This result is consistent with earlier findings that automobile ownership tends to be depressed in the New York region except near its periphery. There is virtually no difference in ownership level between Radburn

Table 42

Car Ownership

	Columbia	Reston	Crofton	Montpelier	Norbeck	Southfield	Lafayette Elmwood	Southwest Washington	Radburn	Glen Rock
Median Family Income (in dollars for all families)	17,100	20,000	19,800	19,300	17,900	18,800	21,800	15,400	16,300	18,900
Car Ownership (percentage distribution)										
No car	-	-	-	-	-	1	2	14	1	-
One car	34	37	28	24	14	17	61	76	42	46
Two or more cars	66	63	72	76	86	82	37	10	57	54
Total	100	100	100	100	100	100	100	100	100	100
Number of families	215	203	98	105	99	110	105	107	103	105

Table 43

Comparison between Observed Level of Auto Ownership and Expected
Level Based on National Average Related to Income[1]

	Columbia		Reston		Crofton		Montpelier		Norbeck	
	Expected	Observed	Expected	Observed	Expected	Observed	Expected	Observed	Expected	Observed
No car	4	-	4	-	4	-	3	-	3	-
One car	31	34	30	37	29	28	29	24	30	14
Two or more cars	65	66	66	63	67	72	67	76	67	86
Total	100	100	100	100	100	100	100	100	100	100

	Southfield		Lafayette Elmwood		Southwest Washington		Radburn		Glen Rock	
	Expected	Observed	Expected	Observed	Expected	Observed	Expected	Observed	Expected	Observed
No car	3	1	3	2	9	14	5	1	6	-
One car	30	17	30	61	36	76	33	42	32	46
Two or more cars	67	82	67	37	55	10	62	57	62	54
Total	100	100	100	100	100	100	100	100	100	100

[1]Expected levels were computed by applying to the family income distribution by community of Table 3 to the vehicle
ownership rates by income found in the 1969 Survey of Consumer Finances and shown in Table 41.

and Glen Rock, implying that the planned features of Radburn such as the super-blocks have little or nothing to do with automobile ownership levels.

B. *Annual Mileage Driven*

Total annual mileage driven is a useful global measure of the total volume of automobile use. In a sample survey people are able to report this statistic with what seems to be tolerable accuracy. Accuracy of report could be improved by asking for an actual odometer reading and then reinterviewing the family at a later date and obtaining a second actual reading. In this study, however, only one interview was taken and the sequence of questions was as follows:

How many cars or trucks do you people have for family use?

What year was the car bought?

Altogether about how many miles has it been driven since you bought it?

In the last 12 months about how many miles has the car been driven?

The results are believed to be good approximations.

Given the difference in the number of cars owned among the peripheral communities, it would be reasonable to expect a difference in annual mileage driven. The average annual mileage for all car owning families, that is, for practically all families, is 22,000 and 21,000 in the two most planned peripheral communities; 23,000 and 21,000, respectively, in the moderately planned; and 20,000 and 24,000 in the least planned areas. An estimate of 22,000 miles per year would be reasonably close for each level of planning.[1]

If the people in the planned communities own fewer cars and drive an equal number of miles, they must put more miles on their cars. We have attempted to find out what the pattern of use may be by estimating average annual mileage for "first," "second," and "third" cars separately (see Table 44). Which of its cars is "first," which is "second," and which "third" for any family is not a matter over which the investigators attempted to exercise any control. The interviewers asked the questions shown above.

The average mileage on the "first" cars turns out to be about the same across the six communities, roughly 13,000 miles per year. The average mileage on the "second" cars also is not very different, 11,000 to 12,000 in the most planned; 11,000 to 14,000 in the moderately planned; and 11,000 to 13,000 in the least planned. About 12,000 miles per year would seem typical. The

---

[1] In a national survey of metropolitan areas (exclusive of New York) the mean mileage on all autos for families whose average income was $15,000 was about 23,000 miles. Lansing and Hendricks, *Automobile Ownership and Residential Density*, p. 27.

Table 44

Mileage Driven on All Cars in the Last Twelve Months

	Columbia	Reston	Crofton	Montpelier	Norbeck	Southfield	Lafayette Elmwood	Southwest Washington	Radburn	Glen Rock
Mileage on All Cars in the Last 12 Months (excluding families with no cars; mean number)	21,700	20,900	23,200	21,400	19,700	24,200	15,700	11,300	14,200	16,600
Number of families	200	174	84	94	73	88	95	84	76	90
Mileage on First Car (mean)	13,500	12,200	13,100	13,000	10,400	13,000	11,600	10,300	9,400	10,600
Number of families with at least one car[1]	198	182	88	96	83	94	96	86	81	97
Mileage on Second Car (mean)	11,100	12,200	13,700	11,300	10,600	12,800	10,200	8,800	9,400	9,900
Number of families with at least two cars[1]	128	110	63	71	65	75	39	9	43	52
Mileage on Third Car (mean)	18,500	14,500	9,200	10,600	8,200	8,500	1,000	a	7,500	10,400
Number of families with three cars[a]	12	17	5	7	9	10	1	a	4	9

[1]Excludes families for whom information on mileage was not ascertained.

[a]No families observed in this category.

Table 45

Average Annual Mileage per Car

Community	Cars per Family	Miles per Car per Year
Columbia	1.73	12,500
Reston	1.73	12,100
Crofton	1.80	12,900
Montpelier	1.87	11,400
Norbeck	2.04	9,700
Southfield	1.93	12,500
Lafayette-Elmwood	1.37	11,500
Southwest Washington	0.96	11,800
Radburn	1.65	8,600
Glen Rock	1.70	9,800

difference seems to be in the miles driven on the "third" car. There are only a few families with "third" cars, but these cars seem to be driven roughly 16,000 miles in Reston and Columbia compared to about 8,000 in Norbeck and Southfield. Both Columbia and Reston are isolated, in the sense that they are located outside the urbanized area in the metropolitan region. It is not surprising that a few people who live in these locations find themselves driving very long distances. The overall picture seems to be one of reduced local mileage, shown by the comparatively low level of multiple ownership in these two communities, offset in the averages by the small group of families with three cars who drive long distances. Thus, total mileage per family works out about constant, but its components are different. We shall look at the data in the next chapters with this interpretation in mind.

The total annual mileage driven in the two centrally located areas is smaller than in the suburban communities, as one might expect. Lafayette-Elmwood and Southwest Washington both are served by freeways in their immediate vicinity. The annual mileage per family is 16,000 in the one and 11,000 in the other, compared to the 22,000 or so observed in the peripheral areas. In the two older communities in Northern New Jersey the average annual mileage is about 15,000. There is a slight difference in the direction of lower mileage per family in Radburn than in Glen Rock.

Finally, in Table 45 we make use of the car ownership and annual mileage rates to obtain an estimate of the average annual mileage driven on cars in each of the communities. When differences in rates of ownership across communities are taken into account in this way, the in-town communities appear much more similar to the new, peripheral areas. Families in the New Jersey communities and in Norbeck (where families averaged more than two cars a piece) tend to drive fewer miles per car per year.

C. *The Journey to Work*

The daily peak loads created by the journey to work are of central importance in the planning of urban transportation systems. If we think of the location of places of work and of residence as fixed, for purposes of this chapter, then the problem of the journey to work is one of moving people between fixed pairs of points. We may begin by considering the distances to be covered. National estimates of the distribution of journeys to work by distance based on data from other surveys can be compared to results from the present study.

Distance to Work (Road Distances)	National Estimate for Metropolitan Areas[1]	Estimates from This Study (Straight Line Distances)[2]	
Less than 1 mile	12		
1.0-1.9 miles	10	One mile or less	14
2.0-3.9 miles	19	2-3 miles	12
4.0-5.9 miles	17	4-5 miles	8
6.0-9.9 miles	18	6-9 miles	13
10.0-14.9 miles	12	10-14 miles	19
15 miles or more	12	15 miles or more	34
Total	100		100
Number of journeys	1516		1136

[1]Lansing and Hendricks, *Automobile Ownership and Residential Density, op. cit.* p. 37. Estimate is for metropolitan areas (exclusive of New York).

[2]Distance based on estimates from measurements on maps. Straight line distances were estimated. Point of origin was taken as the center of the sample population in the community. Location of work was based on a respondent's report of the nearest intersection to his place of employment.

The comparison is an approximate one since the distance estimates in this study are straight line distances estimated from maps while those in the earlier national surveys are road distances reported by the people interviewed. The contrast between the distributions is thus inaccurate: the straight line distances are less than road distances. It is obvious, however, that people in this study typically commute much longer distances than the people in a national sample.

The communities in this study are by no means homogeneous with respect to the distances people live from their work. The average straight line distance from home to work for heads of families is shown in the first column of Table 46. As expected, the average distance is much less for the in-town communities than for the suburban communities. For Lafayette-Elmwood the average distance is 3.7 miles; for Southwest Washington, 2.0 miles. The standard deviations of the distributions also are shown in Table 46. Most people who live in these two centrally located areas have short journeys to work.

In the six suburban communities the average distance to work is much

Table 46

Mean Straight Line Distance from Home to Place of Employment by Community

| | All Methods Combined[1] | | | Method of Making the Journey to Work | | | | | |
| | | | | Always by Car | | Sometimes Car, Sometimes Public | | Always Public | |
Community	Mean	Standard Deviation	N	Mean	N	Mean	N	Mean	N
Columbia	13.3	9.1	203	13.0	184	17.0	12	14.0	1
Reston	13.8	7.8	181	13.4	121	16.3	35	17.3	16
Crofton	15.8	5.7	89	16.1	83	15.8	4	-	-
Montpelier	10.8	5.8	97	10.9	90	10.7	3	15.0	1
Norbeck	9.9	5.0	92	10.2	82	13.5	2	-	-
Southfield	9.9	4.7	102	10.0	95	16.0	2	15.5	2
Lafayette-Elmwood	3.7	4.1	95	4.9	66	1.3	10	1.0	6
Southwest Washington	2.0	1.8	98	2.7	44	2.3	15	1.4	11
Radburn	9.7	7.5	87	7.3	53	14.8	9	17.7	16
Glen Rock	11.4	8.7	91	11.0	56	12.4	7	18.1	17
All communities	10.6	7.8	1135	10.9	874	12.1	99	13.5[a]	70

[1]Includes those who walk to work and a few who use other methods.

[a]Excludes communities where only one person appears in this column.

longer, the average ranging from about 10 to 16 miles. The average distances are high for the two new towns, about 13 to 14 miles. It was intended originally that these communities be self-contained and include both people's homes and their places of work. As of November and December 1969 the plans to develop major local employment centers remained in the future and most people who lived in Columbia and Reston were commuting.

The mode of travel used for the head's journey to work is shown in the first section of Table 47. The six suburban communities present a different type of problem from the in-town communities and the suburbs of New York. Across the six, the percentage who always go to work by car ranges from 93 percent upwards with one conspicuous exception: Reston. In the other five the percentage who always use public transportation is uniformly tiny, 2 percent or less.

The unusual development in Reston is the commuter bus service to downtown Washington. The number of riders on the system during the period of

Table 47

Mode of Travel and Time to Get to Work for Employed Heads of Families by Community

(percentage distribution of heads of household)

	Columbia	Reston	Crofton	Montpelier	Norbeck	Southfield	Lafayette Elmwood	Southwest Washington	Radburn	Glen Rock
Mode of Head's Journey to Work (employed heads with one place of work)										
Always by car	93	71	96	96	96	95	73	49	65	66
Sometimes car, sometimes public	6	19	4	3	2	2	11	16	11	8
Always public transportation	*	8	-	1	-	2	7	13	20	20
Walking	-	-	-	-	1	-	5	12	2	1
Other	1	2	-	-	1	1	4	10	2	5
Total	100	100	100	100	100	100	100	100	100	100
Number of heads	204	188	89	95	86	103	93	96	82	85
Length in Minutes of Head's Journey to Work (employed heads with one place of work)										
Under 10 minutes	5	6	-	1	1	1	12	2	16	4
10-14 minutes	3	5	-	11	6	1	35	17	12	9
15-19 minutes	5	5	2	14	8	15	24	39	10	16
20-29 minutes	12	8	12	26	13	18	19	28	12	6
30-44 minutes	39	25	34	23	33	38	10	12	13	18
45-59 minutes	21	28	39	19	23	19	-	1	5	11
60 minutes or more	13	23	13	6	16	8	-	1	32	36
Total	100	100	100	100	100	100	100	100	100	100
Number of heads	203	184	88	94	86	99	92	94	82	80
Median trip time	39	45	46	43	39	35	15	18	30	42

*Less than one-half of one percent.

the survey was as follows:

Week Period (1969)	Total Riders Both Directions per Week
November 3-7	2233
November 10-14	1816
November 17-21	2174
November 24-28	1623
December 1-5	2350
December 8-12	2408
December 15-19	2213

Source: Letter from Donald A. Morin, Public Transportation Branch, Bureau of Public Roads.

There were seven buses each way each day throughout the survey period. The project is unsubsidized and is operated by the commuters themselves.

It is difficult to make an exact comparison between the survey results and these ridership statistics. The survey data do not indicate exactly the frequency of bus use for people who "sometimes" use it. It is undoubtedly the commuter bus, however, which is taken by the 16 respondents, 8 percent of the total, who always use public transportation to a destination which averages 17 miles away.[2]

In the centrally located communities more people drive to work than use any other mode of travel, but some people do use public transportation, and a few people walk. The "other" methods used include taking a taxi to work.

In the older communities in the New York area, Radburn and Glen Rock, public transportation is well developed. Two family heads in ten always use public transportation to get to work; an additional one in ten sometimes uses it. As shown in the trip reports in Chapter 7 the mix of public transportation used in these communities includes suburban railroads as well as bus and rapid transit.

Public transportation can best serve areas where there are substantial numbers of people who wish to travel between a tight cluster of points or origin and another tight cluster of points of destination. We can indicate the importance of this factor for how people get to work by examining the dispersion of the distribution of distances people travel to work. Our measurements, it will be recalled, are made to the nearest mile from the centers of population of the residential communities studied to the place of work. We do

---

[2]A further problem in making statistical comparisons is that we do not have an estimate for the total number of heads of families in Reston at the time of the survey. Such an estimate, for our purposes would have to exclude people who live in apartment houses, which were excluded from the study. Some people who live in apartments, however, undoubtedly ride the commuter bus.

Table 48

Modal Choice and the Mean and Standard Deviation of

Distances to Work by Community

(straight line distances in miles measured on maps)

Community	Always Public			Sometimes Car, Sometimes Public			Always Car		
	Mean	S.D.	N	Mean	S.D.	N	Mean	S.D.	N
Reston	17.3	1.2	16	16.3	3.0	35	13.4	8.7	121
Radburn	17.7	1.5	16	14.8	4.5	9	7.3	6.9	53
Glen Rock	18.1	0.9	17	12.4	8.2	7	11.0	8.7	56
Southwest Washington	1.4	0.5	11	2.3	1.3	12	2.7	2.3	44
Lafayette-Elmwood	1.0	0.0	6	1.3	0.7	10	4.9	4.4	66

not describe lines of travel except by community of residence and distance in these calculations, so that two places 10 miles from our points of origin could be 20 miles from each other. As a practical matter, however, the long journeys to work from our suburban communities are mostly all in one direction, so that the simple dispersion of distances to work is a rough approximation of the scatter of the destinations. For example, we expect that two men who both go 17 miles from Reston are probably going to about the same spot.

We have computed and shown in Table 48 the mean distance, the standard deviation of the distances (S.D.), and the number of observations for five communities, showing these figures separately for each of the three categories of method of getting to work. We could not include the other communities since virtually nobody in them always uses public transportation. Even as it is we report some statistics based on very few observations.

The most interesting feature of Table 48 is the increase in the dispersion of the distribution of distances to work as one moves from those who always use public transportation to those who sometimes use it and those who always go by car. In Reston, for example, the standard deviation is only 1.2 miles for those who always take the bus; it is 3.0 miles for those who sometimes use public transportation; and it is 8.7 miles for those who always travel by car. For each of the five communities without exception the same increase occurs. For the three suburban communities in Table 48 at the same time that the standard deviation is rising the mean is falling as one moves from left to right across the table, i.e., from public to automotive transportation. The regular riders of the Reston bus, for example, are traveling about 17 miles (straight line distance) to a compact destination area. The regular users of auto transportation from Reston travel an average of 13 miles and the dispersion of the distances they travel is 9 miles.

The two in-town communities, on the other hand, show an association of longer distances to work with automotive transportation. In Southwest Washington, for example, for those who always use public transportation the mean distance is about 1.4 miles, while for those who always travel by car it is

2.7 miles. In the same manner in Lafayette-Elmwood the small group who always use public transportation travel an average of 1.0 miles and all go to the same destination area, namely, the Detroit central business district. Those who travel by car average 4.9 miles to work with a standard deviation of 4.4 miles. These results suggest that it is not distance which is the predominant factor in the market for public transportation so much as the concentration of points of origin and destination.

The long distances commuted by so many people in the communities studied imply long periods of time spent in getting to work. The times reported are shown in the second section of Table 47. Roughly speaking, the people who live in communities which are a longer distance from where they work spend more time to get to work. There are considerable numbers of people who spend an hour or more to get to work in all except the centrally located communities. The communities where it is most common for people to spend a long time getting to work are Glen Rock and Radburn, where one family head in three needs an hour or more to reach his job.

These findings about the journey to work are consistent with existing knowledge on the subject. The finding which stands out is the importance of the commuter bus in Reston.

Annual mileage for the journey to work: We have attempted to estimate the average annual miles driven by the head of the family for the journey to work. This calculation is based on the interview report as to the mode of travel he uses and the straight line distance to his job estimated by us from maps. We have made the following assumptions:

1) one round trip per working day

2) 250 working days per year

3) 15 percent extra mileage to convert straight line to road mileage

4) when several people ride together the miles driven should be reduced in proportion

5) "sometimes" by car and "sometimes" by public transportation means 50 percent each way.

On these assumptions the average annual miles driven per year per family to get the head to work and back is as shown in Table 49, second column. The distances involved are in the range from 4,100 to 6,300 miles for the six peripheral communities, or about 20 to 25 percent of all miles driven. For the other four communities the use of public transportation for the journey to work is more common, and the miles driven for the head's journey are smaller both absolutely and as a proportion of total mileage.

The conclusions reached above about the differences in mileage across

Table 49

Annual Miles Driven Adjusted for the Head's Journey to Work

Community	Mileage on All Cars	Weighted Average Miles for Head's Journey to Work[1]	Mileage for Other Purposes	Percentage of Total Annual Miles for Head's Journey to Work
Columbia	21,700	5,600	16,100	26
Reston	20,900	4,100	16,800	20
Crofton	23,200	6,300	16,900	27
Montpelier	21,400	4,200	17,200	20
Norbeck	19,700	4,100	15,600	21
Southfield	24,200	4,600	19,600	19
Lafayette-Elmwood	15,700	1,600	14,100	10
Southwest Washington	11,300	600	10,700	5
Radburn	14,200	2,200	12,000	15
Glen Rock	16,600	3,100	13,500	19

[1]See text for method of estimation. Average is for all families including those who never drive to work.

communities are not greatly changed when one considers only mileage for other purposes. Radburn and Glen Rock appear more similar. People in Lafayette–Elmwood still drive more than those in Southwest Washington, but both in-town communities still show fewer miles driven than the six suburban areas. The tendency for people in Southfield to average more miles per year than those elsewhere is accentuated, but Norbeck, the other community with a low level of planning, remains at the bottom of the six in miles driven.

7

TRIPS IN THE LAST 24 HOURS
AND THE ACCURACY
WITH WHICH THEY ARE REPORTED

A basic source of information for use in transportation planning is home interviews covering all trips in the 24 hours prior to the interview. One interview is taken per family using a fairly well standardized set of definitions and procedures. The information needed to account for all trips of all members of a large and active family, however, can be complex. To obtain it accurately is not an easy problem in interviewing. The details of the definitions and procedures used in this study are shown in Appendix C and in the questionnaire in Appendix D. Results of a methodological inquiry into the effects of obtaining the trip information from the head of the family or the wife of the head appear in part B of this chapter.

The principal substantive question to which this chapter is addressed is, are there systematic differences in the trips people take which are associated with differences among the types of residential environments?

A. *Variation across Communities in Vehicle Trips*
   and Person Trips

Previous research provides a basis for comparison with the total number of vehicle trips reported in the present study. In 1964 a national survey yielded an estimate of 5.2 vehicle trips per family in metropolitan areas (exclusive of New York). The number rose with income, reaching 8.3 vehicle trips for families with incomes over $15,000 per year, a level roughly comparable in real terms to the median incomes of the residents of the communities in this study.[1]

---

[1]*Residential Location and Urban Mobility,* John B. Lansing and Eva Mueller, Institute for Social Research, The University of Michigan, Ann Arbor, Michigan, June, 1964, p. 54.

Table 50

Vehicle Trips in the Last 24 Hours by Community
(mean number of vehicle trips per family)

	Columbia	Reston	Crofton	Montpelier	Norbeck	Southfield	Lafayette Elmwood	Southwest Washington	Radburn	Glen Rock
A. Origin of Trip										
Work	1.4	1.2	1.0	1.0	1.3	2.0	1.6	.9	1.2	1.2
Home	2.8	2.6	2.6	3.0	3.5	3.3	2.2	1.7	3.4	3.3
Friend's or relative's home	.5	.4	.3	.7	1.1	.5	.4	.2	.7	.9
Store, restaurant, bank	1.4	1.1	.8	1.7	1.5	1.4	.8	.7	1.6	1.9
Doctor's office, hospital	.2	.1	.1	.1	.1	.2	*	*	.1	.2
School	.5	.6	.6	.6	.7	.7	.3	.2	.5	.5
Other; N.A.	.9	.9	.8	1.0	1.2	.9	.8	.5	1.4	1.6
Total	7.7	6.9	6.2	8.1	9.4	9.0	6.1	4.2	8.9	9.6
B. Purpose										
Go home	2.8	2.6	2.7	3.0	3.4	3.2	2.2	1.8	3.3	3.2
Get to work	1.4	1.2	1.0	1.1	1.3	2.0	1.6	.8	1.2	1.2
Shopping	1.0	.9	.7	1.4	1.3	1.0	.5	.5	1.2	1.2
Attend school	.4	.4	.5	.4	.5	.5	.2	.2	.3	.3
Social or recreational	.6	.6	.5	.7	.9	.8	.5	.4	.7	1.0
To take someone somewhere (serve a passenger)	.7	.6	.4	.7	1.3	.7	.5	.3	1.1	1.5
To change mode of travel	.1	.1	.1	.1	.1	.1	*	*	.4	.6
Personal business, medical, dental	.5	.3	.4	.7	.4	.5	.4	.2	.7	.7
Eat meal	.3	.2	*	.2	.2	.4	.2	.1	.3	.3
Other; N.A.	.2	.2	.2	.2	.4	.2	.4	.1	.5	.4
Total[1]	8.0	7.1	6.5	8.5	9.8	9.4	6.5	4.4	9.7	10.4

Table 50 - continued

	Columbia	Reston	Crofton	Montpelier	Norbeck	Southfield	Lafayette Elmwood	Southwest Washington	Radburn	Glen Rock
C. Destination of Trip										
Home	2.8	2.6	2.7	3.0	3.5	3.3	2.2	1.8	3.3	3.3
Work	1.4	1.2	1.0	1.1	1.3	2.0	1.6	.8	1.2	1.2
School	.5	.5	.6	.5	.7	.7	.3	.2	.5	.5
Friend's or relative's home	.5	.4	.2	.7	1.1	.5	.4	.2	.8	.9
Store, bank, restaurant	1.4	1.1	.8	1.7	1.5	1.4	.9	.6	1.6	1.9
Doctor's office, hospital	.2	.1	.1	.1	.1	.2	*	.1	.1	.2
Other; N.A.	.9	1.0	.8	1.0	1.2	.9	.7	.5	1.4	1.6
Total	7.7	6.9	6.2	8.1	9.4	9.0	6.1	4.2	8.9	9.6
D. Mode of Travel										
Auto driver, auto passenger	7.0	6.0	5.5	7.6	8.9	8.6	5.6	3.5	8.3	8.8
Suburban railroad	.1	*	*	-	-	*	-	*	.2	.2
Bus	.6	.8	.7	.5	.5	.4	.4	.4	.2	.3
Rapid transit	-	-	*	*	-	-	*	-	.2	.3
Walk to work	*	-	-	-	-	-	.1	.2	*	*
Taxi	*	.1	*	*	*	*	*	.1	*	*
Other	*	*	*	*	*	*	*	-	-	*
Total	7.7	6.9	6.2	8.1	9.4	9.0	6.1	4.2	8.9	9.6
Standard deviation	4.4	4.0	3.4	4.4	5.3	5.8	3.8	3.0	5.4	5.6

Table 50 - continued

	Columbia	Reston	Crofton	Montpelier	Norbeck	Southfield	Lafayette Elmwood	Southwest Washington	Radburn	Glen Rock
E. Mode of Travel (percentage distribution)										
Automobile (driver or passenger)	90	87	88	94	95	95	92	83	93	91
Bus	8	12	11	5	5	4	6	9	2	3
Walk to work	†	-	-	-	-	-	1	6	†	†
Other (rapid transit, taxi, etc.)	2	1	1	1	†	1	1	2	5	6
Total	100	100	100	100	100	100	100	100	100	100
Number of vehicle trips	1661	1402	610	852	927	992	647	450	917	1019

* .05 or less trips per day.

† Less than one-half of one percent.

1 Trip purpose totals are slightly higher since up to two purposes could be recorded for multi-person trips.

The mean number of vehicle trips per family in each of the ten communities is shown in Table 50. The standard deviation is also shown. The mean for all ten combined is 7.6 vehicle trips per family with a standard deviation of 4.8. The variation within communities is large relative to the variation across communities.[2] Only about 10 percent of the total variance is accounted for by differences among communities. We may note, however, that such variation does exist. The largest difference is that between the two centrally located communities, which average 6.1 and 4.2 trips for Lafayette-Elmwood and Southwest Washington, respectively, and the peripheral communities. Even among the peripheral communities, however, there is a range from 6.2 for Crofton to 9.0 for Southfield, with the most highly planned areas near the middle of that range. There is no evidence that the total number of vehicle trips per family is appreciably influenced by the level of community planning.

The subdivisions of Table 50 present estimates for each community of the average number of vehicle trips per family by origin, purpose, destination, and mode. If two or more family members take a trip together, only one vehicle trip is counted. The most interesting classification in the table is that by mode, and we have indicated both the mean and the percentage distributions of trips on this basis in the last two panels of the table. We expect a higher number of bus trips in the more planned communities. There are some small differences in the predicted direction. The average number of bus trips is about 0.7 per family in Columbia and Reston compared to about 0.4 for residents of the least planned suburban communities. No distinction is made in these statistics between bus trips within the community and outside it.

While the automobile clearly dominates vehicular travel, there is also a slight relationship between automobile use and planning in the new, peripheral communities. On the average about one trip in ten in highly planned Columbia and Reston combined is not by car, while in least planned Norbeck and Southfield only about one trip in twenty is not by automobile. Moderately planned Crofton and Montpelier combined fall in between.

While the mean number of vehicle trips does vary somewhat by community, there is little difference in the proportion of all trips made for specific purposes as shown in Table 51. There is no evidence, in other words, that the range of community planning considered in this study is associated with the purposes of the vehicle trips reported.

Essentially the same data used in Table 50 have been tabulated on a person trip basis in Table 52. Since two or more people often ride in the same vehicle,

[2]The sum of squares divides as follows as between variation within communities and across communities:

Total sum of squares	= 29014
Between means sum of squares	= 2921
Within groups sum of squares	= 26093

Table 51

Purposes of Vehicle Trips in the Last 24 Hours by Community
(percentage distribution of purposes mentioned)[1]

Purpose	Columbia	Reston	Crofton	Montpelier	Norbeck	Southfield	Lafayette Elmwood	Southwest Washington	Radburn	Glen Rock
Go home	35	37	42	36	35	34	33	41	34	31
Get to work	18	17	15	13	14	22	24	18	12	12
Shopping	13	12	12	16	13	11	8	12	13	12
Attend school	5	6	8	5	5	5	3	4	3	2
Social or recreational	7	8	8	8	9	8	8	9	7	9
Take someone somewhere (serve a passenger)	9	8	6	8	13	8	8	7	12	15
Change mode of travel	1	2	1	1	1	1	1	1	4	6
Personal business	6	4	6	8	4	5	6	4	7	6
Eat meal	3	2	*	2	2	4	3	1	3	3
Other	3	4	2	3	4	2	6	3	5	4
Total	100	100	100	100	100	100	100	100	100	100
Number of vehicle trip purposes mentioned	1703	1440	622	873	960	1028	698	462	988	1106

*Less than one-half of one percent.

[1] If more than one person took a trip up to two purposes could be coded for that trip.

Table 52

Person Trips in the Last 24 Hours by Community

(mean number of person trips per family)

	Columbia	Reston	Crofton	Montpelier	Norbeck	Southfield	Lafayette Elmwood	Southwest Washington	Radburn	Glen Rock
A. Origin of Trip										
Work	1.5	1.3	1.0	1.1	1.3	2.0	1.7	.9	1.2	1.3
Home	3.9	3.6	3.6	4.4	5.0	4.5	2.8	2.0	4.6	4.8
Friend's or relative's home	.8	.5	.3	1.1	1.5	.7	.6	.3	1.2	1.1
Store, restaurant, bank	2.0	1.5	1.1	2.6	2.5	2.0	1.0	.8	2.3	2.5
Doctor's office, hospital	.2	.1	.2	.1	.1	.2	*	*	.2	.3
School	.8	.9	.9	.8	1.0	1.0	.4	.3	.6	.9
Other; N.A.	1.3	1.5	1.3	1.8	2.1	1.3	1.0	.6	1.9	2.2
Total	10.5	9.4	8.4	11.9	13.5	11.7	7.5	4.9	12.0	13.1
B. Purpose										
Go home	4.0	3.7	3.7	4.5	5.0	4.3	2.8	2.0	4.4	4.6
Get to work	1.5	1.2	1.1	1.1	1.4	2.1	1.7	.8	1.2	1.3
Shopping	1.5	1.2	1.0	2.1	1.9	1.4	.6	.6	1.7	1.8
Attend school	.6	.6	.7	.5	.6	.8	.3	.2	.5	.6
Social or recreational	1.0	.9	.8	1.1	1.5	1.2	.8	.5	1.0	1.5
To take someone somewhere (serve a passenger)	1.0	.9	.5	1.1	1.9	1.3	.9	.5	2.1	2.7
To change mode of travel	.1	.2	.1	.2	.2	.1	.1	.1	.4	.7
Personal business, medical, dental	.7	.4	.5	.9	.7	.6	.4	.2	.8	.8
Eat meal	.3	.3	*	.3	.3	.5	.2	.1	.4	.4
Other; N.A.	.4	.4	.3	.6	.8	.3	.7	.2	1.0	.5
Total[1]	11.1	9.8	8.7	12.4	14.3	12.6	8.5	5.2	13.5	14.9

Table 52 - continued

	Columbia	Reston	Crofton	Montpelier	Norbeck	Southfield	Lafayette Elmwood	Southwest Washington	Radburn	Glen Rock
C. Destination of Trip										
Home	4.0	3.7	3.7	4.5	5.0	4.4	2.9	2.0	4.5	4.6
Work	1.4	1.2	1.1	1.1	1.4	2.1	1.7	.8	1.2	1.3
School	.8	.9	.8	.7	1.0	1.0	.4	.3	.7	.9
Friend's or relative's home	.8	.5	.3	1.1	1.5	.7	.6	.3	1.3	1.2
Store, bank, restaurant	2.0	1.6	1.1	2.7	2.5	2.0	1.0	.8	2.3	2.6
Doctor's office, hospital	.3	.1	.2	.1	.1	.2	*	.1	.1	.3
Other; N.A.	1.2	1.4	1.2	1.7	2.0	1.3	.9	.7	1.9	2.2
Total	10.5	9.4	8.4	11.9	13.5	11.7	7.5	5.0	12.0	13.1
D. Mode of Travel										
Auto driver, auto passenger	9.5	8.1	7.3	11.3	13.0	11.2	7.0	4.1	11.4	12.2
Suburban railroad	*	*	-	-	-	*	-	*	.2	.2
Bus	1.0	1.2	1.0	.6	.5	.5	.4	.5	.2	.4
Rapid transit	-	-	*	*	-	-	*	-	.2	.3
Walk to work	*	-	-	-	-	-	.1	.3	*	*
Taxi	*	*	.1	*	*	*	*	.1	*	*
Other	*	.1	*	*	*	*	*	-	-	*
Total	10.5	9.4	8.4	11.9	13.5	11.7	7.5	4.9	12.0	13.1
Standard deviation	6.8	5.8	5.4	7.5	9.0	7.7	4.9	3.7	7.9	8.9

* .05 or less trips per day.

[1] Trip purpose totals are slightly higher since up to two purposes could be recorded for multi-person trips.

the number of person trips is greater than the number of vehicle trips. For the combined communities the average number of person trips per family is 10.1 compared to 7.6 vehicle trips, implying about 1.3 persons per vehicle trip. As before, the greatest interest may be in the number of bus trips, which is about 1.0 person trips per family in Columbia and Reston and about 0.5 in Norbeck and Southfield.

B. *Relation of Whether Head or Wife Is Respondent to Number of Trips Reported*

One of the basic problems in survey research in general and reports of trips in particular is the extent to which it is possible for one person to report accurately for an entire family. This study had an experimental manipulation built into the basic procedures by which data were collected which provides some information about this problem. The experimental manipulation consisted in the random designation in advance of the interview of the husband or the wife as the respondent. This manipulation, of course, does not have any meaning when the family does not include a married couple—a single person necessarily answers the questions for himself.

As a result of this random procedure in selecting the respondent we can compare the number of person trips reported in random halves of the sample which we may take to be similar in every respect except who the respondent was. The results are shown in Table 53. Section A of the table includes all families and is of minor interest since the single persons are combined with the heads of families. The main results are those in Section B in which only married couples are considered. On the average, husbands speaking for themselves report 4.61 trips in the preceding 24 hour period, while wives report 3.75 trips for their husbands. It appears that husbands take about 0.86 trips per day more than their wives report. Perhaps the men move about more during the day than their wives realize. This result is more or less what we expected. We also thought it likely that wives speaking for themselves would report more trips, on the average, than would their husbands speaking for them. The results, to our surprise, showed that the average number of person trips taken by wives was almost exactly the same when reported by husbands (3.63) as when reported by the women themselves (3.65). For reports of trips by others in the household, also, it seems to make very little difference whether the husband or the wife is the respondent. The net result is that for the household as a whole the number of person trips reported is about one trip higher when the husband reports than when the wife reports, 11.5 versus 10.4 trips per day.

Households consisting of a single person account for about half as many person trips on the average as households containing a married couple. The single respondents (which include the widowed, separated, and divorced as well as the bachelors) average 5.4 trips per day. It should be kept in mind that all these estimates refer to people living in our selected residential areas and not to

Table 53

Mean Number of Trips Reported by Heads of Families Compared to Wives

	Who is Respondent?	
Type of Trip Taken	Heads and Single Persons	Wives
A. All families		
Number of person trips by head	4.47	3.76
Number of person trips by wife	2.81	3.64
Number of person trips by other family members	2.63	2.92
Number of person trips by visitors	0.16	0.12
Total	10.06[a]	10.44
	n = 710	n = 543
B. Married respondents only	Husbands	Wives
Number of person trips by husbands	4.61	3.75
Number of person trips by wives	3.63	3.65
Number of person trips by other family members	3.07	2.92
Number of person trips by visitors	.20	.12
Total	11.51	10.45
	n = 542	n = 541
C. Single respondents	Single People	
Number of person trips by head	4.02	
Number of person trips by other family members	1.34	
Number of person trips by visitors	.01	
Total	5.37	
	n = 168	
D. Overall mean for all families	10.15	
	n = 1253	

[a]Detail will not add to total owing to rounding.

cross-sections of the general population.

When the purpose of the data collection is to assemble complete information about a family, we may say a priori that the best procedure would be to interview every member of the family, or, at least, every adult member. The need for more than one preson to contribute to the report is greatest when the family is large and active. Interviewers were permitted and encouraged to obtain reports about trips with the assistance of any family member who could help. In 81 percent of the interviews only one person reported. The remaining 19 percent, however, were interviews in which, on the average, the family took a large number of trips. As shown in Table 54, when both respondent and spouse contributed to the report the average was 14.2 trips per family. We interpret this to mean that when the family took a large number of trips the respondent often was aware of that fact and called for assistance, usually from his spouse. We

Table 54

The Effect of Receiving Help on the 24-Hour Trip Reports

(mean numbers of person trips and vehicle trips reported)

Person Trips	Mean Number of Trips	Percent Distribution
Respondent only contributed to trip reports	9.1	81
Respondent and respondent's spouse contributed	14.2	14
Respondent and respondent's child(ren) contributed	14.7	2
Respondent, spouse and child(ren) contributed	18.3	2
Respondent and someone other than spouse or child(ren) contributed	9.4	1
Overall mean	10.1	
Total		100
Number of respondents		1253

Vehicle Trips		
Respondent only contributed to trip reports	6.8	81
Respondent and respondent's spouse contributed	10.5	14
Respondent and respondent's child(ren) contributed	11.1	2
Respondent, spouse and child(ren) contributed	13.3	2
Respondent and someone other than spouse or child(ren) contributed	6.9	1
Overall mean	7.6	
Total		100
Number of respondents		1253

suggest that it may be that the average reports when husbands are designated respondents are more complete because when husbands are interviewed, wives are usually also at home, and can be interrogated if need arises. Wives, however, may be interviewed during the day when husbands are at work and cannot readily be asked about their husbands' trips.

8

WEEKEND TRAVEL

Weekend trips are of increasing importance to transportation planners. The analysis of this type of travel, however, has not received nearly the attention which has been given to the journey to work. The few questions asked on the topic in this study were intended to be exploratory.

There is one issue of special interest in this study with regard to weekend travel. It is sometimes urged that planned residential communities are unusually attractive places to live. People who live in new towns, therefore, might be expected to stay near home on weekends more than those who live in ordinary communities. Why should people leave a new town when so many attractive facilities are available near their homes? Hence, there should be fewer weekend trips by the residents than by comparable people who live elsewhere. One of the purposes of this project is to test the correctness of this reasoning. The remainder of this chapter is occupied with a more general analysis of weekend travel.

A. *Weekend Trips in Highly Planned and Less Planned Communities*

The sequence of questions asked about weekend travel in this study was as follows:

> Last weekend did you go on any trips ten miles or more away from here other than on your vacation?
>
> How many miles away from here did you go?
>
> What was the main reason for the trip?

It is particularly important to keep in mind that it is weekend trips to places ten miles or more away which are being investigated, rather than shorter trips. One reason behind the decision to restrict attention to the longer trips was that the special features of planned communities are not likely to keep people literally at

Table 55

Weekend Trips

(percentage distributions)

	Columbia	Reston	Crofton	Montpelier	Norbeck	Southfield	Lafayette Elmwood	Southwest Washington	Radburn	Glen Rock
Incidence and Length of Reported Trips										
No trip reported	37	31	38	46	50	58	55	64	57	43
Trip reported	63	69	62	54	50	42	45	36	43	57
10-19 miles	11	19	18	17	17	13	13	7	13	19
20-33 miles	36	21	23	23	17	10	19	8	12	13
40-59 miles	7	11	6	4	4	4	3	-	6	7
60 or more miles	9	18	15	10	12	15	10	21	12	18
Total	100	100	100	100	100	100	100	100	100	100
Number of respondents	216	203	98	105	99	110	106	107	103	106
Main Reason for Reported Trips										
To serve a passenger	5	1	1	4	4	2	2	3	2	2
To get to work; business	7	11	10	11	10	11	17	17	18	5
Shopping; personal business	26	26	28	32	14	11	13	14	16	7
To go to public event; concert; etc.	5	10	15	12	21	22	6	5	5	12
Informal social/recreational purpose	51	49	36	39	47	49	58	50	48	73
Other reasons; no defined purpose	6	3	10	2	4	5	4	11	11	1
Total	100	100	100	100	100	100	100	100	100	100
Number of trips	136	138	61	56	49	45	48	36	44	59

home. They may take trips to visit local facilities if trips are defined in the sense used in the 24 hour trip report. It is the longer trips which may be less frequent.

The data needed to test the hypothesis that weekend trips are less frequent in the more highly planned communities are shown in the first section of Table 55. The hypothesis must be rejected. The proportion of the population taking a weekend trip to a place ten miles or more away averages about 66 percent in the most highly planned suburban communities (63 and 69 percent in Columbia and Reston, respectively), about 58 percent in the moderately planned (62 and 54 in Crofton and Montpelier), and about 46 percent in the least planned (50 and 42 percent in Norbeck and Southfield). If anything there are *more* people taking weekend trips in the more highly planned new suburban communities.

In the in-town communities the percentage taking weekend trips is comparatively low, 45 percent in Lafayette-Elmwood and 36 percent in Southwest Washington. We had tentatively expected the contrary, since we thought that high income people who live near the center of a large city would often want to go to the country on weekends. The older communities of Radburn and Glen Rock also show a low to moderate frequency of weekend trips, 43 and 57 percent, respectively.

There are some indications of variations from community to community in the length of the trips people take. In Southwest Washington, where only 36 percent took a trip ten miles or more, over one half of these people took a trip to a place 60 or more miles away. A comparatively high proportion of people in Southfield also took 60 mile trips (15 percent), while the percentage of people who took a trip of any length is low (42 percent). We are uncertain why such differences in trip length should exist, but we do not find much reason to associate them with the degree of planning.

Examination of the results suggests an alternative interpretation: for the high income group being considered, the incidence of weekend trips increases the farther they live from the center of the urbanized area in which they reside. Congestion decreases as one moves outward, and it should be increasingly easy to travel a distance of ten miles or more. We shall consider community location in the next section.

B. *Analysis of Weekend Trips*

To contribute to knowledge of weekend trips to places ten miles or more away we combine in this section data from the ten communities and examine the effects of three basic factors—family income, location in the metropolitan area, and stage in the family life cycle. We shall also look at the purposes of weekend trips in relation to distances travelled.

Since weekend trips involve expenditure for the cost of automotive transportation, as well as possibly for related purposes, one might reasonably suppose that people's outlays on such trips would rise if their income rises.

Table 56

Weekend Trips to Places Ten Miles or More Away by Family Income
(percentage distribution of respondents)

Weekend Travel	All	Family Income					
		Under $12,500	$12,500 -14,999	$15,000 -17,499	$17,500 -19,999	$20,000 -24,999	$25,000 and over
No trip reported	46	51	46	47	44	43	44
Trip reported	54	49	54	53	56	57	56
Distance to destination:							
10-19 miles	14	12	17	15	13	17	14
20-39 miles	20	21	20	19	21	19	20
40-59 miles	6	3	6	5	6	7	6
60 miles or more	14	13	11	14	16	14	16
Total	100	100	100	100	100	100	100
Number of respondents	1249	189	162	163	182	260	245

(Some trips no doubt were by other modes of travel, but the great majority of these trips undoubtedly were by car.) The relation of income to whether people take a weekend trip and how far its destination may be is shown in Table 56. Weekend travel does seem to rise with income but not appreciably in the range over $12,500 a year. The percentage of income spent on weekend travel, thus, declines as income increases; in fact, the income elasticity of expenditure for automotive transportation on weekends must be close to zero.

As suggested above, where people live in a metropolitan area is much more related than their income to their weekend trips (Table 57). Of those who live in in-town communities, Lafayette–Elmwood and Southwest Washington, only 40 percent reported a trip ten miles or more away on the most recent weekend, compared to 63 percent of those who live in new peripheral communities, Columbia, Reston, Crofton, and Montpelier. The built-up suburban areas, Norbeck, Southfield, Radburn, and Glen Rock, fall in between, with 48 percent reporting a weekend trip. We prefer this interpretation to that which would argue that the internal planned features of the former communities grate on people's nerves so that they leave them on weekends. All the evidence in earlier chapters is that people like the planned peripheral communities—but we must add that they are also actively engaged in activities in other parts of the metropolitan region on weekends.

Many of people's activities are influenced by the composition of their families. Weekend travel is not an exception. Young, married couples with no children tend to take weekend trips more often than other people. As shown in Table 58, 68 percent of those in this group reported a weekend trip, including 18 percent who went to a destination 60 miles or more away, which implies a round trip of at least 120 miles. It is more surprising to us that the proportion

Table 57

Weekend Trips to Places Ten Miles or More Away by Location of Community
(percentage distribution of respondents)

Weekend Travel	All	In-town	Community Location in Metropolitan Area Built-up Suburban	Isolated Suburban
No trip reported	46	60	52	37
Trip reported	54	40	48	63
Distance to destination:				
10-19 miles	14	10	15	16
20-39 miles	20	14	14	26
40-59 miles	6	1	5	8
60 miles or more	14	15	14	13
Total	100	100	100	100
Number of respondents	1253	213	418	622

reporting a weekend trip is not very much lower for people at other stages in the family life cycle. Even in families with a child under 5, 50 percent took a trip; even of older people not now married (the widowed, separated, and divorced) 46 percent took a trip 10 miles away. We repeat that these estimates apply to the special communities we are studying, so that we are effectively excluding the low income groups and people who live in apartments which no doubt include elderly people for whom driving a car may seem more of a burden.

The transportation planner's interest in forecasting weekend travel may parallel other people's curiosity as to where all those people are going and for what purposes. We can look at the joint distribution of distance and purpose for the trips reported to us, as is done in Table 59. Of all the weekend trips 50 percent are for informal social and recreational purposes. Shopping and personal business account for 21 percent. Trips to formally scheduled public events account for 11 percent and to get to work (even on the weekend) for 10 percent. In terms of miles travelled the trips for informal social and recreational purposes are more important than their numbers would indicate. Fifteen percent of all weekend trips are trips to places 60 miles or more away for informal social or recreational purposes. Another way to look at the same point is to note that informal social and recreational trips account for three out of four of all weekend trips 60 miles away. Trips for shopping or on personal business are likely to be shorter; nearly half of them are to destinations only 10-19 miles away.

The classification of weekend trips used in Tables 55 and 59 is in some respects too gross. We would like to know in more detail why people take these trips. A closer scrutiny of the trips we do know about may be of assistance for this purpose. The method we have adopted is to list in Table 60 all the available

Table 58

Weekend Trips to Places Ten Miles or More Away by Stage in the Family Life Cycle

(percentage distribution of respondents)

Weekend Travel	All	Young, Single[1]	Young, Married, No Children	Married, with Children			Older, Married, No Children at Home	Older, Single[2]	Single with Children
				Youngest under 5	Youngest 6-14	Youngest 15 or over			
No trip reported	46	47	32	50	45	40	44	54	53
Trip reported	54	53	68	50	55	60	56	46	47
Distance to destination:									
10-19 miles	14	12	11	16	15	20	16	18	8
20-39 miles	20	18	35	20	20	15	16	9	9
40-59 miles	6	3	4	5	5	10	7	3	8
60 miles or more	14	20	18	9	15	15	17	16	14
Total	100	100	100	100	100	100	100	100	100
Number of respondents	1249	85	91	362	398	67	153	57	36

[1]Young is defined as under 45; older as 45 or above.
[2]Single includes widowed, separated, and divorced.

Table 59

Purpose and Distance to Destination of Weekend Trips to Places Ten Miles or More Away

(percentage of weekend trips to destinations 10 miles or more away)

Distance to Destination	Trip Purpose						
	To Serve a Passenger	To Get to Work	Shopping or Personal Business	Attendance at Formally Scheduled Public Event	Informal, Social or Recreational	Other Reasons	Total
10-19 miles	1	2	9	3	11	1	27
20-39 miles	2	3	8	4	19	2	38
40-59 miles	*	5	3	1	5	1	15
60 miles or more	*	*	1	3	15	1	20
Total	3	10	21	11	50	5	100
Total number of weekend trips	19	71	140	71	335	33	669

*Less than one-half of one percent.

Table 60

Selected Examples of Weekend Trips

Type of Purpose	Distance (miles)	Specific Purpose as Stated by Person Interviewed
A. Shopping; personal business	10-19	"To New York City, shopping."
	10-19	"To get apples and cider."
	10-19	"To get a Christmas tree."
	29-39	"Antiquing - we refinish them."
	20-39	"Shopping for antiques."
	20-39	"Visiting relatives and to shop."
	20-39	"Business and pleasure. Take daughter to Washington, D.C. for dancing lessons."
	40-59	"Shopping. We went to Winchester. It was wonderful."
B. To go to a public event	10-19	"To attend church."
	10-19	"A football game."
	10-19	"Educational meetings."
	40-59	"A football game."
	60 or more	"A car rally sponsored by _____ car."
C. Informal social or recreational purpose	10-19	"To visit friends."
	20-39	"A visit to sick friend in hospital then out to dinner."
	20-39	"Out for dinner. To Leesburg."
	20-39	"To go to the airport. I have a plane over there - in Leesburg."
	40-59	"We went to my mother's home for Thanksgiving and a visit with her."
	60 or more	"Visit relatives."
	60 or more	"We went to the mountains to get away from it all."
	60 or more	"Obtaining proficiency flight time."
	60 or more	"See son at Naval Academy."
	60 or more	"Sailing."
	60 or more	"To take a drive along the Skyline Drive."

details about a limited number of actual trips reported to us. The examples selected are limited to three of the categories shown in Table 59: "Shopping and personal business"; "To go to a public event"; and "Informal, social or recreational purposes."

People often state simply that the purpose was "shopping." The examples in Part A of Table 60 suggest that some of the trips for shopping involve going a distance to search for rare or one-of-a-kind goods unlikely to be available everywhere. Antiques would seem to have this character. Other goods and services may be most advantageously purchased in a big city market—as on the trip to New York from one of the New Jersey communities. Any adequate economic analysis would require information about the quantity and character of the items sought. The marketing distinction between shopping goods and convenience goods might prove helpful. The trip "to get a Christmas tree" 10-19 miles away sounds more like an agreeable excursion than a calculated effort to obtain the most tree for a consumer's money.

The specific public events most often mentioned as reasons for trips on the fall weekends studied were football games. People also mentioned other events as diverse as church services and sports car rallies. It seems obvious that the clientele for these events is likely to be very different, and analysis of the probable future demand would seem to require separate consideration of the frequency of trips to attend different types of events. Trips to attend sports events would seem one likely category for separate analysis.

Informal social and recreational purposes, as already emphasized, are the most frequent reasons for weekend trips. Examination of the examples of Part C of Table 60 indicates that they are diverse. One major category consists of trips to visit relatives, often parents or children who have left home. A second category consists of visits to friends. The third major category includes outdoor recreation, ranging from private flying to a trip to the mountains "to get away from it all."

Future inquiry into weekend trips should make use of a more detailed classification by purpose than we were able to use in Table 60. Examination of examples of specific trip purposes suggests that weekend travel is much more diverse in motivation than are the weekday trips, dominated as the latter are by the single purpose of getting from home to work and back. A more adequate typology of reasons for weekend travel is a necessary step toward more satisfactory projections of demand. On the basis of the data at hand the most important predictor of weekend travel is the location of the community where people live within the metropolitan area, with the highest volume of weekend travel associated with a peripheral location.

9

ELEMENTS OF
LOCAL TRANSPORTATION

In this chapter we consider the time it takes residents to get to the grocery store they use most frequently in comparison with similar data based on a national sample. We then present data on the presence, use, and desirability of bus service easily available to the residents. Finally, we conclude with a discussion of the importance of walking and bicycling as both a type of recreation and a mode of purposeful travel in our communities.

A. *Shopping*

From the point of view of a consumer it is preferable to have shopping facilities which are easily accessible which offer a wide selection of merchandise at low prices. In this study, however, we have been able to consider shopping only to a limited extent. We have data only on some aspects of its accessibility to the exclusion of the other basic desiderata.

From the point of view of the transportation planner, shopping is one reason why people take trips. Its importance may be approached by estimating the average number of vehicular trips per day people take to go shopping. This information is shown in the last line of Table 61 based on tabulations of trips in the last 24 hours.

There is considerable range in the average number of person trips per family for this purpose, from 0.6 in the two in-town communities to as high as 2.0 in Montpelier. The fact that the two in-town communities show fewer vehicular shopping trips than the suburban communities may well be due to the proximity of their stores. People may walk to shop frequently rather than drive. Had we included walking trips to shop in our 24 hour report, we would have expected that since a central location implies easy access to shops, a tendency to shop frequently. That walking is a frequent mode for shopping trips in these areas will be indicated later in this chapter. Parking problems and difficulty with

175

Table 61

Shopping Trips and Time to Reach the Grocery Store

(Percentage distribution of families)

Length in Minutes of Trip to Most Frequently Patronized Grocery Store	Columbia	Reston	Crofton	Montpelier	Norbeck	Southfield	Lafayette Elmwood	Southwest Washington	Radburn	Glen Rock
Less than 5 minutes	55	19	5	14	28	28	70	46	71	62
5-9 minutes	27	17	25	44	40	48	18	29	19	21
10-14 minutes	8	34	46	24	20	21	7	7	8	14
15-19 minutes	1	16	14	12	3	3	-	7	2	2
20-29 minutes	7	7	6	6	2	-	4	8	-	1
30 or more minutes	2	7	4	-	7	-	1	3	-	-
Total	100	100	100	100	100	100	100	100	100	100
Number of families	215	200	98	105	98	109	105	105	100	106
Median	4	11	11	8	7	6	3	5	3	3
Percent who spend 15 minutes or more	10	30	24	18	12	3	5	18	2	3
Number of person-trips to go shopping in last 24 hours	1.5	1.2	1.0	2.1	1.8	1.3	0.6	0.6	1.6	1.8

bundles on public vehicles probably contribute to make vehicular shopping more difficult for people in the central city than for people in suburban communities.

As far as time to reach the grocery store is concerned, the people in central locations do have easy access. People were asked how long it usually takes to reach the place where most of the grocery shopping is done for their family. As shown in Table 61 most people do not have to spend much time to get to the grocery store. The median of the times reported is 3 to 5 minutes for the centrally located communities and for the older communities in New Jersey. In the six suburban communities the range is 4 to 11 minutes. The statistics for the two new towns seem to reflect more than anything else the state of construction at the time of interview. Most of the people interviewed in Columbia were close to a village center with a supermarket; some in Reston were close, but others (in Hunters Woods) were at some distance from a shopping center.

We can gain some persepctive on these results by comparing them with data recently reported by Stegman.[1] He uses a national survey with 1476 households in 43 metropolitan areas and reports the mean time to the grocery store as follows:

	Central City	Suburb
Persons who recently moved into large metropolitan areas	8.1 min.	6.8 min.
Nonmovers in large metropolitan areas	8.3 min.	6.2 min.
Persons who recently moved into small metropolitan areas	6.9 min.	11.1 min.

By these standards the people in our in-town communities enjoy unusually quick access to their grocery stores. Our least planned peripheral communities, Norbeck and Southfield, are close to the national averages, with Crofton and Montpelier also close but a bit on the high side with medians of 11 and 8 minutes compared to Stegman's 6.2 to 6.8 in suburbs of large metropolitan areas. Columbia and Reston are below and above these levels, respectively. When construction is further advanced at Reston the time to reach the grocery store may well be equal to or less than Stegman's national average of about six and a half minutes.

B. *Bus Service*

We did not ask people the mode of transportation they use to go shopping as we did the mode for the journey to work. We did ask three questions,

---

[1]Michael A. Stegman, "Accessibility Models and Residential Location," *Journal of the American Institute of Planners,* January 1969, pp. 22-29.

however, about bus service. Although commuter use is also included in the figures, upper limits on the use of the bus to go shopping can be inferred from the data on total frequency of bus use. The sequence of three questions asked about bus service was as follows:

Is there a bus stop within a 10 minutes walk of your home?

How often do you yourself use the bus?

How important is it to you whether there is a bus stop near your home?

The results are shown in Table 62. The communities differ greatly in the percentage of homes with a bus stop within a 10 minute walk. In the two highly planned areas, there is bus service. In the moderatly planned communities, there is practically no bus service. In the communities with a lower level of planning, which also are communities in continuously built-up suburban areas, once again most people report bus service. There are also buses which serve the inner city communities and the older New Jersey communities.

The frequency of reported use of the bus service is comparatively high in Reston, for reasons discussed in earlier parts of this report. Otherwise very few people report using the bus in any of the six suburban communities. This finding is of interest especially for Columbia, where a special effort has been made to provide local bus service within Columbia. The present survey shows that about 22 percent of people interviewed report that they personally do use the bus, but only 5 percent report that they use it as often as one day a week.

The areas of most frequent patronage of the local bus service are the two inner city communities. Of people living in Lafayette-Elmwood 17 percent report using the bus once a week or more; of people in Southwest Washington 25 percent use the bus at least once a week.

People report that they value having bus service available more highly than one might expect on the basis of how often they use it. The proportion who say that it is very important to them to have a bus stop near their home is over 50 percent in the inner city areas and in the range from 17 to 28 percent even in the areas where there now is no service.

The logical implication seems to be that people value the bus, not because they use it so much, but because it is worth something to them to have it available on a standby basis. Further questions on the importance of standby service and what people might be willing to pay for it might be asked in future surveys.

C. *Walking and Riding Bicycles*

Walking and riding bicycles are not often thought of as substitutes for mechanized transportation. Urban planners, however, may adopt this point of view since the possibility exists of so arranging facilities in urban areas that to

Table 62
Bus Transportation
(Percentage distribution of respondents)

	Columbia	Reston	Crofton	Montpelier	Norbeck	Southfield	Lafayette Elmwood	Southwest Washington	Radburn	Glen Rock
Bus Stop Reported within 10 Minute Walk of Home										
Bus stop is present	95	95	-	1	63	75	99	99	98	100
Not present	2	4	98	91	29	11	1	-	2	-
Don't know	3	1	2	8	8	14	-	1	-	-
Total	100	100	100	100	100	100	100	100	100	100
Number of respondents	215	203	98	105	99	110	106	107	103	106
Frequency of Bus Use (for respondents reporting a bus stop within a 10 minute walk of home)										
One day a week or more often	5	14	a	a	-	1	17	25	4	10
2-3 days a month	2	1	a	a	2	-	8	5	1	4
One day a month or less	15	9	a	a	8	2	25	14	33	25
Never	78	76	a	a	90	97	50	56	62	61
Total	100	100	a	a	100	100	100	100	100	100
Number of respondents	202	191	0	1	63	83	105	105	100	104
Importance of Having Bus Stop near Home										
Very important	39	40	17	26	28	17	58	59	46	40
Fairly important	32	25	15	18	27	21	18	14	25	25
Not important at all	29	35	68	56	45	62	24	27	29	35
Total	100	100	100	100	100	100	100	100	100	100
Number of respondents	215	199	98	103	99	110	106	107	103	106

a Too few cases to percentagize.

walk or take a bike is a feasible method of local travel for such purposes as visiting a grocery store. We are interested in the extent to which substitution of this kind does take place in planned communities.

A second approach to walking and bicycle riding is to consider these activities as means of recreation. From this point of view taking a walk is a substitute for other forms of leisure time activity. We have already discussed these activities as forms of outdoor recreation. The distinction between walking or bicycling for pleasure and for the purpose of reaching a destination may be difficult to make, however. It is correspondingly difficult to draw a line between Chapter 4 and the two sections of this chapter which are concerned with walking and riding bicycles.

Walking: Communities differ in how many homes are provided with sidewalks. We shall discuss, first, the sidewalks provided and how important people say they are. We shall then turn to differences in behavior and to the question of whether any observed variation in walking can be associated with variations in the sidewalks provided.

Information about the existence of sidewalks was obtained by observation. Interviewers were asked to answer to the following question:

Is there a sidewalk along the street in front of this home? As it turned out, it was fairly common for an interviewer to note that a sidewalk existed, but not always along the street. In view of the way the item was phrased, however, the frequency of having sidewalks is probably understated. Table 63 shows the percentage of homes which have a sidewalk including those situations where the presence of one not along the street was volunteered.

The contrast between communities could not be greater. In Crofton every home studied has a sidewalk; in Montpelier no home has a sidewalk. The percentage with a sidewalk is very high in the in-town areas—one suspects that if the interviewers had made no errors it would be 100 percent. In Southfield, however, only 38 percent have a sidewalk. In suburban areas, it seems neither the presence nor the absence of sidewalks is unusual.

People were asked about the importance of sidewalks to them in the following way:

How important to you is it to have sidewalks or footpaths going by your home—is it very important, fairly important, or not important at all?

Why do you say so?

Results appear in the second section of Table 63. There is considerable diversity of opinion. The percentage to whom sidewalks near the home is very important ranges from a low of 40 percent in one of the moderately planned suburban communities to a high of 75 percent in one of the in-town areas. There is a minority to whom sidewalks near the home are not important at all, a group

Table 63

Sidewalks

(percentage distribution)

	Columbia	Reston	Crofton	Montpelier	Norbeck	Southfield	Lafayette Elmwood	Southwest Washington	Radburn	Glen Rock
Percent of homes with sidewalks in front of or near house	66	62	100	-	88	38	98	99	67	98
Number of homes	216	203	98	105	98	109	99	99	101	106
Importance of sidewalks going by home (percent distribution of respondents)										
Very important	57	60	70	40	71	39	75	69	47	66
Fairly important	26	18	18	24	19	14	13	22	26	16
Not important at all	17	22	12	36	10	47	12	9	27	18
Total	100	100	100	100	100	100	100	100	100	100
Number of respondents	214	197	98	105	99	110	105	105	101	106
Reasons for importance of sidewalks going by home (percent distribution of first mentions for respondents who gave a reason for importance)										
Safety; safe for children to play	56	38	57	71	71	56	12	33	43	70
Clean to walk on; not messy or muddy	9	12	12	2	6	2	23	25	11	4
Easier to walk on than grass/gravel	9	20	7	12	9	15	24	16	5	10
Protection of lawn; maintenance of privacy	10	3	8	4	2	8	7	4	9	3
Provides a way of getting places	4	12	2	7	1	7	6	5	11	3
Attractive	1	2	8	1	4	-	3	4	1	3
General positive reasons; other	11	13	6	3	7	12	25	13	20	7
Total	100	100	100	100	100	100	100	100	100	100
Number of respondents	176	157	86	69	91	59	94	97	75	92

Table 63 - continued

Reasons for the unimportance of sidewalks going by home (percent distribution of first mentions of respondents who gave a reason for unimportance)	Columbia	Reston	Crofton	Montpelier	Norbeck	Southfield	Lafayette Elmwood	Southwest Washington	Radburn	Glen Rock
Sidewalks not needed; not used	37	45	64	57	30	51	54	38	46	52
Unattractive	14	17	9	19	30	5	-	25	19	5
Too much to maintain	6	-	-	11	10	20	-	-	12	14
Other walkways are available	6	17	-	-	-	11	-	12	4	-
General negative reasons; other	37	21	27	13	30	13	46	25	19	29
Total	100	100	100	100	100	100	100	100	100	100
Number of respondents	35	47	11	37	10	55	13	8	26	21

whose size ranges from about 10 percent in the in-town areas to 47 percent in one of the least planned suburban communities.

This diversity in community opinion seems to be associated with the existing level of facilities. People in places which have sidewalks think them more important than people where there are no sidewalks. The neatest contrast is between the two moderately planned suburban communities one of which has sidewalks while the other does not. In the former, 70 percent think them very important; in the latter, 40 percent. There is the theoretical possibility that people who think sidewalks are important move to places which have them, while those who think the opposite go where there are no sidewalks. It seems unlikely, however, that the presence or absence of sidewalks dominates the choice of destination for many movers. Opinion in the communities with no sidewalks or few sidewalks may more appropriately be interpreted as reflecting how people adjust to that situation.

There are three reasons people give for thinking sidewalks important. The most often mentioned reason by far is that sidewalks contribute to safety. Safety for children is often mentioned. Safety is most important both to people who have sidewalks and people who do not. The other two considerations mentioned fairly frequently are that sidewalks are clean to walk on and easier to walk on than grass or gravel. These latter considerations seem to have to do with sidewalks as part of a transportation system. One thinks of a paved street, for instance, in such terms as these. Only in the two inner city communities are these considerations mentioned more often than safety.

The principal reason people give for thinking sidewalks unimportant is that they are not used. It is perhaps more surprising that the second most common objection to sidewalks is that they are unattractive. Very few people mentioned the opposite view, that is, few favored them because sidewalks are attractive. There seems to be, shall we say, a lack of glamour about sidewalks: they may be useful, they contribute to safety, but they don't seem to be associated with high style.

We were interested in assessing reactions to the walkway systems in the two new towns and our questions were intended to include them as well as more conventional sidewalks. The explicit comment by some respondents in Columbia and Reston that sidewalks are not important because "other walkways available" indicates that the question was sometimes misunderstood and cannot form a solid basis for assessment of the other walkways even though "footpaths" are explicitly mentioned in it. It is instructive that in these people's minds "sidewalks" are so sharply separate from these other surfaced walkways.

We can keep these facilities in mind, however, in comparing the frequency of walking and hiking across communities (Table 64). The questions on which these percentages are based are as follows:

Table 64
Walking and Hiking

	Columbia	Reston	Crofton	Montpelier	Norbeck	Southfield	Lafayette Elmwood	Southwest Washington	Radburn	Glen Rock
Percent who walked to picnic area in last week	4	2	3	-	-	1	6	2	1	-
Number of respondents	214	200	97	105	98	110	105	107	98	105
Percent who walked to a grocery store in last week	15	23	12	-	5	4	40	44	47	8
Number of respondents	213	198	97	105	99	110	105	107	103	105
Percent who walked to other stores in last week	13	24	2	-	3	2	26	32	39	10
Number of respondents	214	198	97	105	99	110	105	107	102	105
Percent who walked to a friend's house in last week	60	58	57	66	52	38	50	46	50	30
Number of respondents	215	201	97	105	99	110	105	107	103	106
Number of places walked to in last week (percentage distribution)										
None	35	33	39	34	47	60	38	35	29	63
One	46	43	50	66	48	36	25	27	26	28
Two	11	12	10	-	3	4	17	18	24	7
Three or four	8	12	1	-	2	-	20	20	21	2
Total	100	100	100	100	100	100	100	100	100	100
Number of respondents	216	203	98	105	99	110	106	107	103	106
Percent who hike or walk for recreation	72	86	66	58	60	60	53	60	68	52
Number of respondents	215	197	97	104	99	106	103	98	102	105

How often in the last week have you walked from your home to any of these places? (a. picnic area; b. grocery store; c. other stores; d. friend's house)

As already discussed, "hiking or walking" is also on the list of outdoor activities about which people were asked.

Anybody who in one week has walked to three or more of the four types of destination about which inquiry was made can be said to be doing a lot of walking. The rank order of the communities on the proportion who walk to three or four of the places listed closely reflects the quality of the walkway system. There are three communities where about 20 percent do that much walking: the two inner city planned communities and Radburn. The two new towns score about 10 percent. In the other communities hardly anybody does that much walking. It is also worth comment that in Montpelier, where there are no sidewalks, nobody in the sample walked to any of the four destinations other than a friend's house. A few people walk to picnic areas in the other communities, but only a few. The greatest variation is in the percentage walking to stores, which ranges up to almost half the population in some communities.

The last row of Table 64 shows the percentage who hike or walk for recreation. Since this question refers to all of last year and the hiking may have been done anywhere, it is not possible to associate it too closely with local facilities. It is still interesting that in Columbia and Reston, the largest percentage report hiking or walking last year not counting when they were on vacation. In Reston this percentage reaches 86 percent, a level much higher than the 53 to 60 percent in the inner city planned communities where so many people walk to their shops.

The evidence at the community level seems strong that the amount of walking people do depends on the available facilities for walking. At the individual level an attempt is made in Table 65 to compare frequency of walking according to type of sidewalk available. The most interesting group is that in the middle column for whom the interviewer volunteered that a sidewalk (or footpath) existed in the vicinity of the home but not along the street. It does turn out, as predicted that 63 percent of the people who live in these situations report walking or hiking more than 10 times last year. Elsewhere the level of this percentage is 44 to 45. People who reside in this situation also seem to score high in number of places walked to in the last week, but the difference between them and the others is too small for statistical reliability.

Do the people who walk more actually drive their cars less? The second column of Table 66 shows the bivariate correlation coefficients between annual mileage on all cars owned by a family and measures of frequency of walking. The correlation coefficients do have negative signs, at least for the measures of

Table 65

The Effect of Having a Sidewalk near
the House on Walking Behavior

(percentage distribution of respondents)

Frequency of Hiking or Walking for Recreation in Last Year	Sidewalk Exists in Front of House	Sidewalk Exists Elsewhere near House	No Sidewalk
Never	36	27	34
Once or twice	3	2	2
Three or four times	5	2	6
Five to ten times	11	6	14
More than ten times	45	63	44
Total	100	100	100
Number of respondents	792	48	360
Number of Places Walked to in Last Week[1]			
None	40	39	40
One	38	23	50
Two	12	20	6
Three or four	10	18	4
Total	100	100	100
Number of respondents	812	49	364

[1]The question was: "How often in the last week have you walked from your
home to any of these places?" (a. Picnic area,
b. Grocery store, c. Other stores, d. Friend's house)

walking in the last week, but they are so small that the substitution of walking
for driving must be regarded as probably very small.

Riding bicycles: The results of the questions about riding bicycles
surprised the investigators more than any other findings. The surprise lay in the
high proportion of adult men and women who reported that they ride a bicycle.
As with walking, there are two sets of questions on which the results are based.
Bicycling was covered in the questions on outdoor recreation and the results
have been discussed in Chapter 4. The percent who said they rode a
bicycle for recreation at least once in the last year (apart from when they were
on vacation) is repeated in the last row of Table 67. The range is 20 to as high as
51 percent. The additional sequence asked was as follows:

Do you ever use a bicycle to get somewhere from your home?

In the last week have you ridden a bicycle from your home to any of these
places? (a. picnic area; b. grocery store; c. other stores; d. friend's house)

When answers to closed-end questions do not match expectations one wonders
whether they were understood as intended. These questions seem clear enough

Table 66

Correlation Matrix of Variable Related
to Walking and Bicycling
(bivariate correlation coefficients)

	1	2	3	4	5	6	7	8	9
1. Number of cars owned	-								
2. Annual mileage, all cars	.59	-							
3. Frequency of recreational walking	.02	.02	-						
4. Number of places walked	-.13	-.13	.25	-					
5. Frequency of recreational biking	.06	.05	.30	.11	-				
6. Number of places biked	-.01	.00	.21	.13	.55	-			
7. Age of respondent	.05	-.01	-.12	-.06	-.18	-.11	-		
8. Family income	.32	.23	.02	-.03	.05	.06	.11	-	
9. Location[1]	.26	.23	.17	-.08	.12	.06	-.13	.05	-

[1]Location is defined as follows: 1. In town
                                          2. Built-up suburban
                                          3. Isolated suburban area

except that there may possibly be ambiguity about the pronoun "you"—a few people may have included other family members besides themselves.

The percentage of heads of families and their wives who say that they used a bicycle in the last week ranges from around 10 percent in the inner city areas (8 percent in Southwest Washington and 12 percent in Lafayette-Elmwood), up to 25 to 30 percent in Crofton, Southfield, and Radburn. The highest percentages of users, in other words, are found in one of the moderately planned and one of the less planned suburban communities as well as in the older planned suburban community. The two most highly planned communities show 21 percent of bicycle users, not the highest level observed.

It happens that one of the most experienced of the interviewers on the Survey Research Center's staff lives near Southfield and took many of the interviews there herself. We asked her if the high proportion of bicycle riders in Southfield seemed reasonable to her. She replied that it did, and that she had noticed it when she moved there some years ago from Virginia. She also commented on the fact that Southfield is flat (it is built on an ancient lake bed) and that bicycle riding is easy. We have not attempted to quantify the degree of hilliness or flatness of the 10 communities, but it is certainly true that the land is flat in some of the communities, including Radburn, while Columbia and Reston are built in rolling countryside. The facilities such as paths available for bicycling should be considered as only one factor; the topography is probably also important in determining how many people ride bicycles.

In Table 68 we consider the relation between the existence of footpaths or sidewalks and the frequency of bicycling. This table is parallel to Table 65 for

Table 67
Bicycling
(percentage distribution of respondents)

	Columbia	Reston	Crofton	Montpelier	Norbeck	Southfield	Lafayette Elmwood	Southwest Washington	Radburn	Glen Rock
Number of places biked to last week (picnic area, grocery store, other stores or friend's house; percent distributions)										
None	79	79	75	84	88	75	88	92	75	92
One	16	16	19	16	12	19	11	3	19	6
Two, three or four	5	5	6	-	-	6	1	5	6	2
Total	100	100	100	100	100	100	100	100	100	100
Percent who ever use bicycle to get somewhere	21	21	28	16	12	26	12	8	25	8
Percent who bicycle for recreation	31	44	39	38	22	51	21	21	37	20
Number of respondents	216	203	98	105	99	110	106	107	103	106

Table 68

The Effect of Having a Sidewalk near
the House on Bicycling Behavior
(Percentage distribution of respondents)

Frequency of Bicycling for Recreation in Last Year	Sidewalk Exists in Front of House	Sidewalk Exists Elsewhere near House	No Sidewalk
Never	70	57	61
Once or twice	4	8	4
Three or four times	4	6	7
Five to ten times	7	4	9
More than ten times	15	25	19
Total	100	100	100
Number of respondents	802	49	363
Number of Places Bicycled to in Last Week[1]			
None	83	74	80
One	13	18	17
Two	2	4	2
Three to four	2	4	1
Total	100	100	100
Number of respondents	812	49	364

[1]The question was: "In the last week have you ridden a bicycle from your home to any of these places?" (a. Picnic area, b. Grocery store, c. Other stores, d. Friend's house)

walking and the same comments about the classification scheme apply. There does not seem to very much difference in frequency of bicycling last week between those who live where there is no sidewalk and those who live where there is a sidewalk or path of some kind near the house but not along the street. Presumably people ride bicycles in the street and the relevant questions would concern the volume of traffic, the width of the street, the condition of the shoulders, and the like.

We can also consider the question of whether the bicycle is a substitute for the automobile using the data in the correlation matrix in Table 66. The results are unambiguous. The correlation between the number of places biked in the last week and annual mileage driven is .00. If there is any substitution, it must be small. What we find, then, is evidence of a substantial number of people riding bicycles, but no indication that the bicycle is about to replace the automobile!

APPENDICES

Appendix A

Sampling Methods and Sampling Error

Sampling methods: The universe sampled includes family heads and wives living in eligible dwellings in the following ten communities: [1]

Baltimore-Washington Metropolitan Area	New York Metropolitan Area	Detroit Metropolitan Area
Southwest Washington, D.C.	Radburn, N.J.	Lafayette-Elmwood, Detroit
Crofton, Maryland	Glen Rock, N.J.	Southfield, Michigan
Columbia, Maryland		
Montpelier, Maryland		
Norbeck, Maryland		
Reston, Virginia		

By eligible dwelling, we mean single family detached houses or multiple dwellings. A multiple dwelling is one which has a separate entrance, no other dwelling above or below it, and is connected to another dwelling by a common structural wall.

The sample was selected in such a manner that every family head or wife who had moved into an eligible dwelling before July 1, 1969, had a known probability of selection. The selection was made in the following way. Visits to several communities during the first two weeks in July were made to identify occupied dwellings. [2] With that information and using large-scale maps for each community in the Ann Arbor office, compact segments or clusters of four, five

---

[1] See Appendix B for a more complete definition of communities.

[2] It was known that residential buildings in Southfield, Montpelier, Glen Rock and Radburn had been completed for some time and that all dwellings were occupied as of July 1. Therefore, site visits to these communities were not made for this purpose.

or six eligible dwellings were outlined. Delineation of clusters considered the eventual analysis of micro-neighborhoods and consequently included dwellings which faced one another on a street or common court. Dwellings strung out in a row were rarely defined as clusters. Having defined the clusters for a community, a probability sample of clusters was selected. This selection aimed at obtaining about 200 interviews from each of Columbia and Reston and about 100 interviews from each of the remaining eight communities.

Within the sample clusters, an interview with the head or the wife of the head of each family unit was attempted. If the dwelling was occupied by more than one family unit, the head (or wife of the head) of each family unit was interviewed.

This procedure left no discretion in the hands of the interviewers. Both dwellings at which interviews were to be taken and the individual respondents to be interviewed within the dwellings were specified.

Sampling error: Even in a properly conducted sample interview survey, estimates are subject to several kinds of errors. These include sampling errors, non-response errors, and errors in reporting and processing. Sampling errors result from the fact that a sample, not the entire population, is being interviewed. Non-response errors arise from failure to interview some individuals who were selected in the sample. Errors due to reporting and processing or response errors arise form the interview itself including inaccuracies in asking, answering, and recording responses. The present discussion is limited to sampling errors.

Sample statistics reflect the random variations arising from interviewing only a fraction of the population. The distribution of individuals selected for a sample will differ by an unknown amount from that of the population from which the sample is drawn. The value that would have been obtained if the entire population had been designated to be interviewed by the same survey procedures is referred to as the population value. If different samples were used under the same survey conditions, some of the estimates would be larger than the population value and some would be smaller. The sampling error is a measure of the chance deviation of a sample statistic from the coresponding population value.

For a given sample design, the larger the sample, the smaller the sampling error. With a sample of a given size, the smallest sampling error would be achieved if the interviews were widely scattered within the communities under study. This kind of sample is usually expensive. Therefore, as with many surveys, we clustered our interviews to achieve acceptable precision at moderate cost as well as for analysis purposes. The clustering process is described in the preceding section. The estimates of sampling presented below are intended to take into account the degree of clustering in the sample.

The sampling errors in the tables are computed in terms of intervals to be used in estimating the true population value.[3] The sampling error used here is equal to two standard errors. That is, in repeated sampling, the sampling error indicates a range on either side of the sample estimate, within which the population value can be expected to be 95 chances in 100. For example, if 50 percent of the population in three communities with 500 interviews are estimated to have some characteristic, the chances are 95 out of 100 that the population value lies within a range of 50 percent plus or minus 5.0 percent or between 45 percent and 55 percent.

Sampling error is also relevant when the observed difference between sub-groups is being considered. Table A-2 gives the number of percentage points required for such a percentage to be considered significant. A significant difference is again defined as one whose size is such that it would be expected to occur by chance 5 times in 100 or less if there were actually no difference between groups in the population.

---

[3]It should be mentioned that these sampling errors were not calculated explicitly for this study. Rather they represent estimates based on experiences with studies in other urban areas similar to the ones in which our communities are located. The figures represent a 15 percent increase over sampling errors used under assumptions of simple random sampling. We speculate that the figures shown in Table A-1 and Table A-2 are conservative estimates of sampling error and consequently should suffice until such time as true sampling errors are calculated for this study.

Table A-1

Approximate Sampling Errors of Percentages

(expressed in percentages)

Reported Percentages	Number of Interviews								
	1250	1000	750	500	300	200	100	50	25
50	3.2	3.6	4.2	5.0	6.7	8.1	11.5	16.5	23.0
30 or 70	3.0	3.3	3.6	4.7	6.1	7.5	10.5	14.9	21.1
20 or 80	1.3	2.9	3.4	4.1	5.3	6.5	9.2	13.0	18.4
10 or 90	2.0	2.2	2.9	3.1	4.0	4.9	6 9	9.8	13.8

Table A-2

Approximate Sampling Errors of Differences between Subgroups

(expressed in percentages)

Size of Subgroup	Size of subgroup				
	500	200	100	50	25
	For percentages around 50 percent				
500	7.3				
200	9.5	11.5			
100	12.6	14.1	16.5		
50	17.0	18.2	19.9	23.0	
25	23.6	25.4	26.7	28.2	32.5
	For percentages around 30 per cent or 70 percent				
500	6.7				
200	8.8	10.5			
100	11.5	12.9	14.9		
50	15.6	16.7	18.2	21.1	
25	21.6	22.3	23.6	25.8	29.8
	For percentages around 10 per cent or 90 per cent				
500	4.4				
200	5.7	6.9			
100	7.6	8.4	9.8		
50	10.2	10.9	12.0	13.8	

Appendix B

Definition of Communities and Their Boundaries

In Chapter 1 we discussed the criteria that were used in the selection of our sample communities and a brief description of the selected communities themselves. This appendix presents in more precise terms the location of these communities and how we defined them for sampling purposes. These descriptions should be read in conjunction with the accompanying maps.

1. *Columbia.* Located along U.S. Route 29 in Howard County, Maryland, Columbia is approximately 25 miles north of Washington, D.C., and 15 miles southwest of downtown Baltimore. The area from which our sample was drawn includes all dwellings excluding apartments that were occupied as of June 30, 1969.

2. *Crofton.* Located along Maryland Route 3 in Anne Arundel County, Crofton is approximately 20 miles east of Washington, D.C., 20 miles south of Baltimore, and 10 miles west of Annapolis, Maryland. The area from which the sample was selected includes all dwellings built and occupied at the time of our site visit in July, exclusive of apartments.

3. *Glen Rock.* This community is located immediately to the north of Fairlawn, New Jersey, approximately 10 miles northwest of the George Washington Bridge. The section of this community from which our sample was drawn is in the vicinity of Maple Avenue and Rock Road. It was gerrymandered to include housing valued at the approximate level of homes in our other sample communities.

4. *Lafayette-Elmwood.* Located approximately one mile east of downtown Detroit, this community consists of two contiguous redevelopment areas. While Lafayette Park has been completed since 1966, Elmwood Park is still in the process of development. The area from which the sample was drawn is bounded by Lafayette Boulevard on the south, Rivard on the west, Antietam on the north and Chene on the east. The high-rise and garden apartments within this area were

excluded as were townhouses that were vacant as of July 1, 1969.

5. *Montpelier.* This community is located south of Laurel, Maryland, off Interstate 95, approximately half way between Baltimore and Washington in Prince Georges County. The entire subdivision represented the population from which our sample was drawn.

6. *Norbeck.* This community is approximately 15 miles northeast of Washington, D.C., and 4 miles east of Rockville, Maryland, in Montgomery County. The area from which our sample was selected is bounded roughly by Norbeck Road on the north, Georgia Avenue on the east, Aspen Hill Road on the south and Rock Creek Regional Park on the west. The precise definition of the sample excluded all dwellings within one-half mile of the park and was gerrymandered to include housing valued at the level found in our other communities.

7. *Radburn.* Located in the center of Fairlawn, New Jersey, approximately 10 miles northwest of the George Washington Bridge, this community was to be the first of several neighborhoods of a new town. The depression in 1929-30 terminated work on the new town but not before the existing neighborhood was completed. The residents of the neighborhood have formed the Radburn Association which includes owners of dwellings built since 1929 according to the original plan. The area covered by the Radburn Association was used as a basis for drawing our sample.

8. *Reston.* This community is located approximately 18 miles west of Washington, D.C., in Fairfax County, Virginia. At the time of the study, the new town consisted of two largely developed neighborhoods; Lake Anne and Hunters Woods. The area from which our sample was drawn included all dwellings occupied as of early July located in the two neighborhoods excluding apartments.

9. *Southfield.* This suburban community is located approximately 18 miles northwest of downtown Detroit. The primary section of this large community from which our sample was drawn was defined by 13 Mile Road on the north, Southfield Road on the east, 12 Mile Road on the south and Evergreen on the west. This area contains garden apartments which were excluded from our sample. In addition, a 2 block section of the area to the west of Evergreen and south of 13 Mile Road was added to include a wider range of home values.

10. *Southwest Washington.* This community is more appropriately called the Southwest Redevelopment Area of Washington, D.C., and is located approximately one mile south of the Capitol. The area under study is part of an expansive redevelopment project which began in the early 1960's and is still in the process of development. The area from which our sample was drawn is approximately bounded by the Southwest Freeway on the north, Delaware Avenue on the east, P Street on the south and the Washington Channel on the west. All dwellings were included except high-rise and garden apartments and

public housing units.

The accompanying maps were used in the interview to elicit certain responses about each community. A complete discussion of the responses is presented in Chapter 3. The use of maps as part of the interview was an attempt to have people in each community respond to the same stimulus. We felt that the mention of a community by name would create problems in interpreting just what a respondent was responding to. The name of a community undoubtedly conjures up a variety of meanings to the people living there. As a means of providing uniformity in the types of community maps used, the maps were prepared according to the following criteria.

1) Where well-defined boundaries such as streets exist, these should delineate the community.

2) In places where sample communities have definite name designations only those portions which contain occupied dwellings built within the past decade and vacant land which will be developed under the name designation should be delineated.

3) In places where boundaries of sample areas are gerrymandered in order to meet selection criteria, the community boundary should be drawn around the sample area and defined by the nearest major thoroughfares on all sides. In no instance should the boundary pass outside the political jurisdiction.

4) Where possible, community boundaries should be straight, clearly discernable, and few in number.

5) Boundary lines should be demarcated by major thoroughfares, railroads, waterbodies, or edges of political jurisdictions.

6) Areas within boundaries should be devoid of local street, building or land use designations, landmarks or other places or elements which could convey special meaning to a respondent and unduly focus his response to the area.

7) Areas beyond boundaries should show major thoroughfares labeled to assist in orienting the sample community within its environment.

8) All maps should be drawn with a north orientation and designated so with a north arrow. Maps should be presented to the respondent with the south orientation toward him. Horizontally written notations should be placed according to this orientation while vertical notations should be read from the right.

Roads, railroads, and boundaries of political jurisdictions were shown with black lines. The particular area of the map to which the respondent's attention was directed was shown with a broken line. This line is shown in black on the following maps but was blue on the maps used in interviewing.

Despite our efforts to present maps to respondents which were believed to be a clear and understandable visual symbol of where they lived, some problems of interpretation and comments about the maps were reported in nearly all communities. The percentages of respondents giving voluntary comments of this sort about the maps in each community were as follows:

Community	Percent
Southwest Washington	16
Reston	8
Glen Rock	8
Columbia	6
Crofton	6
Montpelier	4
Lafayette–Elmwood	3
Radburn	2
Southfield	1
Norbeck	0

The comments recorded about the appropriateness of the mapped area dealt with the size and shape of the area outlined and whether the respondent understood the map. Of the 69 people who made any comment about the map, one in three said explicitly that they had difficulty in understanding the map while another third made comments which also indicated a lack of understanding. Of the remainder most commented on the area selected, with a few objecting to the shape of the area and about equal proportions asserting that the area was too small or too large. Most respondents, however, seemed able to understand the maps and answer the questions based on them.

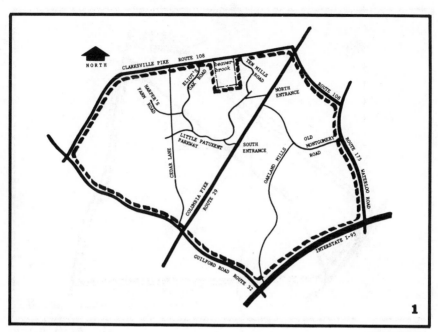

1

COLUMBIA

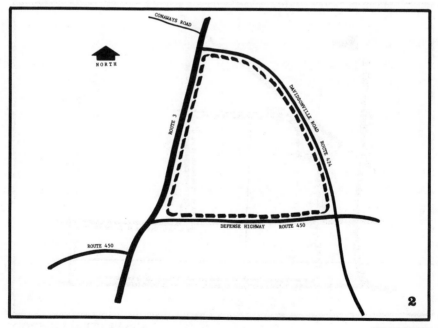

2

CROFTON

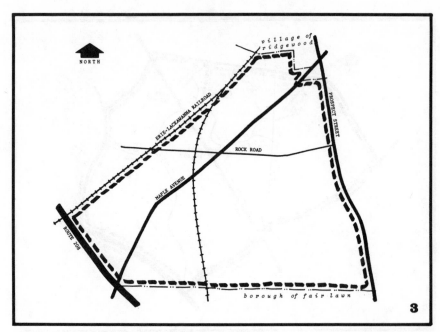

3

GLEN ROCK

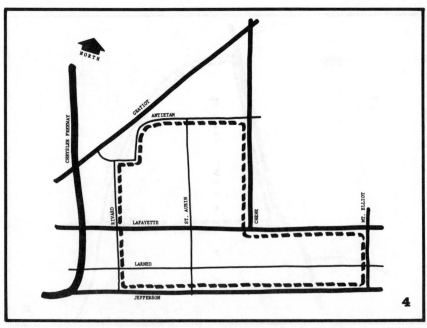

4

LAFAYETTE–ELMWOOD

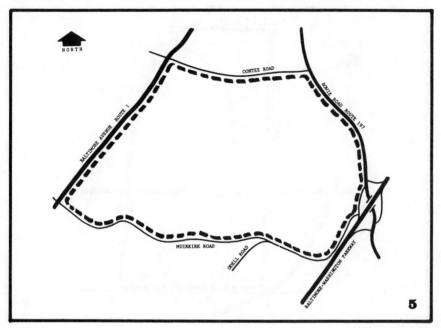

5

MONTPELIER

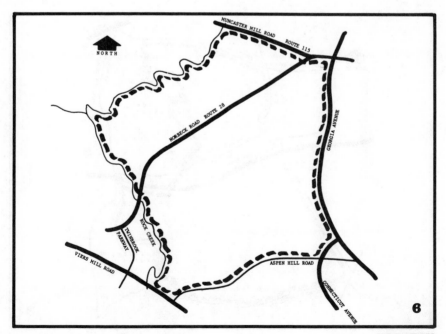

6

NORBECK

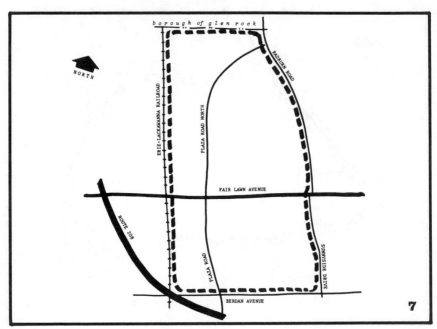

7

RADBURN

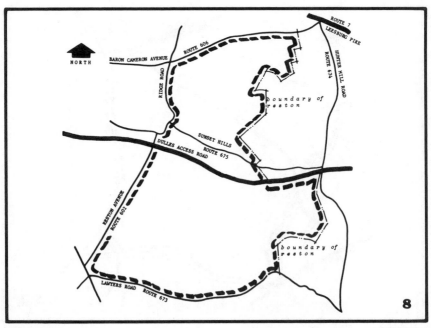

8

RESTON

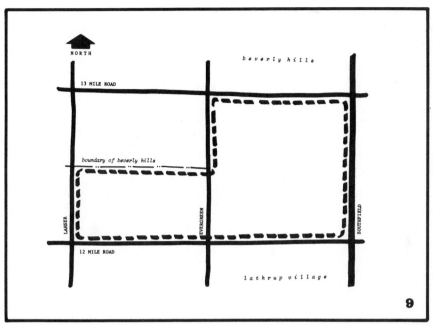

SOUTHFIELD

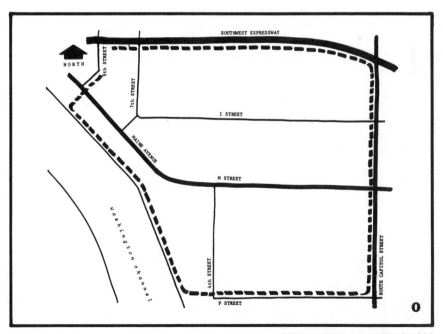

SOUTHWEST WASHINGTON

Appendix C

Definitions Used in the 24-Hour Trip Report

An important consideration in any data collection operation is the accuracy of the information obtained. In the present project the sequence of questions used to elicit 24-hour trip report information is of particular interest not only because of the complexity of the information which must be summarized on the interview form, but also because of the centrality of this data for transportation analysis.

When budget concerns permit, the recommended procedure for collecting home interview travel information includes contacting all family members age 16 or older to obtain the most complete enumeration of trips.[1] In this study, however, only one interview with a single respondent in each sampled dwelling was budgeted. Telephone or in person call backs to assure contacting all family members, in other words, were not possible. As a result, plans were made to maximize and to assess the accuracy of the trip information which would be collected in the one-contact interview situation. Our analysis of the accuracy of trip reporting is included in Chapter 7. This Appendix focuses on efforts made to maximize the quality of the data from interviewing in the field through the coding of the information prior to keypunching.

The most important component of this effort was a codification of the definitions needed to categorize trip behavior. These definitions, adapted from the Bureau of Public Roads' *Procedure Manual*, were included in the project's

---

[1]Treatments of the strengths and weaknesses of various home interview techniques can be found in Frederick W. Memmott, III, "Home Interview Survey and Data Collection Procedures," prepared for presentation before the Origin and Destination Commiteee (No. 2) at the forty-second annual meeting of The Highway Research Board, Washington, D.C., January 1963; the *Manual of Procedures for Home Interview Traffic Study,* Department of Commerce, Bureau of Public Roads, Revised Edition, October 1954 (Reprinted 1957); and publication "1.4 Travel Inventories," U. S. Department of Transportation, Federal Highway Administration, Bureau of Public Roads, mimeo, no date.

"Instruction Booklet for Interviewers." The Survey Research Center interviewers, having read their Instruction Booklets, were to obtain at least one trial interview prior to an additional training session attended by both an interviewing supervisor and a member of the project staff. This training session, lasting an average of two hours, included a discussion of the trip definitions and problems arising in the trial interviews, an extended example of a hypothetical family's trips which interviewers had to work through by themselves, and a final discussion of the points raised by the hypothetical example.

In addition, the first production interviews of each interviewer were carefully monitored by a member of the study staff to identify and correct any errors in interviewing at an early stage. To assure further coding realiability, each interview's trip reports were edited prior to production coding by a single member of the Survey Research Center coding staff to assess the consistency and the logic of the trip sequences recorded. Problems which were identified in the editing were referred back to the interviewer for explication when necessary.

The trip report definitions with which all interviewers and coders were required to be familiar are reprinted here in their entirety, slightly adapted for presentation in this Appendix. The reader may wish to refer to the questionnaire (reproduced in Appendix D) while reading through definitions used for the question sequence.

* *

At this point one of the most important sequences of questions in the interview begins. Its purpose is to obtain information on all trips made by all members of the family unit (except those persons under five years of age) on the day previous to the interview, whether the trip was made as an auto driver or a passenger in an auto, streetcar, bus, truck, or taxi. Walking (*except* walking to work), tricycle, bicycle, uni-cycle, motorcycle, horsedrawn transport, or riding on horseback are not to be included in the survey.

The definitions of terms used in the trip report sequence may seem particularly complex and it is important that they are understood thoroughly before you begin interviewing or coding. You will find that most contingencies are covered by the definitions and explanations which follow, but if there is ever any question, consult your supervisor.

The time period: The 24-hour period for which trip information is to be collected begins at 4 a.m. and extends until 4 a.m. the following day. For example, when interviewing on Saturday to obtain trip data for Friday, include all trips starting between the hours of 4 a.m. Friday and 4 a.m. Saturday. In effect, for most people, what is included is all their waking hours the day before the interview.

Persons to be included: We need to know about all the trips taken by people in this family unit aged five or over. The eligible family members listed in the household composition (Q.1) should be transferred to the areas provided at the bottom of page 16 of the questionnaire. In addition, although *visitors* in the household at the time of the interview should *not* be included in the household composition, *local trips made by visitors should be reported,* provided only that the visitor's customary place of residence is outside the metropolitan area being sampled. Eligible visitors must be entered on the list on page 16 and should be clearly indicated as such along with the city and state of their normal place of residence. (Note that you may have to probe to determine the presence or absence of visitors on the day in question. It is not necessary that a "visitor" be at the respondent's home overnight or longer as a house guest. I.e., the visitor might be "passing through," stop to see the respondent at his home and go out for dinner, and then continue on his trip.)

Defining a "trip":

a) A "trip" is defined as the one-way travel from one point to another for a particular purpose. Thus, round trips to and from work, to and from shopping, or to and from the theater, represent at least two trips in each case; one for the travel to the place of work, shopping, or theater, and one for the return travel. A continuous round trip, such as a pleasure drive through the park, must also be considered as two trips; the most distant point reached during the drive being recorded as the end of the first trip and the beginning of the second.

In general, stops are regarded as the end of one trip and the beginning of another, unless the stops are made for relatively unimportant purposes which do not determine the route of travel, such as to drop a letter in a mail box. buy a package of cigarettes, pick up a hitch-hiker, purchase gasoline, or buy light refreshments. Stops of this nature ordinarliy do not control the route of travel (unless they are the sole purpose for the trip) and should be disregarded. Of course, stops made to avoid conflict with traffic or to comply with directions of traffic officers or traffic control signs and signals also should be disregarded.

Stops which direct the route of travel, such as transacting business at a bank, visiting a friend, eating a meal, shopping, or picking up or discharging a passenger at some specific location should be considered the end of one trip and the beginning of another. In most cases, the person being interviewed will automatically give the proper location to be considered the end of a trip because of his desire to get to a specific location for specific purpose, but it is the responsibility of the interviewer to see that proper information is obtained.

b) If more than one mode of transporation is used in traveling from one point to another in an urban area, each mode used constitutes a separate trip.

c) Certain occupations create travel of a circuitous nature involving several stops for a similar purpose, such as a doctor visiting his patients, a traveling salesman visiting his customers, or a real estate agent visiting properties, and other similar occupations. Travel of this nature is important in a city, and to portray it clearly, the travel between each stop should be recorded as a separate trip, showing the purpose FROM "Work," TO "Work." It is realized that some occupations in this category such as door-to-door salesmen, public utilities meter readers, and certain deliverymen, who use passenger cars, may make a great many stops which are only a few houses apart but which would be classified as trips according to the above definition. Extremely short trips such as these are difficult to obtain accurately, laborious to record, and would not be significant in the subsequent tabulations to be prepared for the analysis. Hence, to avoid these unnecessary complications, *only trips which are approximately two city blocks or greater in length need be recorded.* Disregard entirely any travel between stops which are less than two city blocks apart.

d) Trips by truck, bus, and taxi *drivers* made while driving such vehicles in the course of their day's work, should *not* be reported on the form. However, trips made by *passengers* in such vehicles should be recorded. Also, trips made by the *drivers* in going to and from the point of starting their day's work *should* be recorded.

d) All trips made in company owned automobiles should be included, even if these vehicles were not mentioned as generally available for family use in Q. 37.

f) Trips made by *walking should not be counted* except when the family member is *walking to or from work.* The *entire trip* from home to work must be walking to be counted. Similar trips made to go directly home from work are also to be included and may also be coded under "Walk to work."

Geographic area to be included: Trips made from the metropolitan area in which the respondent lives to some point outside that area (*or* vice versa) are to be included. Trips made between points both of which are *entirely outside* the respondent's metropolitan are are to be excluded. For example, if a businessman flies to a distant city and makes local trips there, exclude those trips. For this study, the relevant metropolitan areas for our ten communities are:

a) *Baltimore-Washington Metropolitan Area*—Columbia, Reston, Crofton, Montpelier, Norbeck, Southwest Washington

b) *New York Metropolitan Area*—Radburn, Glen Rock

c) *Detroit Metropolitan Area*—Southfield, Lafayette-Elmwood

Now I'd like to know about all of the trips taken by people in this family yesterday. By a trip I mean one way—driving to a store and back would be *two* trips.

47. Did (FAMILY MEMBER) go to work or go anywhere by car or public transportation yesterday?

Q47. This must be asked for all family members listed at the bottom of page 16 (and for any house visitors from outside the metropolitan area as well). At the top of each trip column you are to list everyone who took the trip who is included in the list on the bottom of page 16. Thus, if two or more of the persons listed took the same trip together you need to record the trip only once, but each person should be identified in the trip column(s). *Persons are to be identified by their number on the list at the bottom of page 16.* (Note that the Head will always be # 1 as long as you are interviewing a primary family unit member.) For example, the list might consist of:

1. Head
2. Wife
3. Son (5 years old)
4. Son (11 years old)
5. Daughter (9 years old)
6. Aunt Purity (VISITOR from Dubuque, Iowa)

If a trip were reported in which the wife took her two oldest children to school and then returned home, "2, 4 and 5" would be entered at the top of the column for the trip to the school, and "2" at the top of the next column for the mother's return trip.

---

48. Where did (you) begin (your) (next) trip?

Q48. "Priority" for the alternative "WORK" indicates that "WORK" is to be checked if the trip begins where the person works, even if that place is in fact a store, school, hospital or something else. Only *one* may be checked per trip column for this question.

---

49. What was the purpose of this trip?

Q49. When several family members take the same trip, it is quite likely that they will be taking the trip for different purposes. When the Head takes his children to school, the Head's purpose is to take someone somewhere. The children's purpose is to go to school. *If only one person takes a trip, only one "purpose" should be checked.* Note the "SKIP" instruction if "To go home" or "Get to work" is checked. The trip purposes are defined as follows:

a) *Go home*—This refers specifically to the address of the household being interviewed. Trips should never be recorded as proceeding from "home" to "home." This would indicate a round trip, which is not permissible in this study.

b) *Get to work*—This applies to trips made to the location of a person's place of employment, such as factory, a shop, a store, or an office; and, also, to locations that must be visited in performing a normal day's work. Trips made by a doctor in making his calls, and by a salesman calling on prospective customers are classed as trips to work. The purpose "work" would also apply to electricians, carpenters, plumbers, and others who are employed on construction projects and have no regular place of employment

c) *Shopping*—Shopping should be checked whenever a trip is made to do some shopping, regardless of the size of the purchase. Trips made to a store for the purpose of "just looking" are classed as shopping even though no purchase is made.

* *

NOTE: Trips made for repairs to automobiles, radios, or other items, however, and for personal services such as haircuts, beauty treatments, cleaning and pressing clothes, etc., should be recorded as personal business.
The line between "shopping" and "personal business" is somewhat vague, but for our purposes trips made primarily to acquire or look for *tangible products* (e.g., groceries, an automobile, a television, etc.) are to be considered "shopping." Trips made to avail oneself of a *service* (e.g., a haircut, lawnmower repair, etc.), however, are to be classified as "personal business."

* *

however, and for personal services such as haircuts, beauty treatments, cleaning and pressing clothes, etc., should be recorded as personal business.
The line between "shopping" and "personal business" is somewhat vague, but for our purposes trips made primarily to acquire or look for *tangible products* (e.g., groceries, an automobile, a television, etc.) are to be considered "shopping.' Trips made to avail oneself of a *service* (e.g., a haircut, lawnmower repair, etc.), however, are to be classified as "personal business."

It is likely that an expedition made by a housewife around town on a given day will include both purposes. As long as there is at least a two block drive between each store, assigning trip purposes should create few problems. When a single driving trip effectively takes the housewife to several of the stores at once (such as at most shopping centers, for example) and at least one of her stops meets our definition of "shopping," the trip's purpose should be recorded only as "shopping."

d) *Attend school*—This refers to students who are actually attending school. This includes public and private schools, universities, colleges, night schools, etc. Teachers and employees at such institutions would be reported as going to "work."

e) *Social or Recreational*—This purpose includes cultural trips made to church, civic meetings, lectures, and concerts, as well as trips to attend parties or to visit friends. This item also includes trips made for golfing, fishing, movies, bowling, pleasure riding, etc.

f) *To take someone somewhere (serve a passenger)*—This should be checked as the purpose of trips made in an automobile to pick up *or* deliver someone at a specific location. Since "delivering someone somewhere" requires the existence of a passenger, whenever "To take someone somewhere" is checked you will often have to check a purpose box for the passenger as well. (There are two exceptions, however. First, only *one* person may be going to *pick someone up* and in that case only one purpose would be checked. Second, the passenger being served might not be included on the page 16 list. For example, the respondent might have taken a sick neighbor to a hospital. In this case, *only* the respondent would be listed at the top of the column and only his trip purpose would be checked.)

g) *To change mode of travel*—This applies to trips made to locations where a change in the mode of transportation is made. It is applicable as a trip purpose to that portion of the travel which is necessary to reach the location where the change occurs. For example a person going to work drives an automobile from home to a suburban bus stop, parks the automobile, and then rides the bus to a point within walking distance of the place of employment. Two trips are involved. The first, to "change travel mode," as an automobile driver, and the second, to "get to work," as a bus rider. Other combination modes of travel should be recorded in a similar manner. This does not apply to a transfer from one streetcar to another nor from a city bus to a streetcar. Mass transit travel of this nature is to be considered as one continuous trip from the point of origin to the ultimate destination.

h) *Personal business, medical, dental*—Personal business refers to trips made to complete a transaction not considered part of a person's regular employment or to avail oneself of a service. Trips to a doctor's office, to the bank to transact business, to the post office to mail a letter or package, to a dry cleaners, to a hairdressers, and to an office to pay a bill, fall in the category of "personal business." For example, a trip made by a real estate man going to call on a prospect is a trip to work, while a trip to a bank to conduct business not a part of his regular occupation is classed as "personal business."

NOTE: Review carefully the distinction between "shopping" and "personal business" as described in the comments under "shopping."

i) *To eat meal*—This refers to a regular meal and does not include trips for refreshments or light lunches. The purpose of such trips is considered as recreation. *A trip home at noon for the purpose of eating a meal should be considered as an "eat meal" trip instead of a trip "to go home" if the person leaves home again shortly after the meal.*

---

50. Where did you go?

Q50. This question is not to be asked if "Get to work" or "Go home" was checked for Q49. Only *one* box may be checked per trip column for this question.

---

51. How did (you) travel? (IF BY CAR): Did (you) drive?

Q51. We want to know the means of transportation used. If a car was used and two or more people went on this trip, indicate on the line provided which family member drove. In other words, both the "auto driver" and "auto passenger" boxes should be checked if one of the listed persons drive another.

NOTE: Q47-51 must be repeated for each trip. If you run out of columns, use the Supplementary Trip Report Forms provided, being sure to identify each one. Also, if he wishes, the respondent may consult other family members present about their trips.

---

52. Does that include all the trips made any time yesterday by anybody in the family?

Q52. This formal probe should be asked after the respondent has related those trips he remembers and seems ready to go on to another topic. In the interest of completeness, you should jog his memory at least once to look for unreported trips. Depending on the situation in the interview (length, rapport, etc.) and your sense of the completeness of the trips reported you can supplement the general probe by asking "Do you remember any other trips in the morning? . . . in the afternoon? . . . or in the evening?" Another possibility is "Were there any other occasions when the family car(s) was (were) used?"

* *

NOTE: We have tried to design Q48-51 of the questionnaire so that you can record quickly and easily some complicated information. You will need to study these questions and the way the answers are to be recorded in order to do this part of the interview correctly. When you edit your interviews, reread the responses recorded for this section with particular care. If you discover additional trips as you edit, be sure to fill out additional trip columns as necessary at that time.

* *

Finally, to obtain accurate trip generation rates, it is necessary to distinguish between "vehicle trips" and "person trips" in the coding operation. Any journey meeting the definition of a "trip" in the preceeding section should have been recorded in a single column in the questionnaire. For our purposes, each such journey is a "vehicle trip" *regardless* of the mode of transportation used or of the number of persons involved in the journey. While a number of persons may be included on a single "vehicle trip," however, a "person trip" is counted for each person involved. For example, when a mother drives her two children from home to school, there is only one "vehicle trip" but *three* "person trips" to be counted.

There are some cases involving auto passenger travel which may need further explanation. Any passenger who accompanies a driver solely for recreation and without any fixed destination should be considered as making only two "person trips"—one outbound trip from the point of origin to the driver's extreme point of travel, and a return trip to the point of origin, regardless of the number of stops made by the driver. A family unit passenger in a riding pool should be considered as making a single "person trip" from the origin to destination. For example, a wife rides to work with her husband; en route, three stops are made to pick up other members of the riding pool. In cases such as these, the wife makes only one "person trip" to work while the husband makes four trips—three to serve passengers and one to work.

Appendix D

Interview Methods and the Questionnaire

The questionnaire used in this study has been photographically reproduced and appears in the following pages. It is of a general type used in many studies done by the Survey Research Center in different subject matter fields. Detailed questions are asked about a variety of topics relevant to purposes of the study.

The questions asked fall into two broad categories, open end questions, to which the respondent replies in his own words, and closed questions, to which the respondent replies by selecting between alternatives offered to him by the interviewer. To record the reply to an open question the interviewer must write down the answer given as nearly as possible in the actual words spoken. To record the reply to a closed question the interviewer usually need only check a box.

In asking either type of question the interviewer has no choice in phrasing the question. She must use exactly the words written on the questionnaire. The only exception to this rule is on the first page where the interviewer may use her discretion in obtaining the data about the number of adults in the household and their age and sex.

The purpose of the standardization of the questions is to eliminate variation in the data from interview to interview arising out of differences in the way the questions were stated. This procedure requires careful advance planning and pre-testing since the investigator commits himself when he fixes on the wording of a question. Frequently people's situations differ and questions which are appropriate for one family are not at all appropriate for another. It is necessary, therefore, to make extensive use of contingency instructions in the questionnaire. These devices are essential to fit the questions asked to the diverse situations of the people interviewed.

Although most of this interview was administered orally by the interviewer, we also included a self-administered series of questions to be answered

217

by the respondent by checking appropriate responses on a form handed to him. The self-administered series consisted of fourteen short agree-disagree format items plus a semantic differential type question which focussed on seven aspects of the respondent's neighborhood. The decision to present these questions in this manner was based on several considerations. First, given the well educated population we expected to be interviewing, standardized short questions which can be read by the respondent and answered by a simple pencil check take less time to administer than orally presented questions. Second, the use of a "task" midway through an interview can alleviate and possibly prevent the encroachment of monotony and flagging interest for both respondent and interviewer. Third, we expected that respondents would be more candid answering questions about the "friendliness" of neighbors or the importance of a "good name with the right people" if his responses could be pencil checks rather than oral replies. The self-administered form was given to the respondent about half-way through the questionnaire (see the middle of page 13 of the interview) rather than at the end because it was important that the respondent be as little fatigued as possible. Tired respondents tend to give less thought to question content to the detriment of the measurement's validity. The three page self-administered form is reproduced after the last page of the regular interview.

Occasional mention in the interview is also made of cards to be handed to the respondent by the interviewer. The information on the cards corresponds to the categories shown on the questionnaire. An example of this technique occurs in connection with the question on family income, Q66, where we wish to make it clear to the respondent that we do not need his *precise* income, but only the appropriate income range. Handing a respondent a card is also useful if he is to be asked to select one or more responses from a relatively long list of alternatives, as for Q25, memberships in types of clubs and organizations.

The use of a map to elicit responses to the community for questions 12-15 is discussed in detail in Chpater 3 and Appendix B and will not be reiterated here. Similarly, due to their strategic importance in this study, the questions used in the twenty-four hour trip report have been treated in detail in Appendix C.

Because of the particular interest in this study in the highly planned new towns, we have entered percentage distributions of responses by Columbia and Reston residents for questions in the interview where tabulations are available. Unless otherwise indicated, for the percentages shown the base in Columbia is 216 cases; in Reston it is 203 cases.

Project 45789
Fall, 1969

A STUDY OF RESIDENTIAL ENVIRONMENTS

Form Approved
Bureau of the Budget
No. 04-S69003

SURVEY RESEARCH CENTER
INSTITUTE FOR SOCIAL RESEARCH
THE UNIVERSITY OF MICHIGAN

(Do not write in above spaces.)

Interviewer's Label

A. Segment Number _____

B. Your Interview Number _____

C. Date_____

D. Length of Interview_____(Min.)

1. INTERVIEWER: LIST ALL PERSONS, INCLUDING CHILDREN, NOW LIVING IN THE DWELLING UNIT BY
THEIR RELATION TO THE HEAD. CONSULT ITEM 5 ON THE COVER SHEET AND INDICATE
RESPONDENT BY A CHECK (√) IN RIGHT COLUMN BELOW. THE RESPONDENT MUST BE
THE HEAD OF HOUSEHOLD OR HIS WIFE. MAKE NO SUBSTITUTIONS.

	C.	R.			C.	R.	
FOR ADULTS' AGE (CARD 1):	-	-	A. 18-24		1	6	E. 55-64
	44	33	B. 25-34		2	1	F. 65-74
	39	38	C. 35-44		1	-	G. 75 OR OVER
	13	22	D. 45-54				

FOR CHILDREN UNDER 18: ASK AGE IN YEARS.

a. All persons, by relation to head	b. Sex	c. Age (See above: for adults age 18+, enter letter)	d. Family Unit Number	e. Indicate R by "√"
1. HEAD OF HOUSEHOLD				
2.				
3.				
4.				
5.				
6.				
7.				
8.				

2

2.   Where did you live most of the time while you were growing up -- in the country, in a small town, in a suburb, or in a city?

C.   12 ☐1 COUNTRY   28 ☐2 SMALL TOWN   24 ☐3 SUBURB   36 ☐4 CITY
R.   10   28   20   42

3.   During that time did you usually live in a single family house or an apartment, or what?

C.   84 ☐1 SINGLE FAMILY   11 ☐2 APARTMENT   5 ☐ OTHER (SPECIFY)_____
R.   83   10   7

4.   Could you tell me when the house you are living in <u>now</u> was built?

C.	R.			C.	R.			C.	R.		
-	-	☐1 1939 OR BEFORE	-	19	☐5 1965	34	8	☐9 1969
-	-	☐2 1940-1949	-	17	☐6 1966
-	-	☐3 1950-1959	13	19	☐7 1967			☐0 DON'T KNOW
-	7	☐4 1960-1964	53	30	☐8 1968

5.   And when did you move into it?

C.	R.			C.	R.			C.	R.		
-	-	☐1 1939 OR BEFORE	-	6	☐5 1965	42	24	☐9 1969
-	-	☐2 1940-1949	-	14	☐6 1966
-	-	☐3 1950-1959	10	21	☐7 1967
-	-	☐4 1960-1964	48	35	☐8 1968

> 5a.   What month did you move in?
>
> ☐1 JAN.   ☐2 FEB.   ☐3 MARCH   ☐4 APRIL   ☐5 MAY
>
> ☐6 JUNE   (IF LATER, DO NOT INTERVIEW)

6.   Just before you moved to your present home were you living in a single family house or an apartment or what?

C.   50 ☐1 SINGLE FAMILY HOUSE   47 ☐3 APARTMENT   3 ☐ OTHER (SPECIFY)_____
R.   57   34   9

7.   Was that in the country, in a small town, in a suburb, or in a city?

C.   6 ☐1 COUNTRY   15 ☐2 SMALL TOWN   51 ☐3 SUBURB   28 ☐4 CITY
R.   5   14   58   23

8.   When you were looking for a place to live what especially appealed to you about coming here?

_____

_____

8a.   Anything else?_____

_____

3

☐ MOVED HERE IN 1964 OR EARLIER (SEE Q. 5) ➛ GO TO Q. 10

5 MOVED HERE IN 1965-1969

↓

9. Would you say that living here has worked out about as you expected, or better than you expected, or not as well?

C. R.
25 30 ① BETTER THAN EXPECTED

C. R.
57 43 ② ABOUT AS EXPECTED

9 15 ④ BETTER IN SOME WAYS, NOT IN OTHERS   9 15 5 NOT AS WELL AS EXPECTED

    9a. Why do you say that? _____

    _____

    9b. Anything else?_____

    _____

10. TYPE OF DWELLING - BY OBSERVATION:
C. R.
76 45 ☐ R LIVES IN A SINGLE FAMILY HOUSE ON A SEPARATE LOT ➛ GO TO Q. 12

24 55 5 R LIVES IN A TOWNHOUSE

↓

11. If you could do as you pleased, would you prefer to live in a single family house, a townhouse, or an apartment?

C.	12	12	-	-
	① SINGLE FAMILY HOUSE	② TOWNHOUSE	③ APARTMENT	N.A.
R.	27	25	1	2

    11a. Why do you say so?_____

    _____

4

12. I'd like to ask you how you feel about this area as a place to live - I mean
    the area outlined on the map (SHOW MAP). From your own personal point of view,
    would you rate this area as a place to live as excellent, good, average, below
    average, or poor?

C. 52 |1| EXCELLENT 40 |2| GOOD 6 |3| AVERAGE 1 |4| BELOW AVERAGE 1 |5| POOR
R. 61   33   4   2   -

    12a. In what ways?_____

    _____

    _____

    _____

INTERVIEWER: IF R MAKES ANY VOLUNTARY COMMENTS ABOUT THE APPROPRIATENESS OF THE
              MAPPED AREA PLEASE NOTE THEM.

C. R.
-   3 |1| MAPPED AREA TOO SMALL   C. R.
-   - |2| MAPPED AREA TOO LARGE   2 2 |7| OTHER_____
-   1 |3| MAPPED AREA WRONG SHAPE   95 92 0. NO COMMENT
3   2 |4| DON'T UNDERSTAND IT   _____

                                       _____

C. R.
93 90 |1| HOUSEHOLD CONTAINS NOBODY AGED 55 AND OVER ➤ GO TO Q. 14

7 10 |5| HOUSEHOLD INCLUDES SOMEONE AGED 55 AND OVER

---

13. For retired people how would you rate this area as a place to live? Would you
    say it was excellent, good, average, below average, or poor?

C. 44 |1| EXCELLENT 31 |2| GOOD 13 |3| AVERAGE 12 |4| BELOW AVERAGE - |5| POOR (N = 16)
R. 61   17   -   11   11   (N = 18)

    13a. In what ways?_____

    _____

    _____

    _____

C. R.
76 70   ☐ HOUSEHOLD CONTAINS NOBODY 12-17 → GO TO Q. 15

24 30   5 HOUSEHOLD CONTAINS SOMEONE 12-17

---

14. From teenagers' point of view how would you expect them to rate this area as a place to live - would you say it was excellent, good, average, below average, or poor for them?

C. 30 ☐ EXCELLENT 46 ☐ GOOD 10 ☐ AVERAGE 8 ☐ BELOW AVERAGE 6 ☐ POOR (N = 50)
R. 15   37   17   20   11   (N = 54)

14a. In what ways?_____

_____

_____

C. R.
27 33   ☐ HOUSEHOLD CONTAINS NO CHILDREN AGED UNDER 12 → GO TO Q. 17

73 67   5 HOUSEHOLD CONTAINS ONE OR MORE CHILDREN UNDER 12

---

15. As a place to raise children under 12 how would you rate this area - would you say it was excellent, good, average, below average, or poor?

C. 77 ☐ EXCELLENT 19 ☐ GOOD 3 ☐ AVERAGE 1 ☐ BELOW AVERAGE - ☐ POOR
R. 78   16   4   1   1

15a. In what ways?_____

_____

_____

16. How do you feel about the places <u>right near your home</u> for children under 12 to play out of doors - would you say they are excellent, good, average, below average, or poor?

C. 56 ☐ EXCELLENT 26 ☐ GOOD 12 ☐ AVERAGE 3 ☐ BELOW AVERAGE 3 ☐ POOR (N = 157)
R. 68   21   7   2   2   (N = 135)

16a. Why do you say so?_____

_____

6

17. How many times in the last week have you yourself spent an afternoon or evening with friends or gone to a meeting or social event or something like that?

C. R.

22 24   [0] NOT AT ALL

18 24   [1] ONCE

20 21   [2] TWICE

27 24   [3] THREE OR FOUR TIMES

13 7   { [5] FIVE OR SIX TIMES

           [7] SEVEN OR MORE TIMES

18. Now I'd like to ask you just about your close neighbors - I mean the half dozen families living nearest to you. How many of the adults in these families would you know by name if you met them on the street - all of them, nearly all, half of them, just a few of them, or none of them?

C. R.

63 62   [4] ALL

25 24   [3] NEARLY ALL

 7 6   [2] HALF OF THEM

 5 8   { [1] JUST A FEW OF THEM

           [0] NONE OF THEM → SKIP TO Q. 20

19. How often do you talk to any of the half dozen families who live closest to you just to chat or for a social visit - would it be every day, several times a week, once a week, 2-3 times a month, once a month, a few times a year, or never? (HAND R CARD A)

C. R.

27 22 [6] EVERY DAY

44 41 [5] SEVERAL TIMES A WEEK

14 22 [4] ONCE A WEEK

 8   9 [3] 2-3 TIMES A MONTH

         ⎧ [2] ONCE A MONTH
 7   6 ⎨ [1] A FEW TIMES A YEAR; RARELY
         ⎩ [0] NEVER

20. Do you people have a place where you can be out in your yard and feel that you can really have privacy from your neighbors if you want it?

C. 38   62
R. 58 [1] YES   42 [5] NO

    20a. Why do you say so?_____

    _____

    _____

21. Some homes are close enough together so that even when people are indoors they hear their neighbors and their neighbors hear them. Do you and your neighbors hear each other very often, occasionally, or almost never?

C. 2 [1] VERY OFTEN   11 [2] OCCASIONALLY   87 [3] ALMOST NEVER
R. 4   16   80

8

22. How much do you care whether you hear each other - a great deal, somewhat, or don't you care?

C. 48
R. 46   ☑ A GREAT DEAL   24/28 ☑ SOMEWHAT   28/26 ☑ DON'T CARE

23. How do you feel about the amount of outdoor space near your home which members of your family can use for their different activities - do you people have more space than you need, or about the right amount, or too little space?

C. 14
R. 21   ☑ MORE THAN NEED   71/69 ☑ RIGHT AMOUNT   15/10 ☑ TOO LITTLE

24. Why do you say so?_____

_____

_____

25. Now here is a list of clubs and organizations that many people belong to. Please look at this list (SHOW R CARD B), and tell me which of these kinds of organizations you yourself belong to. (PAUSE) Are there any others you're in that are not on this list? (<u>CHECK AT LEFT</u> EACH KIND OF ORGANIZATION R BELONGS TO, <u>THEN</u> ASK Q. 26 FOR EACH KIND OF ORGANIZATION MENTIONED.)

26. Would you say you are very involved, somewhat involved, or not very involved in _____ ? (CHECK RESPONSE IN "INVOLVEMENT" COLUMN BELOW.)

Percent
Members

C.	R.	25. ORGANIZATION		26. INVOLVEMENT		
				-1-	-2-	-3-
60	50	a. ☐ Church or synagogue	a.	/Very/	/Somewhat/	/Not very/
18	12	b. ☐ Church-connected groups (but not the church itself)	b.	/Very/	/Somewhat/	/Not very/
12	8	c. ☐ Hobby clubs	c.	/Very/	/Somewhat/	/Not very/
24	28	d. ☐ College alumni (alumnae) associations	d.	/Very/	/Somewhat/	/Not very/
11	9	e. ☐ Fraternal lodges or organizations	e.	/Very/	/Somewhat/	/Not very/
24	19	f. ☐ Business or civic groups	f.	/Very/	/Somewhat/	/Not very/
43	42	g. ☐ Parent-teachers associations	g.	/Very/	/Somewhat/	/Not very/
19	18	h. ☐ Community centers	h.	/Very/	/Somewhat/	/Not very/
21	11	i. ☐ Regular card playing group	i.	/Very/	/Somewhat/	/Not very/
12	12	j. ☐ Sport teams	j.	/Very/	/Somewhat/	/Not very/
8	8	k. ☐ Country clubs	k.	/Very/	/Somewhat/	/Not very/
13	14	l. ☐ Youth groups (Girl Scout Leaders, Little League Managers, etc.)	l.	/Very/	/Somewhat/	/Not very/
28	36	m. ☐ Professional groups	m.	/Very/	/Somewhat/	/Not very/
7	12	n. ☐ Local political clubs or organizations	n.	/Very/	/Somewhat/	/Not very/
5	5	o. ☐ State or national political clubs or organizations	o.	/Very/	/Somewhat/	/Not very/
33	42	p. ☐ Neighborhood improvement associations	p.	/Very/	/Somewhat/	/Not very/
9	11	q. ☐ Charity or welfare organizations	q.	/Very/	/Somewhat/	/Not very/
17	14	r. ☐ Other (Specify)_____	r.	/Very/	/Somewhat/	/Not very/
5	4	s. ☐ Other (Specify)_____	s.	/Very/	/Somewhat/	/Not very/

☐ NONE (IF NONE, CONTINUE WITH QUESTION 27.)

3.5　3.5　Mean number of memberships

10

27. Thinking of your involvement in clubs and community organizations in the past 2 years - would you say you are more involved now, or less involved now than you were 2 years ago?

C.   45 _____   29   26
R.   39 [*1*] MORE INVOLVED NOW 29 [*2*] SAME AS BEFORE   32 [*3*] LESS INVOLVED NOW

28. Some people would like to be more involved in clubs and community activities than they are while others would like to be less involved. How about you, would you like to be more involved, less involved, or about as involved as you are now?

C.   34 _____   61   5
R.   25 [*1*] MORE INVOLVED   66 [*2*] SAME AS NOW   9 [*3*] LESS INVOLVED

   28a. Why do you say so?_____

   _____

   _____

29. Here is a list of outdoor activities. (HAND R CARD C) I'd like to know which of these you yourself have taken part in within the last year , not counting when you were away from here on vacation. (COMPLETE Q. 29 FOR ALL ACTIVITIES, THEN ASK Q: 30-31 SEQUENCE FOR EACH ACTIVITY R MENTIONS.)

☐ NO LISTED ACTIVITIES PARTICIPATED IN ➞ GO TO Q. 32

29. ACTIVITIES PARTICIPATED IN	30. How often did you _____ in the last year not counting when you were on vacation? (READ ALTERNATIVES)	31. Where did you go (most often)? Was it within 10 miles of here?
A. Outdoor swimming at a pool C. R. 77 73 ☐ Participated	C. R. 7 2 [*1*] Once or twice 8 9 [*3*] Three or four times 17 ·12 [*5*] Five to ten times 45 50 [*7*] More often	C. R. 4 3 [*1*] More than 10 miles 67 66 [*2*] Within 10 miles ↓ Where?_____ 6 4 N.A. (NEAREST INTERSECTION OR EQUIVALENT)
B. Tennis 19 23 ☐ Participated	3 1 [*1*] Once or twice 5 2 [*3*] Three or four times 4 6 [*5*] Five to ten times 7 14 [*7*] More often	4 1 [*1*] More than 10 miles 13 22 [*2*] Within 10 miles ↓ Where?_____ 2 - N.A. (NEAREST INTERSECTION OR EQUIVALENT)
C. Hiking or walking 72 85 ☐ Participated	2 1 [*1*] Once or twice 5 9 [*3*] Three or four times 20 14 [*5*] Five to ten times 45 61 [*7*] More often	5 4 [*1*] More than 10 miles 63 76 [*2*] Within 10 miles ↓ Where?_____ 4 5 N.A. (NEAREST INTERSECTION OR EQUIVALENT)

(CONTINUED ON NEXT PAGE) ⟶

11

29. ACTIVITIES PARTICIPATED IN	30. How often did you _____ in the last year not counting when you were on vacation? (READ ALTERNATIVES)	31. Where did you go (most often)? Was it within 10 miles of here?
D. Picnicking C. R. 64 50☐ Participated	C. R. 15 8 /1/ Once or twice 19 13 /3/ Three or four times 19 13 /5/ Five to ten times 11 16 /7/ More often	C. R. 15 18 /1/ More than 10 miles 46 31 /2/ Within 10 miles ↓ Where?_____ 3 1 N.A. (NEAREST INTERSECTION OR EQUIVALENT)
E. Golfing 18 21☐ Participated	4 2 /1/ Once or twice 1 1 /3/ Three or four times 5 6 /5/ Five to ten times 8 12 /7/ More often	3 4 /1/ More than 10 miles 14 17 /2/ Within 10 miles ↓ Where?_____ 1 - N.A. (NEAREST INTERSECTION OR EQUIVALENT)
F. Boating 38 36☐ Participated	9 8 /1/ Once or twice 12 5 /3/ Three or four times 10 9 /5/ Five to ten times 7 14 /7/ More often	11 14 /1/ More than 10 miles 25 19 /2/ Within 10 miles ↓ Where?_____ 2 3 N.A. (NEAREST INTERSECTION OR EQUIVALENT)
G. Bicycling 31 43☐ Participated	3 5 /1/ Once or twice 7 7 /3/ Three or four times 6 9 /5/ Five to ten times 15 22 /7/ More often	1 1 /1/ More than 10 miles 28 39 /2/ Within 10 miles ↓ Where?_____ 2 3 N.A. (NEAREST INTERSECTION OR EQUIVALENT)

/1/ MOVED HERE IN 1964 OR EARLIER (SEE Q. 5) ➤ GO TO Q. 33

/5/ MOVED HERE IN 1965-1969
↓

32. Since you came to live here have you participated in outdoor activities like these more than you did before, or less, or about the same?
C. 62 /1/ MORE NOW   26 /2/ ABOUT THE SAME   12 /3/ LESS NOW R. 66   24   10

12

33. How often in the last week have you walked from your home to any of these places?
(SHOW R CARD D)

		Not at all in last week			Once or twice			3-4 times			5+ times	
		C. 96	☐0	R. 98	C. 2	☐*I*	R. 1	C. -	☐3	R. -	C. 2	☐5	R. 1
a.	Picnic area												
b.	Grocery store	85	☐0	77	12	☐*I*	13	2	☐3	8	1	☐5	2
c.	Other stores	87	☐0	76	11	☐*I*	16	1	☐3	6	1	☐5	2
d.	Friend's house	40	☐0	42	28	☐*I*	30	18	☐3	19	14	☐5	9

34. Do you ever use a bicycle to get somewhere from your home?

C. R.
79 79 ☐5 NO, NEVER → GO TO Q. 35

21 21 ☐*I* YES

> 34a. In the last week have you ridden a bicycle from your home to any
> of these places? (SHOW R CARD D) (CHECK EACH PLACE BICYCLED TO)
>
> C. R.   C. R.
> 3 - ☐ a. Picnic area   5 12 ☐ c. Other stores
>
> 13 17 ☐ b. Grocery store   18 10 ☐ d. Friend's house

35. How important to you is it to have sidewalks or footpaths going by your
home - is it very important, fairly important, or not important at all?

C. 57 ☐*I* VERY IMPORTANT   26 ☐2 FAIRLY IMPORTANT   17 ☐3 NOT IMPORTANT AT ALL
R. 60   18   22

35a. Why do you say so?_____

_____

_____

36. <u>Last weekend</u> did you go on any trips ten miles or more away from here other than on your vacation?

C. 63
R. 69 [1] YES   36 29 [5] NO → (GO TO S-SERIES)   1 2 [6] NO - WAS AWAY ON VACATION → (GO TO S-SERIES)

> 36a. How many miles away from here did you go? (LONGEST TRIP)
>
> C. 11
> R. 19 [1] 10-19 miles   35 21 [3] 20-39 miles   7 11 [5] 40-59 miles   10 18 [7] 60 or more
>
> 36b. What was the main reason for the trip?
>
> _____
>
> _____

****
* **S-SERIES:**
*
* Thank you. This next section goes better if you fill it out yourself. Here are
* some statements that some people agree with and others disagree with. Please mark
* each one according to whether you agree or disagree, and how strongly. (EXPLAIN
* BY USING FIRST ONE AS AN EXAMPLE, IF NECESSARY.)
****

		None	One	Two	Three or More
37. How many cars or trucks do you people have for family use?	C.	-	34	60	6
	R.	-	37	53	10

_____ (NUMBER)   ☐ NONE → GO TO Q. 41

ASK ABOUT EACH CAR OR TRUCK OWNED OR USED

	First	Second	Third
38. What year was the car bought?			
39. Altogether about how many miles has it been driven since you bought it?			
40. In the last twelve months about how many miles has the car been driven?			

14

41. Is there a bus stop within a 10 minute walk of your home?

C. 95
R. 95 ⬜ *I* YES   2 ⬜ *5* NO ➝ GO TO Q. 43   3 ⬜ *B* DON'T KNOW ➝ GO TO Q. 43
                          4   1

> 42. How often do you yourself use the bus?
> C. R.
> 1   7 ⬜ 1. Daily or almost every day (5-7 days a week)
> 4   6 ⬜ 2. 1-4 days a week
> 2   1 ⬜ 3. 2-3 days a month
> 15 9 ⬜ 4. One day a month or less
> 73 72 ⬜ 5. Never

43. How important is it to you whether there is a bus stop near your home?

C. 39   32   29
R. 46 ⬜ *I* VERY IMPORTANT ⬜ *2* FAIRLY IMPORTANT ⬜ *3* NOT IMPORTANT AT ALL
                       25   29

44. Where is most of the grocery shopping done for your family these days?

NAME OF STORE OR SHOPPING CENTER:_____

LOCATION (E.G., STREET INTERSECTION:_____

TOWN:_____

45. How long does it usually take to get there from here? (ONE WAY)
C. R.
55 19 ⬜ *I* Less than 5 minutes
27 17 ⬜ *2* 5-9 minutes
 8 34 ⬜ *3* 10-14 minutes
 1 16 ⬜ *4* 15-19 minutes
 7   7 ⬜ *5* 20-29 minutes
 2   7 ⎰ ⬜ *6* 30-39 minutes
       ⎱ ⬜ *7* 40+ minutes

PLANNED RESIDENTIAL ENVIRONMENTS 233

15

46. Now I'd like to know about all of the trips taken by people in this family yesterday. By a trip I mean one way - driving to a store and back would be <u>two</u> trips.

47. Did (FAMILY MEMBER) go to work or go anywhere by car or public transportation yesterday?

☐ YES ➤ GO TO Q. 48   ☐ NO ➤ REPEAT Q. 47 FOR NEXT FAMILY MEMBER

☐ NO FAMILY MEMBER TOOK ANY TRIP YESTERDAY ➤ SKIP TO Q. 52

```
***************************************************************************
*                                                                         *
* IMPORTANT:  QUESTION 47 MUST BE ASKED FOR ALL FAMILY MEMBERS LISTED.  BEGIN WITH *
*             HEAD.  IF OTHER FAMILY MEMBERS WENT ALONG ON A TRIP, INDICATE WHO AT *
*             THE TOP OF COLUMN FOR THAT TRIP.                            *
*                                                                         *
***************************************************************************
```

16

WHO IS THIS TRIP FOR? ENTER EACH PERSON BY RELATIONSHIP TO HEAD →	Family Member(s) Who Went: _____	Family Member(s) Who Went: _____
48. Where did (you) begin (your) (next) trip?	[1] Work (Priority) [2] Home [3] Friend's or Relative's Home [4] Store, Restaurant, Bank [5] Doctor's Office, Hospital [6] School [7] Other	[1] Work (Priority) [2] Home [3] Friend's or Relative's Home [4] Store, Restaurant, Bank [5] Doctor's Office, Hospital [6] School [7] Other
49. What was the purpose of this trip? (CHECK TWO BOXES IF NECESSARY)	[1] Go home [2] Get to work } (GO TO Q. 51) [3] Shopping [4] Attend school [5] Social or recreational [6] To take someone somewhere (serve a passenger)-(CHECK ALSO THE PURPOSE OF HIS TRIP) [7] To change mode of travel [8] Personal business, medical, dental [9] Eat meal [0] Other	[1] Go home [2] Get to work } (GO TO Q. 51) [3] Shopping [4] Attend school [5] Social or recreational [6] To take someone somewhere (serve a passenger)-(CHECK ALSO THE PURPOSE OF HIS TRIP) [7] To change mode of travel [8] Personal business, medical, dental [9] Eat meal [0] Other
50. Where did (you) go?	[1] Home [2] School [3] Friend's or Relative's Home [4] Store, Bank, Restaurant [5] Doctor's Office, Hospital [6] Other	[1] Home [2] School [3] Friend's or Relative's Home [4] Store, Bank, Restaurant [5] Doctor's Office, Hospital [6] Other
51. How did (you) travel? (IF BY CAR): Did (you) drive? (CHECK TWO BOXES IF ONE FAMILY MEMBER DROVE ANOTHER)	[1] Auto driver-WHICH FAMILY MEMBER DROVE? _____ [1] Auto passenger [2] Suburban Railroad [3] Bus [4] Rapid Transit [5] Walk to work [6] Taxi [7] Other	[1] Auto driver-WHICH FAMILY MEMBER DROVE? _____ [1] Auto passenger [2] Suburban Railroad [3] Bus [4] Rapid Transit [5] Walk to work [6] Taxi [7] Other

INTERVIEWER: REPEAT QUESTIONS 46-51 FOR EACH TRIP.   INCLUDE TRIPS BY ANY FAMILY MEMBER AGED 5 AND OVER.   LIST THE FAMILY MEMBERS AGED 5 AND OVER BELOW.   (SEE Q. 1)

1. _____   4. _____   7. _____

2. _____   5. _____   8. _____

3. _____   6. _____   9. _____

17

Family Member(s) Who Went:	Family Member(s) Who Went:	Family Member(s) Who Went:
_____	_____	_____
[1] Work (Priority) [2] Home [3] Friend's or Relative's Home [4] Store, Restaurant, Bank [5] Doctor's Office, Hospital [6] School [7] Other	[1] Work (Priority) [2] Home [3] Friend's or Relative's Home [4] Store, Restaurant, Bank [5] Doctor's Office, Hospital [6] School [7] Other	[1] Work (Priority) [2] Home [3] Friend's or Relative's Home [4] Store, Restaurant, Bank [5] Doctor's Office, Hospital [6] School [7] Other
[1] Go home [2] Get to work } (GO TO Q. 51) [3] Shopping [4] Attend school [5] Social or recreational [6] To take someone somewhere (serve a passenger)-(CHECK ALSO THE PURPOSE OF HIS TRIP) [7] To change mode of travel [8] Personal business, medical, dental [9] Eat meal [0] Other	[1] Go home [2] Get to work } (GO TO Q. 51) [3] Shopping [4] Attend school [5] Social or recreational [6] To take someone somewhere (serve a passenger)-(CHECK ALSO THE PURPOSE OF HIS TRIP) [7] To change mode of travel [8] Personal business, medical, dental [9] Eat meal [0] Other	[1] Go home [2] Get to work } (GO TO Q. 51) [3] Shopping [4] Attend school [5] Social or recreational [6] To take someone somewhere (serve a passenger)-(CHECK ALSO THE PURPOSE OF HIS TRIP) [7] To change mode of travel [8] Personal business, medical, dental [9] Eat meal [0] Other
[1] Home [2] School [3] Friend's or Relative's Home [4] Store, Bank, Restaurant [5] Doctor's Office, Hospital [6] Other	[1] Home [2] School [3] Friend's or Relative's Home [4] Store, Bank, Restaurant [5] Doctor's Office, Hospital [6] Other	[1] Home [2] School [3] Friend's or Relative's Home [4] Store, Bank, Restaurant [5] Doctor's Office, Hospital [6] Other
[1] Auto driver-WHICH FAMILY MEMBER DROVE?	[1] Auto driver-WHICH FAMILY MEMBER DROVE?	[1] Auto driver-WHICH FAMILY MEMBER DROVE?
[1] Auto passenger [2] Suburban Railroad [3] Bus [4] Rapid Transit [5] Walk to work [6] Taxi [7] Other	[1] Auto passenger [2] Suburban Railroad [3] Bus [4] Rapid Transit [5] Walk to work [6] Taxi [7] Other	[1] Auto passenger [2] Suburban Railroad [3] Bus [4] Rapid Transit [5] Walk to work [6] Taxi [7] Other

INTERVIEWER: REPEAT QUESTIONS 46-51 FOR EACH TRIP. INCLUDE TRIPS BY ANY
FAMILY MEMBER AGED 5 AND OVER.

18

WHO IS THIS TRIP FOR? ENTER EACH PERSON BY RELATIONSHIP TO HEAD ⟶	Family Member(s) Who Went: _____	Family Member(s) Who Went: _____
48. Where did (you) begin (your) (next) trip?	1 Work (Priority) 2 Home 3 Friend's or Relative's Home 4 Store, Restaurant, Bank 5 Doctor's Office, Hospital 6 School 7 Other	1 Work (Priority) 2 Home 3 Friend's or Relative's Home 4 Store, Restaurant, Bank 5 Doctor's Office, Hospital 6 School 7 Other
49. What was the purpose of this trip? (CHECK TWO BOXES IF NECESSARY)	1 Go home ⎫ 2 Get to work ⎬ (GO TO Q. 51) 3 Shopping 4 Attend school 5 Social or recreational 6 To take someone somewhere (serve a passenger)-(CHECK ALSO THE PURPOSE OF HIS TRIP) 7 To change mode of travel 8 Personal business, medical, dental 9 Eat meal 0 Other	1 Go home ⎫ 2 Get to work ⎬ (GO TO Q. 51) 3 Shopping 4 Attend school 5 Social or recreational 6 To take someone somewhere (serve a passenger)-(CHECK ALSO THE PURPOSE OF HIS TRIP) 7 To change mode of travel 8 Personal business, medical, dental 9 Eat meal 0 Other
50. Where did (you) go?	1 Home 2 School 3 Friend's or Relative's Home 4 Store, Bank, Restaurant 5 Doctor's Office, Hospital 6 Other	1 Home 2 School 3 Friend's or Relative's Home 4 Store, Bank, Restaurant 5 Doctor's Office, Hospital 6 Other
51. How did (you) travel? (IF BY CAR): Did (you) drive? (CHECK TWO BOXES IF ONE FAMILY MEMBER DROVE ANOTHER)	1 Auto driver-WHICH FAMILY MEMBER DROVE? _____ 1 Auto passenger 2 Suburban Railroad 3 Bus 4 Rapid Transit 5 Walk to work 6 Taxi 7 Other	1 Auto driver-WHICH FAMILY MEMBER DROVE? _____ 1 Auto passenger 2 Suburban Railroad 3 Bus 4 Rapid Transit 5 Walk to work 6 Taxi 7 Other

INTERVIEWER: REPEAT QUESTIONS 46-51 FOR EACH TRIP. INCLUDE TRIPS BY ANY FAMILY MEMBER AGED 5 AND OVER. LIST THE FAMILY MEMBERS AGED 5 AND OVER BELOW. (SEE Q. 1)

1. _____   4. _____   7. _____

2. _____   5. _____   8. _____

3. _____   6. _____   9. _____

Family Member(s) Who Went:	Family Member(s) Who Went:	Family Member(s) Who Went:
_____	_____	_____
[1] Work (Priority) [2] Home [3] Friend's or Relative's Home [4] Store, Restaurant, Bank [5] Doctor's Office, Hospital [6] School [7] Other	[1] Work (Priority) [2] Home [3] Friend's or Relative's Home [4] Store, Restaurant, Bank [5] Doctor's Office, Hospital [6] School [7] Other	[1] Work (Priority) [2] Home [3] Friend's or Relative's Home [4] Store, Restaurant, Bank [5] Doctor's Office, Hospital [6] School [7] Other
[1] Go home [2] Get to work } (GO TO Q. 51) [3] Shopping [4] Attend school [5] Social or recreational [6] To take someone somewhere (serve a passenger)-(CHECK ALSO THE PURPOSE OF HIS TRIP) [7] To change mode of travel [8] Personal business, medical, dental [9] Eat meal [0] Other	[1] Go home [2] Get to work } (GO TO Q. 51) [3] Shopping [4] Attend school [5] Social or recreational [6] To take someone somewhere (serve a passenger)-(CHECK ALSO THE PURPOSE OF HIS TRIP) [7] To change mode of travel [8] Personal business, medical, dental [9] Eat meal [0] Other	[1] Go home [2] Get to work } (GO TO Q. 51) [3] Shopping [4] Attend school [5] Social or recreational [6] To take someone somewhere (serve a passenger)-(CHECK ALSO THE PURPOSE OF HIS TRIP) [7] To change mode of travel [8] Personal business, medical, dental [9] Eat meal [0] Other
[1] Home [2] School [3] Friend's or Relative's Home [4] Store, Bank, Restaurant [5] Doctor's Office, Hospital [6] Other	[1] Home [2] School [3] Friend's or Relative's Home [4] Store, Bank, Restaurant [5] Doctor's Office, Hospital [6] Other	[1] Home [2] School [3] Friend's or Relative's Home [4] Store, Bank, Restaurant [5] Doctor's Office, Hospital [6] Other
[1] Auto driver-WHICH FAMILY MEMBER DROVE?	[1] Auto driver-WHICH FAMILY MEMBER DROVE?	[1] Auto driver-WHICH FAMILY MEMBER DROVE?
[1] Auto passenger [2] Suburban Railroad [3] Bus [4] Rapid Transit [5] Walk to work [6] Taxi [7] Other	[1] Auto passenger [2] Suburban Railroad [3] Bus [4] Rapid Transit [5] Walk to work [6] Taxi [7] Other	[1] Auto passenger [2] Suburban Railroad [3] Bus [4] Rapid Transit [5] Walk to work [6] Taxi [7] Other

INTERVIEWER: REPEAT QUESTIONS 46-51 FOR EACH TRIP.   INCLUDE TRIPS BY ANY
FAMILY MEMBER AGED 5 AND OVER.

20

52. Does that include all the trips made anytime yesterday by anybody in the family?

    [1] YES → GO TO Q. 53

    [5] NO → ADD THESE TRIPS ON THE TRIP RECORD FORM

53. Do you own this home, pay rent, or what?

C. 97   2   1

R. 90 [1] OWNS OR IS BUYING 10 [2] RENTS - [3] NEITHER OWNS NOR RENTS

> 53b. How is that?_____
>
> _____
>
>   GO TO Q. 56

> 53a. (HAND R CARD E-1) Could you tell me the letter of the group on this card that would indicate about how much rent you pay a month, not including utilities?
>
> | C. | R. | | | C. | R. | | |
> |----|----|----|----|----|----|----|----|
> | 25 | - | A. [1] Under $100 | | - | 75 | E. [5] $250-$299 | |
> | - | - | B. [2] $100-$149 | | - | 15 | F. [6] $300-$349 | |
> | - | - | C. [3] $150-$199 | | - | - | G. [7] $350-$399 | |
> | 75 | 10 | D. [4] $200-$249 | | - | - | H. [8] $400 and over | |
>
> C. (N = 4)
> R. (N = 20)
>
>   GO TO Q. 56

54. (HAND R CARD E-2) Could you tell me the letter of the group on this card that would indicate about what the present value of this home is? What would it bring if you sold it today?

C.	R.			C.	R.		
5	-	A. [1] Under $20,000		5	21	F. [6] $44,000-$49,999	
8	-	B. [2] $20,000-$25,999		3	19	G. [7] $50,000-$61,999	
24	7	C. [3] $26,000-$31,999		1	5	H. [8] $62,000-$73,999	
39	22	D. [4] $32,000-$37,999		1	2	I. [9] $74,000 and over	
14	24	E. [5] $38,000-$43,999					

C. (N = 212)
R. (N = 183)

55. Compared to other homes you considered at the time you were buying do you think that this home will be a better financial investment, a worse investment, or about the same?

C. 76   22   2

R. 73 [1] BETTER   20 [2] SAME   7 [3] WORSE

C. (N = 212)
R. (N = 183)

    55a. Why do you feel that way?_____

_____

_____

56. As far as you're concerned, do you think it's a good idea for neighborhoods -- and here again I'm thinking of clusters of five or six homes -- to have people of different religious backgrounds or the same religious backgrounds, or doesn't it matter?

C. 51
R. 47 [1] Good if different   46/50 [2] Doesn't matter   3/3 [3] Good if the same

57. And as far as you're concerned, do you think it's a good idea for neighborhoods to have people of different racial backgrounds or the same racial background or doesn't it matter?

C. 57
R. 57 [1] Good if different   37/38 [2] Doesn't matter   6/5 [3] Good if same

58. What is (HEAD'S) (your) main job at the present time? What kind of work (does HEAD) (do you) do? (IF RETIRED OR UNEMPLOYED, GET LAST MAIN JOB. PROBE CAREFULLY FOR SPECIFIC JOB. E.G., BANK TELLER, VICE-PRESIDENT IN CHARGE OF RESEARCH AND DEVELOPMENT, ETC.)

HEAD IS: (CHECK)

C. 99
R. 96   [1] EMPLOYED   [2] UNEMPLOYED   1/2 [3] RETIRED;DISABLED   2 [4] HOUSEWIFE → GO TO Q,65

JOB DESCRIPTION FOR HEAD:

59. What kind of business is (was) that in? (MAIN JOB) _____

60. Does (HEAD) work for himself or someone else?

C. 4
R. 9 [1] SELF-EMPLOYED   96/91 [5] SOMEONE ELSE

22

⑤ HEAD IS <u>NOT</u> NOW WORKING ➤ GO TO Q. 65

① HEAD IS NOW WORKING

61. What are the names of the two streets at the intersection nearest (HEAD'S) place of work?

a. _____

b. _____

☐ HEAD DOES NOT HAVE ONE REGULAR PLACE OF WORK→GO TO Q. 65

62. (Just a few minutes ago you told me how (HEAD) got to work yesterday. Now I'd like you to tell me if this is how (HEAD) usually makes the trip to work.)

Does (HEAD) always go by car, sometimes by car and sometimes by public transportation, always by public transportation, or some other way?

C. R.

93 71 ① Always car

6 19 ② Sometimes car, sometimes public

- 8 ③ Always public ➤ GO TO Q. 64

1 2 ⑦ Other:_____

_____

(GO TO Q. 64)

63. When (HEAD) does go by car, does (HEAD) usually drive to work alone or do other people ride in the same car with (HEAD)?

☐ Shares trip C.73
R.69 ① Goes alone ➤ GO TO Q.64 (N = 200)
(N = 165)

63a. (IF SHARES:) How many people other than (HEAD) ride in the same car?
C. 16   4   7
R. 18 ② One other 5 ③ Two others 8 ④ Three or more others

64. What time does (HEAD) usually leave home to go to work?   _____

64a. And what time does (HEAD) usually get to work?   _____

64b. Then it takes about   _____ minutes, is that right?

INTERVIEWER: CALCULATE NUMBER OF MINUTES, CHECK WITH R, RECORD ANY CORRECTIONS IN MARGIN AT RIGHT.

<u>C. R.</u>

8 9 [5] HEAD HAS NO WIFE LIVING AT HOME ➡ GO TO Q. 66

92 91 [/] WIFE LIVING AT HOME

---

65. Is (WIFE) doing any work for pay at this time (too)?

C.   34 [/] YES   66 [5] NO ➡ GO TO Q. 66   (N = 199)
R.   36   64   (N = 185)

    65a. On the average about how many hours a week does (WIFE) work?

C.   4 [/] Less than 10 2 [2] 10-19 6 [3] 20-29 4 [4] 30-39 18 [5] 40 or more
R.   4   6   7   5   14

---

66. Please tell me the letter of the group on this card (HAND R CARD F) that would
     indicate about what the total income for you and your family was last year --
     1968 -- before taxes, that is.

<u>C. R.</u>   <u>C. R.</u>

 2 1 A. ☐ Under $5000   19 19 F. ☐ $17,500-$19,999

 3 5 B. ☐ $5000-$9999   16 24 G. ☐ $20,000-$24,999

13 2 C. ☐ $10,000-$12,499   8 15 H. ☐ $25,000-$29,999

22 8 D. ☐ $12,500-$14,999   5 12 I. ☐ $30,000 and over

12 14 E. ☐ $15,000-$17,499

    66a. Does that include the income of everyone in the family?

       [/] YES   [5] NO -- ASK FOR "EVERYONE'S" INCOME, MAKE CORRECTION ABOVE.

67. What was (HEAD'S) <u>father's</u> usual occupation while (HEAD) was in grade school?

_____

    67a. What kind of business was that in? _____

_____

    67b. Was he self-employed? [/] YES   [5] NO
                           C.   24   76
                           R.   32   68

24

68. How many years of school or college did you complete?

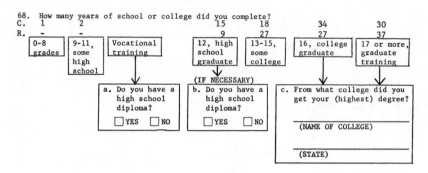

69. (IF MARRIED) How many years of school or college did your (SPOUSE) complete?

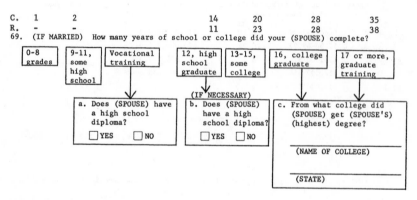

BY OBSERVATION:

70. RACE:
   C. 85   14   1
   R. 93 [1] WHITE   6 [2] BLACK   1 [3] OTHER:_____

71. Is there a sidewalk along the street in front of this home?

C. R.
65 62 [1] SIDEWALK EXISTS ALONG THE STREET

34 38 [5] NO SIDEWALK

1 - [ ] HARD TO TELL - EXPLAIN:_____

_____

Survey Research Center
The University of Michigan
Project 45789

INTERVIEWER'S LABEL

Your Int. No. _____

Please indicate for each of the following sentences whether you agree or disagree with it and how much. Do this by placing an (X) over the appropriate alternative under the sentence.

1. When I go outside and look around me at the street and the neighbors' homes I like what I see.

OTHER, N.A., D.K.

	1. AGREE STRONGLY	2. AGREE SOMEWHAT	3. DISAGREE SOMEWHAT	4. DISAGREE STRONGLY	
C.	49	40	10	1	-
R.	66	26	4	3	1

2. A modern style of architecture is more attractive for a new home than a colonial style.

	1. AGREE STRONGLY	2. AGREE SOMEWHAT	3. DISAGREE SOMEWHAT	4. DISAGREE STRONGLY	
C.	18	29	39	13	1
R.	31	30	26	8	5

3. Whenever an opportunity arises I like to try doing things in new ways.

	1. AGREE STRONGLY	2. AGREE SOMEWHAT	3. DISAGREE SOMEWHAT	4. DISAGREE STRONGLY	
C.	36	56	7	1	-
R.	37	55	5	1	2

4. The raising of one's social position is one of the more important goals in life.

	1. AGREE STRONGLY	2. AGREE SOMEWHAT	3. DISAGREE SOMEWHAT	4. DISAGREE STRONGLY	
C.	5	26	38	31	-
R.	2	25	32	39	2

5. I would enjoy living for a year or two in a foreign country.

	1. AGREE STRONGLY	2. AGREE SOMEWHAT	3. DISAGREE SOMEWHAT	4. DISAGREE STRONGLY	
C.	49	35	9	7	-
R.	58	30	6	3	3

6. Most people in this community really care what happens to it.

	1. AGREE STRONGLY	2. AGREE SOMEWHAT	3. DISAGREE SOMEWHAT	4. DISAGREE STRONGLY	
C.	62	31	4	3	-
R.	61	32	6	-	1

7. We need a lot more freeways in and around our big cities.

	1. AGREE STRONGLY	2. AGREE SOMEWHAT	3. DISAGREE SOMEWHAT	4. DISAGREE STRONGLY	
C.	28	38	21	12	1
R.	22	36	20	19	3

8. I don't like to belong to clubs that get new members all the time.

	1. AGREE STRONGLY	2. AGREE SOMEWHAT	3. DISAGREE SOMEWHAT	4. DISAGREE STRONGLY	
C.	3	14	49	33	1
R.	6	12	38	37	7

1

2

9. As a rule you can tell quite a bit about a person by the way he dresses.

OTHER, N.A., D.K.

C. 3	1. AGREE STRONGLY 41	2. AGREE SOMEWHAT 33	3. DISAGREE SOMEWHAT 22	4. DISAGREE STRONGLY	1
R. 3	42	30	23		2

10. I have as many friends as I want.

C. 12	1. AGREE STRONGLY 35	2. AGREE SOMEWHAT 35	3. DISAGREE SOMEWHAT 17	4. DISAGREE STRONGLY	1
R. 14	37	37	8		4

11. I enjoy working on a project with people I don't know.

C. 17	1. AGREE STRONGLY 53	2. AGREE SOMEWHAT 26	3. DISAGREE SOMEWHAT 3	4. DISAGREE STRONGLY	1
R. 17	58	18	4		3

12. It is worth considerable effort to assure one's self of a good name with important people.

C. 9	1. AGREE STRONGLY 31	2. AGREE SOMEWHAT 37	3. DISAGREE SOMEWHAT 21	4. DISAGREE STRONGLY	2
R. 5	26	39	26		4

13. Most people around here would like to spend more time with their neighbors.

C. 10	1. AGREE STRONGLY 54	2. AGREE SOMEWHAT 28	3. DISAGREE SOMEWHAT 4	4. DISAGREE STRONGLY	4
R. 6	39	39	6		10

14. In general, how satisfying do you find the way you're spending your life these days? Would you call it _completely_ satisfying, _pretty_ satisfying, _not very_ satisfying, or _not at all_ satisfying?

C. 18	1. COMPLETELY SATISFYING 73	2. PRETTY SATISFYING 7	3. NOT VERY SATISFYING 1	4. NOT AT ALL SATISFYING	1
R. 17	75	4	2		2

3

15. Here are some words and phrases which we would like you to use to describe
this <u>neighborhood</u> as it seems to you. By neighborhood we mean just what
you can see from your front door, that is, the five or six homes nearest
to yours around here. For example, if you think the neighborhood is
"noisy," please put a check right next to the word "noisy." If you think
it is "quiet," please put a check right next to the word "quiet," and if
you think it is somewhere in between, please put a check where you think
it belongs.

							Others, N.A., D.K.
Noisy	: ___: ___: ___: ___: ___:					Quiet	
(C)	1	5	17	27	48		2
(R)	1	4	15	23	56		1
Attractive	: ___: ___: ___: ___: ___:					Unattractive	
(C)	52	29	14	2	1		2
(R)	58	33	6	2	-		1
Unfriendly people	: ___: ___: ___: ___: ___:					Friendly people	
(C)	-	1	12	26	59		2
(R)	1	4	12	28	53		2
Poorly kept up	: ___: ___: ___: ___: ___:					Well kept up	
(C)	1	1	6	27	63		2
(R)	1	3	11	31	53		1
People similar to me	: ___: ___: ___: ___: ___:					People dissimilar to me	
(C)	21	25	35	11	6		2
(R)	18	25	39	7	7		4
Pleasant	: ___: ___: ___: ___: ___:					Unpleasant	
(C)	70	23	4	1	1		1
(R)	73	17	7	1	1		1
Very poor place to live	: ___: ___: ___: ___: ___:					Very good place to live	
(C)	1	1	6	22	68		2
(R)	2	2	4	21	70		1

Appendix E
Supplementary Tables

Table E-1:

Why the Area Appealed for Those Who Moved to Their Community [1]

(reasons cited by 10 percent or more of the respondents)

	Percent
Columbia	
Liked the town's concept, idea, philosophy, plan	51
Nearness to work	22
Nearness to shopping, entertainment, downtown facilities	19
Liked the type of people, neighbors	18
Good schools	11
Good price on home, lot	11
Number of respondents	216
Reston	
Nearness to country, outdoor recreation, "nature"	38
Liked the town's concept, idea, philosophy, plan	36
Desire for peace and quiet, small neighborhoods, no congestion	20
Nearness to shopping, entertainment, downtown facilities	12
Contemporary architecture, newness of home	11
Nearness to work	11
Liked type of people, nice neighbors	11
Number of respondents	203
Crofton	
Nearness to country, outdoor recreation, "nature"	39
Liked the town's concept, idea, philosophy, plan	22
Nearness to shopping, entertainment, downtown facilities	22
Nearness to work	18
Good price on home, lot	17
Desire for peace and quiet, small neighborhoods, no congestion	13
General or unspecified appeal of town, area	10
Number of respondents	98
Montpelier	
Nearness to work	48
Good price on home, lot	37
Nearness to shopping, entertainment, downtown facilities	21
House (lot) had plenty of space for play, activities	21
House (lot) well planned, well laid out	18
Nearness to country, outdoor recreation, "nature"	13
Liked type of people, nice neighbors	12
Desire for peace and quiet, small neighborhoods, no congestion	10
General or unspecified appeal of town, area	10
Number of respondents	105

Table E-1 - continued

	Percent
Norbeck	
Good price on home, lot	23
Good schools	23
Nearness to work	20
House (lot) has plenty of space for play, activities	17
Nearness to shopping, entertainment, downtown facilities	16
Nearness to country, outdoor recreation, "nature"	15
Liked type of people, neighbors	14
House (lot) well planned, well laid out	12
Number of respondents	99
Southfield	
Nearness to work	30
Good schools	26
Nearness to shopping, entertainment, downtown facilities	20
Good price on home, lot	16
General or unspecified appeal of town, area	16
House (lot) well planned, well laid out	14
Liked type of people, neighbors	14
House (lot) has plenty of space for play, activities	12
Nearness to country, outdoor recreation, "nature"	10
Number of respondents	110
Lafayette-Elmwood	
Nearness to work	53
Nearness to shopping, entertainment, downtown facilities	42
Liked type of people, neighbors	26
Few(er) maintenance problems	18
House (lot) has plenty of space for play, activities	16
Number of respondents	106
Southwest Washington	
Nearness to work	43
Nearness to shopping, entertainment, downtown facilities	36
Liked type of people, neighbors	36
House (lot) has plenty of space for play, activities	10
Contemporary architecture, newness of home	10
Number of respondents	107

Table E-1 - continued

	Percent
Radburn	
Recreation facilities available, playgrounds	26
Liked type of people, neighbors	23
Nearness to shopping, entertainment, downtown facilities	21
Nearness to country, outdoor recreation, "nature"	20
Liked the town's concept, idea, philosophy, plan	18
Nearness to work	15
Good price on home, lot	12
General or unspecified appeal of area, town	10
Number of respondents	103
Glen Rock	
Good schools	44
Nearness to shopping, entertainment, downtown facilities	25
Nearness to work	21
Liked type of people, neighbors	21
General or unspecified appeal of town, area	18
Desire for peace and quiet, small neighborhoods, no congestion	17
Nearness to country, outdoor recreation, "nature"	12
House (lot) has plenty of space for play, activities	11

---

[1]The question was: "When you were looking for a place to live, what especially appealed to you about coming here?"

Table E-2:

Reasons Why Residents Evaluated the Mapped Area of Their Community Positively

(reasons cited by 10 percent or more of the respondents)

	Percent
Columbia	
Accessibility of job, stores, downtown, entertainment, etc.	47
Physical facilities in the area are planned, provided for, accessible, town is planned	22
Area has trees, hills, lakes, etc.	13
Plenty of space, little or no congestion	12
General beauty or attractiveness of area	11
Number of respondents	216
Reston	
Accessibility of job, stores, downtown, entertainment, etc.	28
Physical facilities in the area are planned, provided for, accessible, town is planned	27
Area has trees, hills, lakes, etc.	24
Plenty of space, little or no congestion	23
General beauty or attractiveness of area	13
Neighbors are "friendly," "desirable," "nice"	12
Area is safe from crime, traffic	10
Number of respondents	203
Crofton	
Accessibility of job, stores, downtown, entertainment, etc.	48
Physical facilities in the area are planned, provided for, accessible, town is planned	15
Plenty of space, little or congestion	14
Number of respondents	98
Montpelier	
Accessibility of job, stores, downtown, entertainment, etc.	49
Good schools	15
Good access to freeways	13
Physical facilities in the area are planned, provided for, accessible, town is planned	10
Neighbors are "friendly," "desirable," "nice"	10
Number of respondents	105
Norbeck	
Accessibility of job, stores, downtown, entertainment, etc.	48
Good schools	24
Neighbors are "friendly," "desirable," "nice"	23
Physical facilities in the area are planned, provided for, accessible, town is planned	13
Good access to freeways	11
Number of respondents	99

Table E-2 - continued

	Percent
Southfield	
Accessibility of job, stores, downtown, entertainment, etc.	56
Good schools	27
Neighbors are "friendly," "desirable," "nice"	24
Good access to freeways	20
Property is well kept up	11
Physical facilities in the area are planned, provided for, accessible, town is planned	10
General or unspecified appeal of the area	10
Number of respondents	110
Lafayette-Elmwood	
Accessibility of job, stores, downtown, entertainment, etc.	63
Neighbors are "friendly," "desirable," "nice"	33
Physical facilities in the area are planned, provided for, accessible, town is planned	14
Good access to freeways	13
Good bus service or other public transportation	12
Neighbors are heterogeneous	11
Number of respondents	106
Southwest Washington	
Accessibility of job, stores, downtown, entertainment, etc.	58
Attractive architecture	19
Neighbors are "friendly," "desirable," "nice"	17
Area is safe from crime, traffic	10
Number of respondents	107
Radburn	
Accessibility of job, stores, downtown, entertainment, etc.	53
Neighbors are "friendly," "desirable," "nice"	25
Good bus service or other public transportation	19
Physical facilities in the area are planned, provided for, accessible, town is planned	14
Area is safe from crime, traffic	11
Recreation facilities available, playgrounds	11
Number of respondents	103
Glen Rock	
Accessibility of job, stores, downtown, entertainment, etc.	46
Neighbors are "friendly," "desirable," "nice"	22
Good schools	19
Good bus service or other public transportation	17
Area has good public services	13
Area is quiet, free of pollution	12
General or unspecified appeal of the area	12
Physical facilities in the area are planned, provided for, accessible, town is planned	10
Number of respondents	106

Table E-3:

Relationship between Frequency of Participation in Recreation Activities

and Distance to Nearest Public or Semi-Public Recreation Facilities

(Percentage distribution of respondents)

Frequency of Participation in-	Distance to Nearest Facility (miles)							
A. Swimming in an outdoor pool	Less than .125	.125- .249	.25- .49	.50- .74	.75- .99	1.00- 1.49	1.50- 1.99	2 miles or more
not at all	28	25	33	38	42	46	49	37
one to four times	11	15	10	12	13	11	7	21
five times or more	61	60	57	50	45	43	44	42
Total	100	100	100	100	100	100	100	100
Number of respondents	261	99	289	217	165	144	41	19
B. Tennis								
not at all	74	73	79	83	84	79	82	78
one to four times	8	2	6	6	6	8	10	5
five times or more	18	25	15	11	10	13	8	17
Total	100	100	100	100	100	100	100	100
Number of respondents	63	85	375	305	173	161	62	23

	Less than .50	.50- .99	1.00- 1.99	2.00- 2.99	3.00- 3.99	4.00- 4.99	5.00- 9.99	10 miles or more
C. Golfing								
not at all	76	73	81	78	73	84	94	-
one to four times	4	7	5	6	9	-	-	-
five times or more	20	20	14	16	18	16	6	-
Total	100	100	100	100	100	100	100	-
Number of respondents	25	135	473	358	218	19	18	-
D. Boating								
not at all	40	66	71	53	73	71	69	83
one to four times	20	16	15	22	16	19	17	9
five times or more	40	18	14	15	11	10	14	8
Total	100	100	100	100	100	100	100	100
Number of respondents	70	233	150	53	94	63	269	310

Table E-4

Relationship between Frequency of Participation in Recreation Activities
and Distance to Place Where Respondent Engaged in Activities

(Percentage distribution of respondents)

Frequency of Participation in-	Distance to Place Where Respondent Engaged in Activity (miles)						
A. Swimming in an outdoor pool	Less than .125	.125-.249	.25-.49	.50-.99	1.00-1.99	2.00-9.99	10 miles or more
one to four times	15	12	12	14	12	26	46
five times or more	84	88	87	86	87	74	53
Total	99	100	99	100	99	100	99
Number of swimmers	181	61	167	173	75	39	74
B. Tennis							
one to four times	27	13	30	28	34	50	35
five times or more	73	87	70	72	66	50	65
Total	100	100	100	100	100	100	100
Number of tennis players	22	15	46	47	50	18	23

	Less than .50	.50-.99	1.00-1.99	2.00-4.99	5.00-9.99	10 miles or more
C. Golfing						
one to four times	a	26	26	17	41	31
five times or more	a	74	74	83	59	66
Total	a	100	100	100	100	97
Number of golfers	4	27	43	52	27	110
D. Boating						
one to four times	34	14	56	73	a	52
five times or more	66	86	44	24	a	47
Total	100	100	100	97	a	99
Number of boaters	35	14	32	33	7	214

Table E-4 - continued

Frequency of Participation in-	Distance to Place Where Respondent Engaged in Activity (miles)			
	Less than 1.0	1.00-1.99	2.00-9.99	10 miles or more
E. Hiking or walking				
one to four times	8	10	16	29
five times or more	91	90	78	70
Total	99	100	94	99
Number of hikers or walkers	518	115	32	116
F. Bicycling				
one to four times	25	24	46	38
five times or more	73	76	54	62
Total	98	100	100	100
Number of bikers	305	66	11	16
G. Picnicking				
one to four times	30	27	55	59
five times or more	70	52	45	41
Total	100	79	100	100
Number of picnickers	138	86	117	312

[a]Too few observations to percentagize.

Table E-5

Comparison of Findings on Frequency of Participation in Outdoor Recreation
between the Planned Residential Environments Survey and Other Surveys

(Percentage distributions)

	1969 Planned Residential Environments	1960 ORRRC National Survey[1]		1968 Oakland County Survey[2]		1965 Detroit Regional Survey[3]	
	All Groups	All Groups	$10,000 and Over	All Groups	$15,000 and Over	All Groups	$15,000 and Over
Outdoor Swimming		a		b		b	
Not at all	34	54	33	43	29	61	47
One to four times	12	19	20	14	16	10	53
More often	54	26	47	43	55	27	
Total	100	99*	100	100	100	98*	100
Number of cases	1253	2759	264	1000	227	466	116
Tennis							
Not at all	80	data not		93	86	data not	
One to four times	6	available		2	4	available	
More often	14			5	10		
Total	100			100	100		
Number of cases	1253			1000	227		
Golfing							
Not at all	78	data not		82	62	88	78
One to four times	6	available		5	11	3	22
More often	16			13	27	9	
Total	100			100	100	100	100
Number of cases	1253			1000	226	128	116
Boating		c					
Not at all	70	71	53	61	56	84	62
One to four times	15	16	23	17	19	12	38
More often	15	12	22	22	25	14	
Total	100	99*	98*	100	100	100	100
Number of cases	1253	2759	264	1000	226	351	116
Hiking or Walking		d					
Not at all	34	82	72	59	51	37	46
One to four times	8	8	13	11	9	23	54
More often	58	9	10	30	40	40	
Total	100	99*	95*	100	100	100	100
Number of cases	1253	2759	264	1000	227	466	116

Table E-5 - continued

Picnicking	1969 Planned Residential Environments All Groups	1960 ORRRC National Survey[1] All Groups	1960 ORRRC National Survey[1] $10,000 and Over	1968 Oakland County Survey[2] All Groups	1968 Oakland County Survey[2] $15,000 and Over	1965 Detroit Regional Survey[3] All Groups	1965 Detroit Regional Survey[3] $15,000 and Over
Not at all	45	33	27	39	52	37	44
One to four times	27	35	37	26	20	23	56
More often	28	31	35	35	28	40	
Total	100	99*	99*	100	100	100	100
Number of cases	1253	2759	264	1000	227	699	116

---

*Totals exclude respondents whose participation rates were not obtained.

[1] Source: ORRRC Study Report 20, Table 10, p. 12.

[2] Source: Leisure Time in Oakland County, 1969, Tables 3-6, 10 and 14.

[3] Source: Living Patterns and Attitudes in the Detroit Region, 1967, pp. 20-21, 224-225.

[a] Outdoor swimming or going to the beach.

[b] Outdoor swimming.

[c] Boating and canoeing.

[d] Hiking.

Note: Comparative studies of annual participation rates in outdoor recreation activities include participation at all times including vacations.

Table E-6:

Participation in Selected Outdoor Recreation Activities,
September 1964 through August 1965; United States Totals[1]
(Percentage of population 12 years and over who participated)

	All Groups	Family Income $15,000-$25,000	Family Income $25,000 and Over
Swimming	49	73	69
Boating[2]	26	41	34
Sailing	3	9	-
Canoeing	4	8	-
Hiking	9	15	-
Walking for pleasure	51	67	59
Bicycling	19	26	23
Picnicking	60	62	52

---

[1] Abstracted from Table H, Bureau of Outdoor Recreation, U.S. Department of the Interior, The 1965 Survey of Outdoor Recreation Activities, October 1967, mimeographed.

[2] excluding sailing and canoeing.

Appendix F

List of Tables

Bibliography

Allen, Muriel I. (ed.), *New Communities: Challenge for Today,* American Institute of Planners, Background Paper, No. 2, October 1968, Washington, D.C.

Alonso, William, "The Mirage of New Towns," The Public Interest, No. 19 (Spring 1970), 3-17.

Berger, Bennett M., *Working Class Suburb,* Berkeley: University of California Press, 1960.

Bracey, H. E., *Neighbors,* London: Routledge and Kegan Paul, 1964.

Bradburn, Norman M., and David Caplovitz, *Reports on Happiness,* Chicago: Aldine, 1965.

Bureau of Outdoor Recreation, *Outdoor Recreation Trends,* Washington, D.C.: Government Printing Office, April, 1967.

Bureau of Outdoor Recreation, *The 1965 Survey of Outdoor Recreation Activities,* Washington: October, 1967, (Mimeo).

Campbell, Angus, and Howard Schuman, *Racial Attitudes in Fifteen American Cities,* Institute for Social Research, The University of Michigan, Ann Arbor, Michigan, 1968.

Caplow, Theodore, and Robert Forman, "Neighborhood Interaction in a Homogeneous Community," *American Sociological Review,* Vol. 15, No. 3, (June 1950), 357-366.

Clark, S. D., *The Suburban Society,* Toronto: University of Toronto Press, 1966.

Clawson, Marion, and Jack Knetsch, *Economics of Outdoor Recreation,* Baltimore: The Johns Hopkins Press, 1966.

265

Derthick, Martha, "Defeat at Fort Lincoln," *The Public Interest,* No. 20 (Summer 1970), 3-39.

Dobriner, William M., *Class in Suburbia,* Englewood Cliffs: Prentice-Hall, 1963.

Downs, Anthony, "Alternative Forms of Future Urban Growth in the United States," *Journal of the American Institute of Planners,* Vol. 36, No. 1 (January 1970), 3-11.

Driver, Beverly L. (ed.), *Elements of Outdoor Recreation Planning,* Ann Arbor, Michigan: University Microfilms, Inc., 1970.

Eichler, Edward, and Marshall Kaplan, *The Community Builders,* Berkeley: University of California Press, 1967.

Fava, Sylvia F., "Contrasts in Neighboring: New York City and a Suburban Community," in *The Suburban Community,* William M. Dobriner (ed.), New York: Putnam, 1958, 122-131.

Festinger, Leon, Stanley Schachter and Kurt Back, *Social Pressures in Informal Groups,* New York: Harper and Brothers, 1950.

Foote, Nelson N., J. Abu-Lughod, M. Foley and L. Winnick, *Housing Choices and Housing Constraints,* New York: McGraw-Hill, 1960.

Gallion, Arthur B., and Simon Eisner, *The Urban Pattern* (Second edition), Princeton: Van Nostrand, 1963.

Gans, Herbert J., *The Levittowners,* New York: Random House, 1967.

Gans, Herbert J., *People and Plans,* New York: Basic Books, 1968.

Goldsmith, Harold F., and Janice Munsterman, "Neighborhood Homogeneity and Community Satisfaction," paper presented at the Annual Meetings of the Rural Sociological Association, San Francisco, California, August, 1967.

Gutman, Robert, "Site Planning and Social Behavior," *Journal of Social Issues,* Vol. 22, No. 4 (October 1966), 103-115.

Howard, Ebenezer, *Garden Cities of To-Morrow,* 1902; reprinted as an M.I.T. Press Paperback Edition, Cambridge: M.I.T. Press, 1965.

Kaplan, Marshall, "The Roles of Planner and Developer in the New Community," *Washington University Law Quarterly,* Vol. 1965 (February 1965), 88-106.

Katona, George, William Dunkelberg, Jay Schmiedeskamp, and Frank Stafford, *1968 Survey of Consumer Finances,* Institute for Social Research, The University of Michigan, Ann Arbor, Michigan, 1969.

Katona, George, William Dunkelberg, Gary Hendricks and Jay Schmiedeskamp, *1969 Survey of Consumer Finances,* Institute for Social Research, The University of Michigan, Ann Arbor, Michigan, 1970.

Keller, Suzanne, *The Urban Neighborhood: A Sociological Perspective,* New York: Random House, 1968.

Kuper, Leo, (ed.), *Living in Towns,* London: The Gresset Press, 1953.

Ladd, William M., and Oleh Dub, *Leisure Time Activity in Oakland County,* a report prepared for the Oakland County Planning Commission and the Oakland County Parks and Recreation Commission by the Center for Urban Studies, The University of Michigan, Dearborn Campus, Dearborn, Michigan, January 1969.

Lansing, John B, *Residential Location and Urban Mobility: The Second Wave of Interviews.* A report prepared for the U.S. Department of Commerce, Bureau of Public Roads by The Survey Research Center, Institute for Social Research, The University of Michigan, Ann Arbor, Michigan, 1966.

Lansing, John B., and Nancy Barth, *Residential Location and Urban Mobility: A Multivariate Analysis.* A report prepared for the U.S. Department of Commerce, Bureau of Public Roads, by the Survey Research Center, Institute for Social Research, The University of Michigan, Ann Arbor, Michigan, 1964.

Lansing, John B., Charles Wade Clifton, and James N. Morgan, *New Homes and Poor People,* Institute for Social Research, The University of Michigan, Ann Arbor, Michigan, 1969.

Lansing, John B., and Gary Hendricks, *Automobile Ownership and Residential Density.* A report prepared for the Bureau of Public Roads, Federal Highway Administration, U.S. Department of Transportation by the Survey Research Center, Institute for Social Research, The University of Michigan, Ann Arbor, Michigan, 1967.

Lansing, John B., and Gary Hendricks, *Living Patterns and Attitudes in the Detroit Region,* Detroit Regional Transportation and Land Use Study, 1967.

Lansing, John B., and Robert W. Marans, "Evaluation of Neighborhood Quality," *Journal of American Institute of Planners,* Vol. 35, No. 3 (May 1969), 195-199.

Lansing, John B., and Eva Mueller with Nancy Barth, *Residential Location and Urban Mobility.* A report prepared for the U.S. Department of Commerce, Bureau of Public Roads by the Survey Research Center, Institute for Social Research, The University of Michigan, Ann Arbor, Michigan, 1964.

Lemkau, Paul V., "Human Factors in the New Town," *Building Research,* Vol. 3, No. 1 (January-February 1966), 29-32.

Marans, Robert W., "Social and Cultural Influences on New Town Planning: An Israeli Experiment," *Journal of the Town Planning Institute,* Vol. 56, No. 2 (February 1970), 60-65.

Mayor's Committee for Community Renewal, *Detroit: The New City,* Detroit: Report and Information Committee, City of Detroit, 1966.

Michelson, William, *Man and His Urban Environment: A Sociological Approach,* Reading, Massachusetts: Addison-Wesley, 1970.

Mueller, Eva, and Gerald Gurin, *Participation in Outdoor Recreation: Factors Affecting Demand Among American Adults,* ORRRC Study Report 20, Washington: Government Printing Office, 1962.

New Town Development Research Project, New Towns Research Seminar Series I, (Fall, 1969). New Towns Research Seminar Series II, (Spring, 1970). Center for Urban and Regional Studies, University of North Carolina, Chapel Hill (mimeo).

Outdoor Recreation Resources Review Commission, *Outdoor Recreation for America,* Washington: Government Printing Office, 1962.

Perloff, Harvey S. (ed.), *The Quality of the Urban Environment: Essays on "New Resources" in an Urban Age,* Baltimore: The Johns Hopkins Press, 1969.

The Reston Virginia Foundation for Community Programs, Inc., *Social Planning and Programs for Reston, Virginia,* March 1967.

Rossi, Peter H., *Why Families Move,* Glencoe: The Free Press, 1955.

Rouse, James W., "The City of Columbia, Maryland," in *Taming Megalopolis,* Vol. II, H. W. Eldredge (ed.), Garden City: Anchor Doubleday, 1967: 838-848. (Abridged from a statement before the Housing Sub-Committee, House Banking and Currency Committee on HR1296, Title II, Land Development and New Communities, March 25, 1966.)

Stegman, Michael A., "Accessibility Models and Residential Location," *Journal of American Institute of Planners,* Vol. 35, No. 1 (January 1969), 22-29.

Stein, Clarence, *Toward New Towns for America,* New York: Reinhold, 1957.

United Nations, *Planning of Metropolitan Areas and New Towns,* Meeting of the United Nations Group of Experts on Metropolitan Planning and Development, Stockholm, 14-30 September 1961. United Nations Symposium on the Planning and Development of New Towns, Moscow, 24 August-7 September 1964. United Nations Publication, Sales No.: 67 IV.5.

Von Eckardt, Wolf, "The Case for Building 350 New Towns," *Harper's Magazine,* December 1965, 85-94.

Werthman, Carl, Jerry S. Mandel, and Ted Dienstfrey, *Planning and the Purchase Decision: Why People Buy in Planned Communities.* A pre-publication of the Community Development Project. University of California, Berkeley: Institute of Regional Development, Center for Planning and Development Research. Preprint No. 10, July 1965.

Willmott, Peter, and Michael Young, *Family and Class in a London Suburb,* London: Routledge and Kegan Paul, 1960.

Wilson, Robert L., "Livability of the City: Attitudes and Urban Development," Chapter 11 in *Urban Growth Dynamics,* F. Stuart Chapin, Jr. and Shirley F. Weiss (eds.), New York: Wiley and Sons, 1962, 359-399.

Wolf, Eleanor P., and Charles N. Lebeaux with Shirley Terreberry, and Helen Saperstein, *Change and Renewal in an Urban Community: Five Case Studies of Detroit,* New York: Praeger, 1969.

Young, Michael, and Peter Willmott, *Family and Kinship in East London,* Middlesex, England: Penguin Books, 1967.

Zehner, Robert B., "Satisfaction With Neighborhoods: The Effects of Social Compatibility, Residential Density, and Site Planning," unpublished Ph.D. dissertation, The University of Michigan, 1970.